HOW TO
LEAD

Wisdom from the World's
Greatest CEOs, Founders,
and Game Changers

DAVID M.
RUBENSTEIN

Simon & Schuster
New York London Toronto Sydney New Delhi

Simon & Schuster
1230 Avenue of the Americas
New York, NY 10020

First Simon & Schuster hardcover edition September 2020

SIMON & SCHUSTER and colophon are registered
trademarks of Simon & Schuster, Inc.

For information about special discounts for bulk
purchases, please contact Simon & Schuster Special Sales at
1-866-506-1949 or business@simonandschuster.com.

The Simon & Schuster Speakers Bureau can bring authors to
your live event. For more information or to book an event, contact
the Simon & Schuster Speakers Bureau at 1-866-248-3049
or visit our website at www.simonspeakers.com.

Interior design by Lewelin Polanco

Manufactured in the United States of America

1   3   5   7   9   10   8   6   4   2

Library of Congress Cataloging-in-Publication Data is available.

ISBN 978-1-9821-3215-6
ISBN 978-1-9821-3218-7 (ebook)

To Bettie and Bob, my late parents,
and to Camille and Grant, my young grandchildren

Contents

Introduction

I have always been fascinated with leadership—specifically, what individual leaders can accomplish by the power of their intellect, level of their unique skill, force of their personality, or effectiveness of their ability to persuade.

That fascination has no doubt been shared by nearly everyone on the planet during the COVID-19 crisis, as they looked to see whether certain individuals would rise to the occasion by developing the health, medical, financial, social, and political solutions to guide humanity through that unprecedented crisis. And clearly some did.

Similarly, during the protests following George Floyd's death, many Americans looked for leaders to calm the racial tensions and address the anguish felt in the country. And again, there were those who heroically rose to the occasion.

Leadership comes in many forms and is exercised in many ways. Some leaders can command military troops in war. Others can conceive of and build large companies. Some leaders can develop scientific breakthroughs that improve the lives of millions of people, or use their expertise to help guide the public response to dangerous new diseases. Others can create works in the visual or performing arts that trigger deep emotions and showcase human expression at its highest level. Some can master athletic skills that unite fans around the world, while other leaders can transform an existing organization or develop solutions to complicated problems. Still others are able to create new ways of communicating or thinking.

I have long been interested in how these different types actually become and stay leaders. As a result of my fascination with the human trait of leadership, I have always had a habit—maybe bad manners—of asking leaders, whenever I first meet them, how they became leaders. What were the key factors? Was it luck, drive, talent, training, experience, or some other factor? How was this ability found and cultivated? How did they put it into action, and what happened when it was tested? Not everyone has been prepared to respond immediately to my barrage of questions.

That habit became more publicly visible when I became the president of the Economic Club of Washington, D.C., in 2008 and began almost monthly interviewing a prominent business, government, or cultural leader. For better or worse, I continued my interest in knowing what makes leaders tick when I began the *Peer to Peer* interview show on Bloomberg TV in 2016 (broadcast on PBS as well since 2018).

This book, an outgrowth of these interviews, is designed to provide the reader with the perspectives of different kinds of leaders, with the hope that readers might be inspired to develop or enhance their own leadership skills. How did Jeff Bezos and Bill Gates build global tech empires, against all odds? How did Phil Knight take an idea from his business school thesis and build the largest athletic-shoe company? How did Ruth Bader Ginsburg overcome legal roadblocks to gender equality and later become the Supreme Court's rock star? How did Tim Cook follow the legendary Steve Jobs and build an even stronger company? How did Jack Nicklaus become the world's greatest golfer? How did Condoleezza Rice rise to the highest levels of government, defying the segregated South of her youth? How did Bill Clinton and George W. Bush overcome the severe challenges they faced as president? How did Dr. Anthony Fauci become one of the world's most respected authorities on infectious diseases such as Ebola, HIV/AIDS, and now COVID-19?

Obviously, more than just reading a book about leadership is necessary to become a leader. But the stories of some of the best-known living leaders show how leadership grows over the course of a life and career. Many of those featured in this book started with little else than an idea and their own drive. Their stories also reveal the value that a leader can bring to a challenge, often affecting humanity in profoundly positive ways. Every story is inspirational.

A fair question might be: Why should anyone really want to be a leader?

First, a leader can create the type of change or results that will improve the lives of others. Second, a leader can motivate others to become leaders, and in turn improve others' lives. And third, a leader can feel a sense of accomplishment and achievement that provides human fulfillment and happiness.

I have written *How to Lead* because I care a good deal about the positive impact that strong, decisive, and talented leaders can bring to a society. But I did not honestly feel that my own specific leadership story was sufficient to inspire others. I felt that the story of really extraordinary leaders, as told through frank interviews, would be far more helpful.

That said, I have gained some perspective from my own more modest and increasingly eclectic "leadership" journey: from an only child in a blue-collar family, to a scholarship student, lawyer, White House aide, private equity cofounder, philanthropist, nonprofit organization chair, public speaker, television show interviewer and commentator, and author. (Not being a really good leader in any one area, I suppose I tried many different areas.)

From an early age, children seem to realize that some adults are doing things that are particularly impressive. Indeed, nearly all children seem to look up to leaders—or "heroes"—and want to be like them. In my own childhood, those individuals were probably such historic figures as George Washington, Abraham Lincoln, Theodore and Franklin Roosevelt, and Winston Churchill; more contemporary figures like John Wayne, Jonas Salk, and Martin Luther King Jr.; and, more typical for a boy in my hometown, Baltimore sports stars like the Orioles' third baseman Brooks Robinson or the Colts' quarterback Johnny Unitas.

But no leader in my boyhood rivaled the youthful, charming, and charismatic President John F. Kennedy, who showed leadership in the Cuban Missile Crisis in 1962 that kept the U.S. and the Soviet Union from a nuclear war—one that could have killed more than 100 million people (including me). My ninth-grade teacher was so convinced that a nuclear confrontation was likely that she assigned no homework for a few days. She said we would probably not be around—not the most comforting reason to avoid homework.

I wondered then, and now, what made individuals rise up and become extraordinary leaders. How did they make something happen that would not otherwise have happened? Was it their personality, mental or physical skills, or the good fortune of being in the right place at the right time? And why did so many who became great leaders later in their lives *not* exhibit signs of this type of leadership in their youth? Why were they not student body presidents, Rhodes Scholars, athletic team captains? I wondered about this in the hope that—not being much of a great leader in my own youth—there might be some chance later in life, when I thought and hoped it might matter more.

When I talk to student or young adult leaders, I often say that life generally can be divided into thirds. The first third is getting an education or training for a future career; the second third is focusing on building your career, perfecting skills, and rising to a senior position or a position of responsibility and leadership; and the final third involves receiving the benefits—financial, psychic, public recognition—from the level of achievement attained in the second of these phases.

I have told students that "winning" during the first third of life can be pleasurable, but often the winners of that phase do not become the leaders that might have been predicted from those early results. And, I add, leadership in the second and third parts of life can be more meaningful and enduring for the individual and society.

Why do so many first-third leaders not become the world leaders that they seem, at a young age, destined to be? Perhaps it is that those who are the Rhodes Scholars, student body presidents, newspaper editors in chief, All-American athletes, Supreme Court clerks, and the equivalent may be burned out a bit by the time the first third of life is over. Maybe they coast a little after the first third. Or perhaps they conclude that being a great leader is not all that it is cracked up to be, so why push oneself in the other two-thirds of life?

By contrast, with some obvious exceptions, those who are often the leaders in the second and final thirds are generally not the superstars in the first third. Why is that?

Some people mature later. Others may have disadvantages in their younger years—family issues, lack of financial resources, health challenges, poor education opportunities, etc. Still others may just not have had the motivation or ambition, perhaps because of a lack of role models or opportunities.

I would perhaps be in a somewhat interesting but not wholly unique category: I would have liked to be a real leader in my first third of life—I had no lack of ambition—and tried; but honestly did not have the talent, ability, or other requisite attributes then valued by my peers (e.g., outgoing personality, athletic skills, family wealth, specialized talent in a particular area). Later I had some unexpected, and probably undeserved, luck to become a leader in the financial services, philanthropic, and nonprofit worlds toward the end of the second third and beginning of the final third of my life. All of this later-life success no doubt has been a surprise (or shock) to my classmates or other childhood friends, though many have been too polite to say so.

In my youth, I was a reasonably good student, but no academic superstar, if grades or board scores are the measurement. I was a reasonably good athlete until age eight, when my peers shot past me in size and ability and I became a mediocre athlete. I was involved in a great many extracurricular activities and was a member of an impressive youth group in Baltimore, but was never the dynamic leader who rose to the top in those settings.

All that said, I did receive a partial scholarship (not for basketball) to attend Duke University and a full-tuition scholarship to attend the University of Chicago Law School. (I needed scholarships; my father worked for the post office, earning a modest salary.) And I did get a job at the well-known New York law firm of Paul, Weiss, Rifkind, Wharton & Garrison, which was appealing to me because of the presence of prominent individuals who had served in government, like Ted Sorensen, counsel to President Kennedy. As a young lawyer, I had the chance to work with the firm's most senior lawyers, and New York's top business leaders and government officials, when I was assigned to work on the pending bankruptcy of New York City.

I enjoyed that government-related work, and felt that working in government would be more rewarding. The lower compensation was of no real concern, for money held no real interest to me; I had never had much money, and did not honestly aspire to make too much. Politics and public policy were much more alluring.

Had I stayed at Paul, Weiss, I might have developed a specialty, become partner, and remained there for the next forty-plus years, until the forced retirement that such firms now impose on their sixty-five- to seventy-year-old partners. But that platform, enviable perhaps for serious lawyers, would probably not have given me the opportunity to become much of a player in the world of government service or politics. So I left after just two years to chase the dream of working in the federal government and ultimately being a White House staffer and presidential advisor—like Ted Sorensen.

That was a bit of a pipe dream; I had no political contacts or track record, and I was barely out of law school. But I was enamored with politics, public service, and the presidency, and business was the furthest thing from my mind.

That dream probably started when I watched President Kennedy give his eloquent inaugural address on January 20, 1961. He called on the nation to meet the new challenges facing the world, and he inspired a generation to become engaged with government and the public good. The speech was poetry in prose form, and his words about trying to do something for the country stayed with me throughout my youth.

Sometimes lightning strikes for those who take chances.

With the help of a recommendation from Ted Sorensen, I left Paul, Weiss to become chief counsel to the U.S. Senate Judiciary Committee's Subcommittee on the Constitution, which was a long title for being Senator Birch Bayh's legislative assistant on Judiciary Committee matters. But he was running for president, seemed to me qualified for that position, and would surely ask me to join his White House staff after his inevitable election.

Unfortunately, fate intervened: Senator Bayh dropped out of the race (though probably not because of his poor selection of a Judiciary Committee staffer), ending what I thought was my chance to work in the White House. But while working in the Senate, I had a chance to sit on the floor of the Senate and watch the greats of that era—Senators Scoop Jackson, Warren Magnuson, Phil Hart, Jacob Javits, Howard Baker, and Ted Kennedy—show their leadership skills.

As the 1976 primaries were ending, I received a call from someone working for another candidate, the likely nominee, Governor Jimmy Carter, and was invited to interview for a job on his post-nomination policy staff. I thought a peanut farmer's chances of getting elected were modest, but I had nothing better to do. I got the job, moved to Atlanta, and proceeded to do what I could to help Governor Carter's policy leader, Stuart Eizenstat.

When I joined the campaign team, Carter was more than thirty points ahead of the incumbent, President Gerald Ford. After my handiwork, Carter won by one point.

Fortunately, I was not blamed for the decline in his fortunes, and ultimately became a deputy domestic policy assistant to President Carter—

a job, needless to say, I was not really qualified to hold. White House jobs are often filled by those who worked on the campaign; it is not necessarily who is best qualified.

I held that position for the entire four years of the Carter administration, and thoroughly relished it. How could someone from a blue-collar background, a first-generation college graduate, not love working in the West Wing, traveling on Air Force One and Marine One, meeting with the president and vice president, and helping my boss, Stuart Eizenstat, run the domestic policy team at the White House, all while in my late twenties and early thirties? Does life get any better?

I am not sure that experience really made me a "leader" in the first third of my career, but I had managed, through lots of luck, to elevate my career over what it might otherwise have been if pure talent, intellect, and leadership qualities were the only criteria.

Eventually, as often happens in life, reality hit. I thought President Carter would win reelection and I might be elevated to a more senior White House position in his second term—to become a real "leader." The Election Gods did not think that was a great idea, and Carter lost decisively to Ronald Reagan.

I had not thought that was possible, for Ronald Reagan would turn seventy shortly after becoming president. How could the American people elect such an old person? I was then thirty-one. I am now seventy-one. This age now seems a bit younger than I had once thought.

I was a junior leader around the White House one day, with the potential to be a senior leader. And the next day I was unemployed. Law firms were not dying to hire a thirty-one-year-old ex–Carter White House aide, with two years of law practice under his belt. Humility came quickly, and fortunately never left.

It took me many months to find a law firm willing to take a chance. (I told my mother I had so many offers that I was just taking my time sifting through them.) When I finally found one, I realized why law firms were not dying to hire me. I was not experienced in practicing law; no one wanted insights on the Carter White House in the Reagan era; and, with no specialty or real legal training, I was likely to be an average lawyer, at best, for the remainder of my career.

So I decided to take a career risk—abandon the practice of law to start a new (and really the first) private equity firm in Washington, D.C.

I suppose I was motivated by five factors:

1. I did not enjoy the practice of law—and recognized that real career success depends on having a passion for what one is doing.
2. I read about a highly successful buyout that former secretary of the treasury Bill Simon had done of Gibson greeting cards, achieving financial results far beyond what is possible in the law. (A $300,000 investment became worth $70 million in just eighteen months.)
3. I saw law practice increasingly as a business more than a passion, and thought that, if I was going to be in business, I might try something that seemed more interesting, and lucrative, than practicing law. (My earlier disdain for making money had disappeared with a new family.)
4. I thought there was little competition in the buyout world in Washington—there were no buyout firms—and thus it was an open field in a growing area.
5. I read that entrepreneurs tend to start their companies by the age of thirty-seven, and after that age individuals are much less likely to start companies—and I read that when I was thirty-seven.

There was no reason my new buyout firm should have succeeded. These firms were generally in New York; none of my partners had Wall Street or private equity experience; we had no money at the outset; and we had no clear business plan or prospects for raising capital.

But the firm, The Carlyle Group, did find a way to get off the ground. I recruited three partners who had investment experience; I was able to raise the initial $5 million to launch the firm in 1987; and our early deals tended to work—giving us the credibility to raise dedicated pools of capital, to expand beyond buyouts to other types of private equity investments, and to eventually expand into a global firm. To everyone's surprise, including mine, we became one of the world's largest and best-known private equity firms over the ensuing thirty-plus years, and that helped to make me a second- and final-third-of-life "leader," despite the modest leadership skills I displayed early on.

Beyond my becoming a "leader" in the burgeoning private equity world, Carlyle's success also gave me the ability, and perhaps the self-confidence, to get involved in the philanthropic world and the somewhat related nonprofit world.

In the realm of philanthropy, I was one of the original signers of the Giving Pledge (created by Bill and Melinda Gates and Warren Buffett), and essentially fostered the concept of "patriotic philanthropy," i.e., taking actions to remind people of the history and heritage of our country: buying Magna Carta and providing it to the National Archives; preserving rare copies of the Declaration of Independence and the Emancipation Proclamation; helping to repair the Washington Monument, the Lincoln Memorial, the Jefferson Memorial, Monticello, Montpelier, and the Iwo Jima Memorial.

In the nonprofit world, I have served as the chairman of the board of Duke University, the Smithsonian Institution, and as cochair of the Brookings Institution; and I currently serve as the chairman of the board of the John F. Kennedy Center for the Performing Arts and the Council on Foreign Relations; president of the Economic Club of Washington, D.C.; a fellow of the Harvard Corporation; and a trustee of the National Gallery of Art, the University of Chicago, Johns Hopkins Medicine, the Memorial Sloan Kettering Cancer Center, and the Institute for Advanced Study. I have also focused my energies on education, having served on four major university boards and created scholarship programs at Duke, Harvard, the University of Chicago, and the D.C. Public and Charter Schools.

So what were the attributes that enabled me to go from something of a nonleader in my first phase of life to a leader in the second and third?

Self-analysis is always fraught with risk, and there is the danger of patting oneself on the back unduly, but the attributes I would cite are the same ones that I repeatedly hear from those I interview on my show:

1. *Luck.* There is no doubt that successful leaders seem to have luck along the way. It was a chance encounter that led to my interview with Stuart Eizenstat, which in turn led to my White House position. While the administration did not end well, the position probably gave me enough visibility, self-confidence, and ambition to start a private equity firm with no financial experience. And I had the luck to select two partners whom I did not previously know, Bill Conway and Dan D'Aniello, who had much more financial experience and credibility than I did. That we have stayed together as partners for more than thirty years is unusual in the business world—and lucky.

2. *Desire to Succeed.* A leader also has to possess a desire to

succeed—to achieve something of note, to make a mark in the world, to create a product or service of real interest and value to others. Perhaps I had that desire for the same reason many individuals from modest economic and social roots do—to have a more interesting and fulfilling life than the one experienced as a youth. (My parents were not high school or college graduates; we lived in a modest eight-hundred-square-foot row house in a Jewish blue-collar section of Baltimore.)

3. *Pursuit of Something New and Unique.* A leader is typically a person who desires to build or create something—to go where others have not yet tried to go. The idea that a private equity firm could be built in Washington by individuals who had no Wall Street experience seemed a bit ridiculous to many. But the typical reaction to that idea was actually favorable compared to the reaction to my subsequent idea that we should build a firm that offered all types of private equity investments, not just buy-outs, and do this around the world. That had not been done yet.

4. *Hard Work/Long Hours.* There is no shortcut to becoming a leader. Performing a job and being a real leader of note at that job takes many hours of hard work. It is impossible to develop the requisite skills for this five days a week, nine to five.

   I always had the view that there were more brilliant and clever individuals than myself, and the only way to compete with them was to work longer and harder than they did. My "workaholic" tendencies did draw attention during my career, but I suppose they also kept me out of the typical youth or adult temptations not designed to be career-enhancing. A modest plus for workaholics.

   But in truth, workaholism is a plus, I have learned, only if one has some outside unrelated interests that can provide different, less tension-filled experiences, pleasures, and intellectual joy. Even Einstein felt the need to play the violin daily and to sail regularly in the summer.

5. *Focus.* Focus your energies on truly mastering one skill or subject; broaden your areas of focus only after credibility has been established with peers and others in the one area where you are the master. At Carlyle, I decided to focus on raising the capital needed for the increasing number of investments the firm was

making in the U.S. and around the world. Once my fund-raising abilities had been established, I was able to expand my focus to other needs of my firm.

6. *Failure.* Any leader has failed at something, or many things. Learn from this experience, and be motivated to prove the failure was an aberration. My having been part of a "failed" White House certainly fueled my ambition to succeed in the next part of my career. Too, failure teaches humility, and exponentially enhances the desire to succeed the next time.

7. *Persistence.* Almost by definition, a leader is doing something new, different, unique, etc., and will therefore encounter resistance from those who like or respect the status quo. The key is to persist when others say no or fight against the change you want to make.

   Everyone told me that Carlyle could not become the global firm that I wanted to build from the non–financial capital of Washington, D.C. The more I was told this, the more I was determined to persist with my dream and ambition.

8. *Persuasiveness.* It is impossible to lead if no one is following. A leader can persuade others to follow through one of three basic means of communication: writing something that inspires readers; saying something that motivates listeners; or doing something that sets an example for others to follow.

   More specifically, people follow individuals who can persuade them of the merits or wisdom of their view or actions. Few leaders can lead equally well through all of these means, but I have actually tried over the years, through much practice and trial and error, to improve my basic writing and speaking skills, and to pursue actions that I hoped would lead others to follow, especially in philanthropy.

9. *Humble Demeanor.* Some leaders allow their position of authority to develop into an arrogant demeanor; other leaders recognize that they are not omnipotent or all-knowing and that luck has helped them, and the result is a more humble demeanor. The latter is more effective in earning respect from followers.

   Clearly some of the world's most famous leaders have not been pleasant individuals, in part because of their overwhelming arrogance. My own view has been that the more effective and enduring leaders have a humility that shows they recognize their own weaknesses and their own good luck. I have tried to conduct my own life with an eye toward remaining humble; that both fits my personality and turns out to be a more effective way to get others to want to follow.

10. *Credit-Sharing.* The most effective leaders inevitably realize that they can accomplish a great deal more if they are willing to share the credit with others.

   As John F. Kennedy famously said, "Victory has a hundred fathers, and defeat is an orphan." Of course everyone would like to get credit for successful outcomes, and there is nothing wrong with that if the credit is appropriately shared. Ronald Reagan said much the same: "There is no limit to what humans can accomplish if they are willing to share the credit." I have found it to be extremely effective to share as much credit as possible when success occurs, and to take or share the blame when failure arises.

11. *The Ability to Keep Learning.* Leaders need to expand their knowledge every day—to exercise their most unique muscle: their brain. Failing to do so makes it difficult to keep up with a rapidly changing world and with the increasingly large amounts of information that can be helpful in being an informed, knowledgeable leader.

   I have tried to continue to learn by somewhat obsessive reading: six newspapers a day, at least a dozen weekly periodicals, and at least one book a week (though often trying to juggle three to four books simultaneously). Nothing focuses the mind like a well-written book.

12. *Integrity.* Leaders vary in their commitment to integrity and ethical behavior, but the most effective leaders are seen as committed to highly ethical behavior—and that commitment enhances their leadership capabilities.

   When I started the practice of law, the leader of Paul, Weiss, former judge Simon Rifkind, told all of the new lawyers: "It takes a lifetime to build a reputation, and five minutes to destroy it. So do not take ethical risks that can ruin your reputation—and life." What more can be said? Do not cut ethical corners, and you will be a much more effective leader.

13. *Responding to Crises.* Leaders are most needed when crises occur, as we have been reminded this year during the COVID-19 pandemic and the nationwide protests over the death of George Floyd. Rising to the occasion when an existential crisis occurs can mark a leader forever—Lincoln holding his country together during the Civil War or Churchill rallying his country to fight the Nazi attacks. On a much lesser scale, I have tried, by working harder and communicating better, to motivate our employees at a time of enormous, unprecedented financial stress.

My own experiences with and observations of leadership provided me with the perspectives just described. Others will inevitably have different perspectives because of their different experiences, and because there is more than one type of leadership.

In my professional career, my leadership experience involved starting, building, growing, and running an entrepreneurial investment firm. That type of leadership is different from the types of leadership experiences that many of those interviewed for this book have had.

For simplicity's sake, I have divided the leadership experience of those in this book into six categories:

1. **Visionaries:** Jeff Bezos, Bill Gates, Richard Branson, Oprah Winfrey, and Warren Buffett
2. **Builders:** Phil Knight, Ken Griffin, Robert F. Smith, Jamie Dimon, and Marillyn Hewson
3. **Transformers:** Melinda Gates, Eric Schmidt, Tim Cook, Ginni Rometty, and Indra Nooyi
4. **Commanders:** George W. Bush and Bill Clinton, Colin Powell, David Petraeus, Condoleezza Rice, and James A. Baker III
5. **Decision-Makers:** Nancy Pelosi, Adam Silver, Christine Lagarde, Anthony S. Fauci, and Ruth Bader Ginsburg
6. **Masters:** Jack Nicklaus, Mike "Coach K" Krzyzewski, Renée Fleming, Yo-Yo Ma, and Lorne Michaels

In each of the interviews in this book, I have tried to ask the interviewee about how he or she became and remains a leader. Their stories are all different, but inevitably the qualities that they cite as key to their success tend to revolve around the attributes I mentioned above as vital to being an effective leader. The interviews have been edited for length and consistency and updated as needed, in consultation with the interviewees.

My hope is that readers will recognize that leadership has its challenges, and mere interest in being a leader is not enough. But those from any background can become leaders—and strong leaders can make some part of the world a better place.

David M. Rubenstein, June 2020

VISIONARIES

Jeff Bezos

Bill Gates

Sir Richard Branson

Oprah Winfrey

Warren Buffett

JEFF BEZOS

Founder and CEO, Amazon;
Owner, the *Washington Post*

"When you can make a decision with analysis, you should do
so. But it turns out in life that your most important decisions
are always made with instinct, intuition, taste, heart."

J eff Bezos did not invent the idea of selling books over the Internet. Others were already doing that when he established Amazon in 1994. But he did have a vision of how he could use better
software to make the sales process work more efficiently. Even more
significantly, Jeff ultimately had the vision of selling almost anything over the Internet—at a time when it was still somewhat in its
infancy.

I first met Jeff Bezos in 1995 in Amazon's very modest start-up offices in Seattle. I went to see if I could renegotiate a deal that one of
Carlyle's companies—Baker & Taylor, the country's second-largest book
distributor—had cut with him about two years earlier. Under that deal,

Baker & Taylor would allow Amazon to use its bibliography of books in print, enabling Bezos to sell books over the Internet.

When Jeff first approached Baker & Taylor, he was not flush with cash, and offered them an equity ownership in the new company. (Some remember the number as 20 to 30 percent.) Our representative wanted cash, and ultimately reached an agreement for $100,000 a year for five years.

When I began to realize an equity ownership might be better than cash, I decided to visit Jeff in Seattle. He politely said he no longer was dependent on the bibliography, and that his company had progressed a fair bit. But he did say that Baker & Taylor had been helpful at the outset and that he would provide some equity to us—roughly 1 percent of Amazon—in lieu of the annual cash payments. Unfortunately, we did not have the requisite confidence in Amazon, and we sold our equity shortly after the IPO in 1996 for about $80 million.

My biggest business mistake. That stake today, after stock splits and new stock issuances, would be worth about $4 billion.

Since that time, Jeff has rewritten the world of retailing and computing and space exploration, and become the world's wealthiest and one of its best-known individuals. Amazon has achieved a market value in excess of $1 trillion, with more than 840,000 full- and part-time employees in early 2020, one of the world's best-known brand names, and a seemingly ubiquitous presence in the United States and increasingly around the world.

Over the years, I have come to know Jeff a fair bit and have interviewed him on a few occasions. (Once was in a private setting with Bill Gates—the first time these two neighbors and business leaders had been interviewed jointly. I wish there were a recording or transcript. It was probably my favorite interview ever.) In addition to being an extraordinary leader, Jeff is an extraordinary interviewee: engaging, frank, insightful, self-deprecating, wise, and interesting—a rare combination.

Everyone wants to know how Jeff built Amazon and became so successful in such a relatively short period. He reveals a few secrets in this interview, held in September 2018 in Washington, D.C.: being willing to take chances and to fail, focusing on the long term, placing customers first, getting a full night's sleep, not making key decisions too early or too late in the day, and having supportive parents.

If only following that pattern were enough, there would be many more Jeff Bezoses and Amazons. I think there are some other ingredients as well—ones unique to Jeff Bezos.

DAVID RUBENSTEIN (DR): Your stock is actually up 70 percent this year [2018]. Is there one thing that you think is responsible for that, or several things?

JEFF BEZOS (JB): We have all-hands meetings at Amazon, and for twenty years, at almost every meeting, I'd say, "When the stock is up thirty percent in a month, don't feel thirty percent smarter. Because when the stock is down thirty percent in a month, it's not going to feel so good to feel thirty percent dumber."

That's what happens. Warren Buffett brings up all the time that great Benjamin Graham quote that in the short run the stock market is a voting machine and in the long run it's a weighing machine. What you need to do is operate your company knowing that it will be weighed one day. Just let it be weighed. Never spend any time thinking about the daily stock price. I don't.

DR: As a result, you have become the wealthiest man in the world. Is that a title you really wanted?

JB: I have never sought that title. It was fine being the second-wealthiest person in the world. I would much rather they said "inventor Jeff Bezos" or "entrepreneur Jeff Bezos" or "father Jeff Bezos"—those things are much more meaningful to me.

I own 16 percent of Amazon. Amazon's worth roughly $1 trillion. That means we have built $840 billion of wealth for other people.

I believe so powerfully in the ability of entrepreneurial capitalism and free markets to solve so many of the world's problems. Not all of them, but so many of them.

DR: You live in Washington State, near Seattle. The man who was the richest man for about twenty years is named Bill Gates. What is the likelihood that the two richest men in the world live not only in the same country, the same state, the same city, but in the same neighborhood? Is there something in that neighborhood we should know about? Are there any more houses for sale there?

JB: I saw Bill not too long ago, and we were joking about the world's-richest-man thing. I basically said, "You're welcome." He immediately turned to me and said, "Thank you."

Medina is a great little suburb of Seattle. I don't think there's anything special in the water there. I did locate Amazon in Seattle because of Microsoft. I thought that big pool of technical talent would provide a good place to recruit talented people from. That did turn out to be true. So it's not a complete coincidence.

DR: Talk to me about your approach to building and decision-making.

JB: Everything I've ever done has started small. Amazon started with a couple of people. Blue Origin [his aerospace firm] started with five people. The budget of Blue Origin was very, very small. Now its budget approaches $1 billion a year. Next year it'll be more than $1 billion.

Amazon literally was ten people. Today it's half a million people. For me it's like yesterday. I was driving the packages to the post office myself, and hoping one day we could afford a forklift.

I've seen small things get big. I like treating things as if they're small. Even though Amazon is a large company, I want it to have the heart and spirit of a small one.

The Day One Families Fund [Bezos's charitable fund, founded in 2018, which makes grants to nonprofits working on homelessness and early childhood education] is going to be like that. We'll wander a little bit too. We have some very specific ideas of what we want to do, but I believe in the power of wandering. All of my best decisions in business and in life have been made with heart, intuition, guts, not analysis.

When you can make a decision with analysis, you should do so. But it turns out in life that your most important decisions are always made with instinct, intuition, taste, heart.

I talk so often to other CEOs and founders and entrepreneurs, and I can tell that even though they're talking about customers, they're really focusing on competitors. It is a huge advantage to any company if you can stay focused on your customer instead of your competitor.

Then you have to identify who your customer is. At the *Washington Post*, for example, are the customers the people who buy advertisements from us? No. The customer is the reader. Full stop.

Where do advertisers want to be? Advertisers want to be where there are readers. So it's really not that complicated.

With a school, who are the customers? Is it the parents? Is it the teachers? No. It is the child. That's what we're going to do at Day One. We're going to be focused on the child. We're going to be scientific when we can be, and we're going to use heart and intuition when we need to.

DR: Why did you buy the *Washington Post*? What convinced you to do that? You had no background in that area.

JB: I had no intention of buying a newspaper, had never thought about the idea. It wasn't like a childhood dream.

My friend Don Graham—I've known him for twenty years now—approached me through an intermediary and wanted to know if I would be interested in buying the *Post*. I sent back word that I would not, because I didn't really know anything about newspapers.

Over a series of conversations, Don convinced me that was unimportant, because inside the *Washington Post* was so much talent that understands newspapers. What they needed was somebody who had an understanding of the Internet.

I did some soul-searching. My decision-making process on something like this would definitely be intuition and not analysis.

The financial situation of the *Washington Post* at that time—2013—was very upside down. It's a fixed-cost business, and they had lost a lot of revenue over the previous five or six years. I said, "Is this something I want to get involved in? If I'm going to do it, I'm going to put some heart into it and some work into it." I decided I would only do that if I really believed it was an important institution.

As soon as I started thinking about it that way, I was like, "This *is* an important institution. It's the newspaper in the capital city of the most important country in the world. The *Washington Post* has an incredibly important role to play in this democracy."

Today, with the Internet, you get that gift of free distribution. We had to take advantage of that gift. That was the basic strategy. We had to switch from a business model where we made a lot of money per reader, with a relatively small number of readers, to a tiny bit of money per reader on a very large number of readers. That's the transition we made.

I'm pleased to report that the *Post* is profitable today. The newsroom is growing.

DR: When you agreed to buy it, the asking price was $250 million. Did you negotiate?

JB: No. I asked Don how much he wanted. He said, "Two hundred fifty million." I said, "Fine." I didn't negotiate with him. I did no due diligence. I wouldn't need to with Don.

DR: I have something I'd like to sell. . . . You grew up in Texas?

JB: I was born in Albuquerque, but I left when I was three or four and moved to Texas.

DR: And from an early age were you a pretty smart student?

JB: I have always been academically smart. The older I get, the more I realize how many kinds of smart there are. There are a lot of kinds of stupid too. I see people all the time who wouldn't have gotten A-pluses on their calculus exams but who are incredibly smart. But yes, I was a very good student.

DR: You graduated as valedictorian. How did you decide to go to Princeton?

JB: I wanted to be a theoretical physicist, so I went to Princeton. I was in the honors physics track, which starts out with a hundred students. By the time you get to quantum mechanics it's, like, thirty.

So I'm in quantum mechanics, and I've been taking a bunch of computer-science classes and electrical engineering classes, which I'm also enjoying. And I can't solve this partial differential equation. It's really, really hard. I've been studying with my roommate, Joe, who also is really good at math.

The two of us worked on this one homework problem for three hours and got nowhere. We finally look at each other over the table at the same moment and say, "Yasantha," because Yasantha was the smartest guy at Princeton.

We go to Yasantha's room, and we show him this problem. He looks at it. He stares at it for a while and he says, "Cosine." "What do you mean?" "That's the answer." "That's the answer?" "Yeah, let me show you." He writes out three pages of detailed algebra. Everything crosses out, and the answer is cosine.

I said, "Yasantha, did you just do that in your head?" He said, "No that would be impossible. Three years ago, I solved a very similar problem and I was able to map this problem onto that problem, and then it was immediately obvious that the answer was cosine." That was an important moment for me, because that was the moment I realized I was never going to be a great theoretical physicist.

In theoretical physics, you have to be one of the top fifty people in the world or you're really just not helping out much. I saw the writing on the wall, and I changed my major very quickly to electrical engineering and computer science.

DR: But you graduated summa cum laude.

JB: I graduated summa cum laude.

DR: Phi Beta Kappa.

JB: Phi Beta Kappa.

DR: And then you went into the highest calling of mankind—finance.

JB: Yes. I went to New York City and ended up working at a quantitative hedge fund run by a brilliant man named David Shaw—D. E. Shaw and Company. I started there when there were only thirty people. When I left there were about three hundred.

David's still one of the most brilliant people I've ever met. I learned so much from him. I used a lot of his ideas and principles on things like HR and recruiting and what kind of people to hire when I started Amazon.

DR: You were a star there, I understand. What propelled you to say, "I'm quitting this. I'm going to start a company selling books over the

Internet and I'm going to do it from Seattle"? Where did that idea come from?

JB: This is 1994. Nobody has heard of the Internet. Very, very few people. It was used at that time by scientists and physicists. We used it a little bit at D. E. Shaw for some things, but not much.

I came across the fact that the World Wide Web was growing at something like 2,300 percent a year. This is in 1994. Anything growing that fast is going to be big. I looked at that and I was like, "I should come up with a business idea and get it on the Internet, then let the Internet grow around us. And we can keep working on it."

I made a list of products that I might sell online. I started force-ranking them, and I picked books. Books are super unusual in one respect, which is that there are more items in the book category than there are in any other category. There are three million different books in print around the world at any given time. So the founding idea of Amazon was to build a universal selection of books. The biggest bookstores only had 150,000 titles.

So that's what I did. I hired a small team, we built the software, and I moved to Seattle.

DR: Why did you pick Seattle—because of Microsoft?

JB: It was two things. The largest book warehouse in the world at that time was nearby in a town called Roseburg, Oregon—and then also the recruiting pool that was available from Microsoft.

DR: You told your parents you were going to quit D. E. Shaw, where you were successful, making presumably a fair amount of money. You told your wife, MacKenzie, that you were going to move across the country. What did they all say?

JB: They were immediately supportive—right after they asked the question "What's the Internet?" With your loved ones, you bet on them. You're not betting on the idea. You are betting on the person.

When I told my boss, David Shaw, that I was going to do this thing, we went on a long walk in Central Park. Finally, after a lot of listening, he said, "I think you're onto a good idea here. But this would be a better idea for somebody who didn't already have a good job." That actually made so much sense to me that he convinced me to think about it for two days before making a final decision.

It's one of those decisions I made with my heart and not my head. I basically said, "When I'm eighty, I want to have minimized the number of regrets that I have in my life." Most of our regrets are acts of omission. They're things we didn't try. It's the path untraveled. Those are the things that haunt us.

DR: I remember when I went out there and you were telling me that you had to go deliver the books to the post office yourself.

JB: I was doing that for years. The first month, I was packing boxes on my hands and knees on the hard cement floors, with somebody else kneeling next to me. I said, "You know what we need? Kneepads. This is killing my knees." This guy packing alongside me said, "We need packing tables." I was like, "That's the most brilliant idea I've ever heard." The next day I went and bought packing tables, and it doubled our productivity.

DR: Where did the name Amazon come from?

JB: Earth's biggest river, earth's biggest selection.

DR: That seems simple. Was that an easy choice, or were there other candidates?

JB: I first named it Cadabra. It's really hard to impress upon you how small this beginning was. But when I was driving to Seattle, I wanted to hit the ground running. I wanted to have a company incorporated, and I wanted to have a bank account set up.

So I called a friend, and he recommended his lawyer to me. Turned out this guy was actually his divorce attorney. But he incorporated the company for me and set up bank accounts. He said, "I need to know what name you want the company to have for the incorporation papers." I said—this is over the phone—"Cadabra." Like *abracadabra*. He said, "Cadaver?" And I was like, "Okay, that's not going to work." I said, "Go ahead with Cadabra for now, and I'll change it." Three months later, I changed it to Amazon.

DR: If you'd only sold books, today you wouldn't be the richest man in the world, presumably. When did you first get the idea to sell other things?

JB: After books, we started selling music, and then we started selling videos. Then I got smart and e-mailed a thousand randomly selected customers and asked them, "Besides the things we sell today, what would you like to see us sell?"

That answer came back incredibly long-tailed. Basically, the way they answered the question was with whatever they were looking for at that moment. I remember one of the answers was, "I wish you sold windshield wiper blades because I really need windshield wiper blades."

I thought, "We can sell anything this way." Then we launched electronics and toys and many other categories over time. You read the original business plan, it's just books.

DR: Your stock at one point went to $100, then went down to $6, or something like that.

JB: At the peak of the Internet bubble, our stock peaked somewhere around $113. Then after the bubble busted open, our stock went down to $6. It went from $113 to $6 in less than a year. My annual shareholder letter that year starts with a one-word sentence: "Ouch."

DR: Most of the Internet companies of the dot-com era are out of business. What was it that made you survive while virtually all the rest of them are gone?

JB: That whole period is very interesting, because the stock is not the company and the company is not the stock. As I watched the stock fall from $113 to $6, I was also watching all of our internal business metrics, number of customers, profit per unit, everything you could imagine. Every single thing about the business was getting better, and fast.

So as the stock price was going the wrong way, everything inside the company was going the right way. We didn't need to go back to capital markets, we didn't need more money. A financial bust like the Internet bubble bursting makes it really hard to raise money, but we already had the money we needed. We just needed to continue to progress.

DR: Wall Street kept saying, "Amazon's not making any money. They're just getting customers. Where are the profits?" Wall Street kept beating you up on that. Your response was: "I don't really care what you think."

JB: I was on television with Tom Brokaw. He pulled together half a dozen Internet entrepreneurs from that era. This was right before the bubble burst, or maybe right after.

He was interviewing all of us, and he finally turned to me and he said, "Mr. Bezos, can you even spell *profit*?" Tom, by the way, is now one of my good friends. He's like, "Can you even spell *profit*?" I said, "Sure. P-r-o-p-h-e-t." And he burst out laughing.

People always accused us of selling dollar bills for ninety cents, and said, "Look, anybody can do that and grow revenue." That's not what we were doing. We always had positive gross margins. It's a fixed-cost business. What I could see from the internal metrics was that at a certain volume level, we would cover our fixed costs and the company would be profitable.

DR: Amazon Prime seems to be a great way to get money in advance of people actually getting goods and services. Whose idea was that?

JB: Like many inventions, it came up inside a team. I love team inventing; it is my favorite thing. I get to live two to three years in the future. Somebody has an idea, then other people improve the idea, other people come up with objections why it can never work, then we solve those objections. It's a very fun process.

With Prime, there were a couple of things. One of our board members, Bing Gordon, always wanted us to have a loyalty program. We were always wondering, "What could a loyalty program be?" A junior software engineer came up with this idea that we could offer people kind of an all-you-can-eat buffet of fast, free shipping.

The finance team went and modeled that idea. The results were horrifying. Shipping is expensive, and customers love free shipping. There was going to be no order threshold. You could buy a single twenty-dollar item or a single ten-dollar item and get free two-day shipping. When we modeled this, it didn't look pretty. But we could see—again, back to the idea that you have to use heart and intuition—there has to be risk-taking, you have to go by instinct. All good decisions have to be made that way.

You do it with a group, you do it with great humility, because getting it wrong isn't that bad. That's the other thing. We've made doozies, like the Fire Phone and many other things that just didn't work out. We don't have enough time for me to list all of our failed experiments. But the big winners pay for thousands of failed experiments.

So you try something like Prime. It was very expensive at the beginning. It cost us a lot of money. What happens when you offer a free all-you-can-eat buffet? Who shows up to the buffet first? The heavy eaters! It's scary. "Oh my God, did I really say as many prawns as you can eat?"

But we could see the trend lines. We could see that all kinds of customers were coming, and they appreciated that service. That's what led to Prime.

DR: You don't like meetings before 10 a.m.

JB: No.

DR: You like to get eight hours of sleep.

JB: I go to bed early. I get up early. I like to putter in the morning. I like to read the newspaper. I like to have coffee. I like to have breakfast with my kids before they go to school.

So I have my puttering time, which is very important to me. That's why I set my first meeting for ten. I like to do my high-IQ meetings before lunch. Anything that's going to be really mentally challenging, that's a ten-o'clock meeting.

By 5 p.m. I'm like, "I can't think about that today. Let's try this again tomorrow at ten." I need eight hours of sleep. I think better. I have more energy. My mood is better.

And think about it—as a senior executive, what do you really get paid to do? You get paid to make a small number of high-quality decisions. Your job is not to make thousands of decisions every day. If I make three good decisions a day, that's enough. Warren Buffett says he's good if he makes three good decisions a year. I really believe that.

All of our senior executives operate the same way I do. They work in the future, they live in the future. None of the people who report to me should really be focused on the current quarter.

We'll have a good quarterly conference call or something, and Wall Street will like our quarterly results. People will stop me and say, "Congratulations on your quarter," and I say, "Thank you." But what I'm really thinking is, "That quarter was baked three years ago."

Right now I'm working on a quarter that's going to reveal itself sometime in 2021. That's what you need to be doing. You need to be working two or three years in advance.

DR: When you buy over the Internet from Amazon, do you ever get the wrong orders? Do you call up and complain, or you don't have any problems?

JB: I'm a customer of Amazon—hopefully like all of you in this room.

DR: Is there one person who services your account full-time?

JB: If anybody in this room is not an Amazon customer, see me right afterward and I'll walk you through it.

I have problems sometimes. I treat them the same way I treat a problem that I would get from a customer.

My e-mail address is famous. I keep it and I read it. It's Jeff@Amazon.com. I don't see every e-mail that I get anymore, because I get too many, but I see a lot of them. I use my curiosity to pick out certain e-mails. I'll get one from a customer, and there's a defect—we've done something wrong. Usually people are writing us because we've screwed up their order somehow.

So I'll ask the team to do a case study and find the real root cause or causes, and then find real root fixes, so that when you fix it, you're not fixing it for that one customer, you're fixing it for every customer. That process is a gigantic part of what we do. If I have a failed order or some bad customer experience, I would treat it just like that.

DR: You've revolutionized online retail, but now you are in a bricks-and-mortar business. You bought Whole Foods.

JB: I've been asked for years, "Will you ever open physical stores?" For twenty years I've been asked that question. I always say, "Yes, but only when we have the differentiated offering." When we've tried dabbling in something that's a me-too service, we tend to get beaten. It doesn't work. Our culture is much better at pioneering and inventing.

DR: One of your passions is outer space and space travel. You started Blue Origin in secret, then you made it public. You're putting $1 billion or more of your own personal capital into it every year. What are you going to get out of it? Are we going to have people going to space?

JB: This is the most important work I'm doing. I have great conviction about that.

It's a simple argument.

This is the best planet. We have now sent robotic probes to every planet in this solar system. Believe me, this is the good one. But there are all sorts of problems that we are about to face because, for the first time in our history, going back thousands of years, we're now big compared to the size of the planet.

We can fix that problem. But we can fix it in exactly one way, by moving out into the solar system. My role in that is I want to build reusable space vehicles. I want to build space infrastructure so that the next generations of people can use that infrastructure the same way I used UPS and FedEx and so on to build Amazon. That's what Blue Origin is all about.

I would like to take a moment to talk about my parents. You get different gifts in life, and one of the great gifts I got is my mom and dad. My highest admiration is withheld for those people—I know several—who had terrible parents. Maybe they were abusive. Some people so admirably break that cycle.

I didn't have that situation. I was always loved. My parents loved me unconditionally.

She doesn't talk about it that much, but my mom had me when she was seventeen years old. She was a high school student in Albuquerque, New Mexico. I'm pretty sure that wasn't cool in 1964 to be a pregnant mom in high school in Albuquerque, New Mexico.

My grandfather, who is another incredibly important figure in my life, went to bat for her, because the high school wanted to kick her out. You weren't allowed to be pregnant in high school there.

My grandfather said, "You can't kick her out. It's a public school. She gets to go to school." They negotiated for a while, and the principal finally said, "Okay, she can stay and finish high school. But she can't do any extracurricular activities, and she can't have a locker."

My grandfather, being a very wise man, said, "Done. We'll take that deal." So she finished high school. She had me. Then she married my dad—my real dad, not my biological dad. His name is Mike. He's a Cuban immigrant. He got a scholarship to college in Albuquerque, which is where he met my mom.

So I have kind of a fairy-tale story. My grandfather, I'm pretty sure because my parents were so young, would take me every summer to his ranch, starting when I was four. And it was the most spectacular thing. From age four to sixteen I basically spent every summer working along-side him on the ranch.

He was the most resourceful man. He did all his own veterinary work. He would even make his own needles. He would pound the wire and drill a little hole in it and sharpen it and make a needle that he could suture up the cattle with. Some of the cattle even survived.

He was a remarkable man, and a huge part of all of our lives. You don't realize, until you look back, how parents are so important. It's just a really big deal. And my grandfather, he's like a second set of parents for me.

BILL GATES

Cofounder, Microsoft; Cochair, the Bill & Melinda Gates Foundation

"I don't think it's important for me to be remembered specifically. I do hope that infectious disease is largely eliminated as a problem, so that nobody's having to talk about it and people can focus on other issues. That would be a huge, great thing."

For most of the past quarter century, Bill Gates, the cofounder of Microsoft, has been the world's wealthiest individual. And for more than the past decade he has also been—with his wife—the world's largest philanthropist, working principally through the Bill & Melinda Gates Foundation. As a result of these activities, he has also become one of the world's best-known and most admired individuals.

The story is well known but continues to fascinate: Bill was a computer and software nerd who dropped out of Harvard in 1975 to start (with Paul Allen) a company to provide the software to power the computers everyone would soon possess. Bill's brilliance, workaholic dedication to the mission, and business acumen enabled him to lead the process of making Microsoft the world's most significant software company, with a market value of more than $1 trillion and a presence in virtually every personal computer.

Bill has now applied those skills to the mission of philanthropy: leading the effort to improve health in the least-developed countries—the interest in which led him to prescient warnings about pandemics—and improve K–12 education in the U.S., while also starting, with Melinda and with Warren Buffett, the Giving Pledge initiative for the world's wealthiest individuals. (The Giving Pledge is a commitment by individuals with a net worth of at least $1 billion to give away, during their lifetime or upon death, at least half their net worth.)

Despite his high IQ and driven ways, none of this was predictable when Bill was a youth. Who could have foreseen, with the rise of personal computers and software, the building of one of the world's most successful companies, or the accumulation of individual wealth beyond anything seen since the days of John D. Rockefeller?

No one, as Bill would be the first to admit. So how did it all come together this way? His unrivaled success seems to be due to a combination of vision, intellect, drive, and focus. Many individuals have one or two of those elements, but few have all four.

Which of these elements is actually the most significant? In Bill's case, it was the vision that personal computers would become omnipresent and that every one of them would need software. Bill saw that it was the software that would become more valuable than the hardware.

He is clearly a brilliant, driven individual who would have succeeded at almost any activity in which raw intellectual processing power, hard work, and focus are likely to lead to success. Whether another activity would have produced this level of wealth or philanthropic pinnacle cannot be known. What is known is that Bill Gates has been, for at least the past quarter century, one of the world's best-respected individuals, and the subject of endless interest.

I first met Bill when he came to my office in Washington on March 11, 2010, to talk about philanthropy and the soon-to-be-announced Giving

Pledge. Having Bill Gates come to your office for a simple cheeseburger can draw some attention in the office hallways.

Bill is not a publicity seeker, and he does not relish talking about how he has accomplished what he has achieved. But he provides some insights in this interview held in June 2016 in his personal office in the Seattle area.

DAVID RUBENSTEIN (DR): You built one of the great technology companies of the world—one of the great companies of the world. Now you're building and operating one of the great foundations. How do you compare the challenge of building Microsoft to the challenge of running the Bill & Melinda Gates Foundation? Which was more difficult, and which is more pleasurable?

BILL GATES (BG): They have more in common than people might expect: the idea that you find an innovation, really stick to it, build a team behind it, have some setbacks and successes—that theory of change.

My Microsoft work was when I was very young. I started when I was seventeen, and it was my primary focus until I was fifty-three, when I made the transition to working full-time with the foundation. For the early part of that, I was kind of maniacal. I wasn't married, had no kids. I didn't believe in weekends until I was about thirty. I didn't believe in vacations at all.

It was incredibly fulfilling to write the code and be hands-on, stay up all night. For my twenties and thirties, the Microsoft thing was perfect. I didn't have the breadth of knowledge that would let me play my role at the foundation. It was good preparation.

Then, after I met Melinda, got married, started having kids, I was looking at the world more broadly, thinking about where the wealth should go. For this phase of my life, the enjoyment I get—still meeting scientists, although it's not just software, it's biology and lots of other things—this is kind of perfect.

I'd say they're equally difficult. You always know you could be doing better, that you should learn more, be building the team and thinking about things in a better way. You see the positive results, but you always want to do even better.

DR: Let's talk about Microsoft for a moment. You started that when you were in high school. You were driven to be involved with computers. Were there many people who knew about computers in those days?

BG: It was a fairly special time, because computers, when I was young, were super expensive. My friend Paul Allen and I actually snuck into places at the University of Washington where they had computers that weren't being used at night. We were fascinated by what computers could do, but very few people were getting exposure to them. We had to go out of our way, and we were lucky that we did at all.

Then the idea came of moving the computer onto a chip that Intel would make. It would make the computer literally millions of times cheaper than the ones we were using, so both more powerful and more available to people on a personal level.

Then came the idea of, okay, it would be very different—the software you needed, the way the industry would work. We were super lucky to be there when that was happening. Paul was looking at that chip stuff and saying to me, "This is amazing. Why don't other people see this?" Because we were young, and because we took a software point of view, we were able to pursue it in a different way than anyone else.

DR: What did your family think?

BG: When I was young, my parents were great about encouraging me to read, and reading out loud. They were nice enough to send me to a private school, even though the tuition was a meaningful expense for them. So I got a great education. And that's the Lakeside School, where this early—not computer, but terminal that you dialed over the phone to a computer was. And so that was lucky.

They knew I was obsessed with computers, that I would skip athletics, that I'd go in overnight, that I'd leave the house sometimes when they'd prefer I wouldn't go to work at night on these things. I was considered a little strange.

The big moment was when I said that, instead of going to part of my senior year, I wanted to go work for a company writing software. TRW had this amazing network-electrification project that I wanted to work for. They were great about allowing that to be my hobby. When it came time to leave Harvard, although I could have gone back, they were a little worried. But by then I was financing things on my own, and they just sort of watched as it happened.

DR: Did you apply to other schools?

BG: I applied to Princeton, Yale, and Harvard.

DR: Did you get into all of them?

BG: Yeah, I was getting good grades, and doing well on SAT tests.

DR: But did you get perfect SAT scores?

BG: Yes. I'm good at taking tests.

DR: So you went to Harvard, and after your sophomore year you dropped out?

BG: It's actually a little complicated. I went away for a half year to get Microsoft going, and then I went back for a half year. So actually, by the time I left, I'd completed three years, but it was interrupted. I had put a friend in charge of the company, hoping that would work, but the opportunity and the complexity of the business were such that I never went back after the second time.

DR: Have you ever thought how your life could be better if you had gotten your Harvard degree?

BG: I'm a weird dropout, because I take college courses all the time. I love Learning Company courses. I love being a student.

At Harvard, there were smart people around, and they fed you, and they gave you these nice grades that made you feel smart. I feel it was unfortunate that I didn't get to stay there, but I don't think I missed any knowledge, because whatever I needed to learn, I was still in a learning mode.

DR: Had you not dropped out—not that it's the most important thing in your life, dropping out or not—would the computer revolution have gone on, and you would have missed it, and Microsoft would not have become what it became?

BG: At the time I certainly thought so. I thought, "Boy, this is so obvious that software's going to be important. If I don't literally write this software now, and get ahead of everybody, we won't be unique." There was this incredible sense of urgency. As it actually unfolded, if we'd come out a year later, I'm not sure it would have made that much difference.

Because the industry actually started off fairly slowly. What we thought was so clear—the chips had to get better, the original personal computer really didn't do that much. We didn't have disks, we didn't have graphics. That general idea we had to always move quickly was important, but a year later probably still would have been okay.

DR: In the early days, you were just a college dropout. Was it hard to get people to give you work or to hire you? You were very young-looking, you had a high-pitched voice. Did you get taken seriously by businessmen who were much older?

BG: It was very bimodal. For some people, the youth and geekiness was like, "Hey, should we trust them? We've never seen something like that before." But people who looked at the code we had written, saw what we achieved, and listened to this maniacal belief in the importance of software and how we could do things for them quickly, they would almost go overboard in thinking, "Wow, this is something unusual, some sort of genius set of kids here." Sometimes they would expect us to be able to do even more than we could.

Yes, we had to fight for acceptance. I couldn't rent cars, so I had to take cabs around, because I was too young. Some people were a little tough. But then, as we got a little bit of success, people were fascinated by this deep belief we had in software.

DR: There's a story—I don't know if it's true—about when IBM went out to get an operating system for its personal computer. You were competing for the contract. Your mother was on the board of the national United Way, and on that board was the CEO of IBM. Your mother put in a good word for you, and then the CEO of IBM put in a good word for you. Is that how you happened to win the contract?

BG: Whenever my mom would say, "Hey, come over to dinner," I'd say, "I'm too busy." We'd kind of negotiate, and I'd end up coming at least once a week. But in some of those conversations, I said, "Mom, we have this big IBM contract that's super important. We hope this is going to lead to a next generation of personal computers." When she went to a United Way meeting and saw John Opel, who was then the CEO, she said, "Hey, my boy's doing some work for your company." She could tell he'd never heard of me. She came back to me and said, "They've never heard of you." The irony was that when the Florida lab came up to do the review at headquarters, when they said, "We depend on this little company for the software piece," John Opel said, "Oh, that's Mary Gates's son."

DR: You decided to take the company public in—

BG: Nineteen eighty-six.

DR: And at that point, you are a billionaire?

BG: Pretty close to it. Within a year of our going public, there was some *Fortune* cover that said, "The Deal That Made Bill Gates $350 Million."

DR: So you were very wealthy for your age. How old were you when the company went public?

BG: I was thirty.

DR: You had this newfound wealth. Did that all of a sudden make you more famous? Did it make you have a lot more friends? Did the people you knew in high school call up and say, "I really want to get to know you better"? How did it change your life, or didn't it change your life at all?

BG: That whole period of time was amazing because I was hiring people as fast as I could. I'd brought in Steve Ballmer, who was very good at that, and he was helping out. We had a sense of urgency that we wanted to lead the way. There was this graphics-interface thing with Windows that we wanted to do. The idea that I could hire so quickly, invest, and build this worldwide company was fascinating to me.

But I was really busy. If some friend had tried to call me, I wouldn't have had too much time for that. I was really into building this company. I was going out and telling people about the magic of software, which was good for Microsoft, but also helping them understand the opportunities and the huge change agent that software, and eventually software plus the Internet, would become. I was having fun. It was amazing. But I always thought, "We're one step away from not leading here. We've got to keep doing better."

DR: But you had a fair amount of money for anybody your age at that time. Did you say, "I'll go splurge and buy a nice car, I'll buy an airplane, I'll buy a boat"? Or you just didn't really care about that?

BG: I bought one thing that was a tiny bit of a splurge. The car that I owned was a Porsche 911. It was used, but it was an incredible car. That was when I was down in Albuquerque. Sometimes, when I wanted to think at night, I'd just go out and drive around at high speed. Fortunately, I didn't kill myself doing that.

DR: What was your relationship with Steve Jobs in the early days, and how did it change?

BG: We were both there at the very beginning. The Apple 1 was a kit computer that Steve Wozniak designed, and he worked with Steve [Jobs]. They came and offered it at various computer club meetings. We went to lots of computer club meetings.

That Apple computer competed with a computer from my first customer, which was the MITS Altair. Steve [Wozniak] thought that he would do the BASIC interpreter—a fairly key thing that let people program these computers in the early days—himself, but Woz got distracted, so I actually did the BASIC software that went on the Apple II. So I got to work with Steve [Jobs] quite a bit.

We were sort of colleagues in pitching the gospel of personal computing. We were kind of competitors. The time we worked together most intensely was after the IBM PC came out. Steve had a group, a small group at Apple, that was doing the Macintosh. He came to us early on, and asked us if we'd commit resources. We actually put more people on the project than Apple did, and did the early application software that used that mouse graphics interface, and so it was a huge win both for Microsoft and for Apple when the Macintosh became so successful.

DR: When you won the famous IBM contract to produce their operating system, why did they not say, "We want to buy this operating system from you"? Why did they let you, in effect, own it, and they had to license it? Was that a mistake on their part?

BG: Yes, this is before graphics interface, when you still just had text on the screen. The software MS-DOS was a key thing. In fact, when IBM first came to us, they didn't even want to put a disk in. But we pushed them to use a sixteen-byte machine and do a higher-end computer, which actually infringed on another IBM division's work.

It got to be more of a high-end machine, including this MS-DOS. They didn't see how big this machine would be, and their legal department didn't want to take responsibility for the source code. They had a fairly limited license. We understood that this was a seminal machine, and that other people would do similar machines. So that was fairly advantageous to us.

They didn't see the value being in the software. They thought the hardware was the key, and software was just sort of a necessary thing. If they had realized the vision we had, which was that software over time would be way more important than hardware, they would have negotiated probably a different deal.

DR: So your company grows, it becomes successful, it becomes the most valuable company in the world at one point. At what point do you say, "I've made a fair amount of money. I don't need to do this anymore. I want to do something else with my life"? Did it come to you when you were in your forties, or not till you were fifty? When did you realize that you wanted to do something other than just run the company?

BG: Nineteen ninety-five was a big year where we shipped a product, conveniently called Windows 95, and our software was doing well. We had always had the greatest depth of engineering, and we were slightly the biggest. We emerged as the successful company.

So I start thinking, "Wow, there's a lot of value here at Microsoft. What have other philanthropists done historically?" During the '90s, I'm thinking about that. My mom tragically passes away the same year I get married, 1994. My dad is volunteering to help us think about the philanthropy piece.

A Microsoft executive, Patty Stonesifer, was retiring, and available. It was actually in the year 2000 that I decided, "Okay, let's really get this going," so that later, when I went to it, it would have already gotten going. It was in the year 2000 that I put $20 billion into the foundation, and then it became the biggest foundation at that point.

DR: You mentioned you got married in 1994. You married a Duke graduate. How did you have time to woo somebody when you were running your company, and how much time did that take?

BG: Well, she was an employee of Microsoft. We had run into each other in New York City. We ended up sitting together at a dinner. She's an amazing person, and kind of caught me by surprise. That engaged my attention, even with all this exciting Microsoft stuff I was doing. We dated on and off for about five years, and then decided to get married.

DR: You put $20 billion in the foundation initially, and now have much more than that in it. The money that comes to the foundation has largely been the money that you made from Microsoft. But Warren Buffett called you one day and said, "By the way, I'm going to give you most of my money." Were you surprised when he said he wanted to give so much of his wealth to your foundation?

BG: That was a complete surprise, because Warren is the best investor, and he's built this unbelievable company. I was lucky enough to become friends with him in 1991. We became very close friends, and he was giving me advice about all the things I was doing. I was learning so much from him. But his wealth was devoted to a foundation his wife was in charge of. He hadn't funded it that much, but it was all going to go into this Buffett Foundation.

Tragically, she passed away, so he decided his initial plan wouldn't make sense. Much to my surprise, he had decided that a part of the wealth—a little over 80 percent of it—would come to our foundation. In addition, each of his children, in the original foundation he created, all received parts of it in these annual payments.

It was a huge honor, a huge responsibility, and an incredible thing. It let us raise our level of ambition even beyond what we would have done without that, which is, by most definitions, the most generous gift of all time.

DR: When your mother first said, "I'd like you to come and have dinner with me. Warren Buffett will be here. You should meet him," you didn't seem that interested. Why was that?

BG: Warren I thought of as somebody who bought and sold securities, which is a very zero-sum thing. That's not curing disease. It's not a cool piece of software. Looking at volume curves doesn't invent anything. I thought, given my way of looking at the world and what I wanted to figure out and do, and what he looked at, that there wouldn't be much intersection.

That's why it was shocking when I met him. He was the first person to really ask me about software and software pricing, and why wasn't IBM, with all of their strength, able to overwhelm Microsoft? And what was going to happen in terms of how software would change the world.

He let me ask him about why you invest in certain industries, and why some banks are more profitable than others. He was clearly a broad-systems thinker. It started a conversation that has been fun, and enriching—an incredible friendship that was completely unexpected.

DR: And he taught you how to play bridge—or did you already know?

BG: I knew how to play bridge. Our family had done it. Then, because it was a chance to spend time with Warren, I renewed my bridge skill, at first very poorly. But both golf and bridge were things that we did in the hours that we got to goof off together. Warren gave up on golf a few years ago, so my primary excuse to play golf has gone away.

DR: When you were building Microsoft, you did something that I've asked you about before. When somebody restarts their computer today, they have to use three fingers, usually. They put a finger on Control, Alt, and Delete. It seems a little awkward. Why did you do that, and why do people have to have that mechanism to turn on the computer?

BG: Fortunately, most machines nowadays have moved away from that. We knew there was logic in the keyboard that could detect a truly unique single signal that would bypass the software that was running, so you could know it was really starting over. If asked for your password, you would know it wasn't a fake piece of software, it was real.

It clearly ended up being an awkward piece of user interface. If we had to do it over again, we wouldn't do it. It was in the chasm between Microsoft and IBM that it ended up being that way. It's become the poster child of "Hey, couldn't you have made this stuff a little simpler?"

DR: When you were doing Microsoft at the beginning, you were doing the coding yourself, and could presumably know more about coding than just about anybody. Now that you have so many other responsibilities, when Microsoft develops a new piece of software, are you able to really talk to the software engineers at the same level that you could twenty years ago? Have they moved so far past your level of technical expertise that they have a level that you don't possess any longer, or that's not the case?

BG: I'm certainly nowhere near as hands-on as I was when I would either write the code or look it over and hire all the programmers. In my career, this evolution of being an individual performer, then a manager, then a manager of managers, and then setting broad strategy—you have to get used to the fact you don't have as much control.

There are some things that are very complex that you're not digging into in-depth, like the query optimizer, the code generator. But I try to understand enough about software [to grasp] the trade-offs we're making about what features we should put in, what the basic design should be. I still enjoy those discussions.

Even today, over at Microsoft, we get to talk about "What should the next Office do? How can Windows be better? How's the user interface going to change when we have speech, and handwriting, and those things?" I'm able to participate, but it is a way more complex field, and I couldn't actually write all the code myself anymore.

DR: You've been the wealthiest man in the world for twenty years or more. Is that more of a burden than a pleasure? People come up to you all the time, they ask for money, or they expect you to buy them things. How does it feel to be the wealthiest man in the world? Are you getting tired of it or not?

BG: Fortunately, people know that the wealth is dedicated to the foundation, and so they have ideas that are in the foundation's area—fighting infectious disease, improving education. Then it's super interesting to talk to those people. By picking particular causes, and saying, "Hey, that's what we're going to do," we're restricting ourselves to that. It means it's not some type of burden where people are coming up to talk to us.

I have the benefit of being well known. I can go out and meet interesting people, and share my views, and get a lot of attention. I'd say that's a net benefit. When I'm out with the kids, it can be a tiny bit of a drawback, in that you might not get as much privacy as you'd like. But overall, my success has allowed me to get more done, build partnerships, meet the right people.

DR: Do you carry a credit card? You carry cash, or how do you deal with it when you want to go shopping?

BG: I go shop. I go out to the theater.

DR: People don't come up to you all the time for selfies?

BG: They can, yeah, but that's pretty quick. People are usually very nice about it.

DR: Your foundation is not a perpetual foundation. Twenty years after either you or your wife—the last one alive—dies, it will end?

BG: That's right. We're managing the institution and keeping it excellent, and designing it to solve problems that can be totally solved. So we work on malaria. This foundation should be able to participate in getting rid of that—all these infectious diseases that so disproportionally hurt the poor, and really explain most of the difference between why a poor child has a fifty times greater chance of dying than a child in a wealthy country.

In thirty or forty years, those problems should have been brought to an end. Whatever new problems philanthropy should go after, the people who are alive then and picking great executives and building institutions to go solve them, they'll do a much better job than we can by just writing down a little guidance. So it is a limited-time foundation.

DR: In any given period of time, there's always somebody who's the wealthiest person in the world. Historically, people who are the wealthiest in the world have flashed their money. They do a lot of gaudy things. You obviously haven't done that. But whenever you buy something, do you have a sense that people jack up the price when they see you're coming? How do you have a sense of the value of money, given the amount of money you have?

BG: You try to be smart about how to use money. I don't buy many things. My greatest luxury is that I'm able to travel on a jet a lot of the time, which is kind of an outrageous thing. But it gives me flexibility.

So I don't want to waste money on things, but overwhelmingly that's making sure the foundation is run well. As the foundation's giving away money, I'll drop down that wealthy list quite dramatically, because we're giving away more than we're taking in.

DR: You decided that your foundation would focus principally on health in Africa and K–12 education in the United States. How did you come to the conclusion that those are the two things you wanted to work on? Are you comfortable that you have made the right decision?

BG: We talked about it a lot, and that's the decision Melinda and I made. We wanted to take the greatest injustice in the world, something that we could make a huge difference in, and that's health. We broadened that a bit by doing agriculture, and sanitation, and some other things.

Then we wanted to take up a cause that would help the U.S. be as strong as it could. And in that case, trying to help improve educational opportunity is our big thing. We think that focusing on those two things—there's a number of diseases in that health work, and a lot of pieces on how you try to help education improve—that that's enough.

We think it's great to get deep into those things and stay with them, so we feel great about those choices. There's a ton of worthy causes—certain diseases or institutions—that other philanthropists will focus on. We're not saying ours are the only ones, but we love what we're doing.

DR: With Warren and Melinda, you started the Giving Pledge. What is that about, and how has that worked?

BG: Warren was brainstorming with us about how philanthropists figure out what to do, and how they could share with each other without giving up the diversity of what they did. He got us to do some dinners with people who were already doing amazing philanthropy—people like David Rockefeller—and sit down and just hear from them.

At those dinners, a lot of people were saying that we should come up with a way that philanthropists can learn from each other and talk about how they've built staff and picked causes—not that they would give to the same things, but that the quality, and even how early people would get engaged, would be enhanced by people getting together and making a public commitment to give the majority of their wealth away. That's become the Giving Pledge group.

DR: You've now got about 160 people? [That number was 207 as of March 2020.]

BG: Yes, you're a great member. We get together every year, and have very good attendance. I do think it's encouraging people to think about philanthropy at a younger age. It's helping people do it even better. Philanthropy can be hugely impactful if you're getting good ideas from others.

DR: Are there certain issues you care about but just don't have time to get involved with? For example, climate change has been important to you, but is that something your foundation is deeply involved with?

BG: Our foundation is involved in mitigating the effects of climate change—helping people have better savings and more productive seeds, so that agriculture and health work will offset whatever climate-change impacts come along. But the part about changing the energy and transport system so we use zero-emission technologies, including nuclear renewables—that's a gigantic, for-profit business. That kind of high-risk investment—start-up companies, backing innovators in that space—I do that outside the foundation, because the for-profit format makes sense for that piece of it.

DR: You've got a life that most people would love. You're the wealthiest man in the world, one of the most successful businesspeople, the biggest philanthropist. Do you have any regrets about the life you've led?

BG: I feel I've been super lucky, so I'd feel bad to want to go back and change anything. At Microsoft I wish I'd done phones better, or done search better. There are many things where other companies seized the opportunity, and did an amazing job. Microsoft did enough that it's a phenomenal company. But no, I don't think back with remorse, because I think the mistakes help you learn.

DR: And you try not to make the same ones twice.

When people look back twenty years from now, thirty years from now, what would you like to have them say Bill Gates achieved?

BG: I don't think it's important for me to be remembered specifically. I do hope that infectious disease is largely eliminated as a problem, so that nobody's having to talk about it and people can focus on other issues. That would be a huge, great thing.

If our work has helped improve U.S. education, that would be a huge, great thing. Most important is that my kids feel I was a good father and gave them an opportunity to go create their own lives.

SIR RICHARD BRANSON

Founder, Virgin Group

"I never go into a venture with the idea of making a profit.
If you can create the best in its field, generally speaking
you'll find that you'll pay the bills and you'll make a profit."

R ichard Branson has led a life most entrepreneurs, indeed most people, probably dream about: successful creator of many diverse businesses (all under the Virgin brand); legendary daredevil-stunt survivor; wealthy business leader; global philanthropist; forty-plus-year marriage; close relationships with his parents and children; owner and resident of an idyllic Caribbean island; friend of the rich and famous from throughout the world; knighted by Queen Elizabeth II; a face and image recognized and admired throughout the world; and, not inconsequently, a very happy person.

What more could one want from life?

Richard Branson always seems to want more from life, and is always pursuing new—and sometimes dangerous—ventures. His latest has been Virgin Galactic, offering paying passengers a brief trip into space. That seemed a long shot to many when he first announced it, and this undertaking has confronted more than a few challenges. But few have made money over the years betting against Richard Branson.

Some might have thought he could not overcome early obstacles. He dropped out of school at fifteen, had severe dyslexia, and had little money at the outset. But Branson is a born entrepreneur. He has started several hundred different companies, many becoming for a time fabulously successful (e.g., Virgin Records and Virgin Atlantic). Every company was inspired by his vision: be daring; offer something new and exciting; appeal to people's willingness to take a chance; and sell an enjoyable experience as well as a product or service.

What has been the key to Branson's success as an entrepreneur and as a leader? In his view, surrounding himself with talented, innovative, and bold people.

But unlike other entrepreneurs who often say they want to be surrounded by these types of people, Richard Branson is actually willing to listen to these "smarter" individuals, and to make the midcourse changes they might suggest to his initial "brilliant" idea. He is secure enough to recognize that not all of his many ideas will work—a real strength in his success.

No doubt pursuing this worldview is helped by being talented, innovative, and bold. No doubt it also helps to be likable, modest, and self-deprecating—which was what I found him to be when I interviewed him for *Peer to Peer* at a Giving Pledge gathering in May 2018 in the San Francisco area. It was easy to see why Richard Branson, unlike many other self-made, highly successful entrepreneurs, is quite popular and well liked among those who regularly interact with him.

DAVID RUBENSTEIN (DR): You were not a great scholar as a young boy because you had dyslexia. Was it a problem for you early on?

RICHARD BRANSON (RB): In conventional schooling terms, it was a big problem. I would sit at the back of the class and look at the blackboard, and it was just a jumble. I was thought of as a bit lazy, a bit thick, or a mixture of the two.

If I was interested in something, I generally excelled. What I was interested in was what was going on in the world. I decided to start a magazine to campaign against the things that I thought were wrong in the world, in particular the Vietnam War.

DR: You drop out of school at fifteen or so. You start the magazine, and you get interviews with prominent people, one of whom was Mick Jagger. Is it hard to get an interview with Mick Jagger when you're fifteen years old?

RB: In some ways, if you're fifteen you have a better chance of getting interviews with people than if you're thirty or forty or fifty. I would just turn up at people's houses. Because I was young and enthusiastic, they generally took pity on me.

DR: Ultimately you decide to start a record company. Where did you get that idea, and where did the name Virgin come from?

RB: I was fifteen or sixteen years old. We were sitting in the basement with a bunch of girls, and we were throwing out ideas. We got down to either Slipped Disc Records, because of the black vinyls that always had scratches and slipped, or Virgin. One of the girls laughed and said, "Well, we're all virgins, and you're a virgin at business. Why don't you call it Virgin?"

DR: Did she get a finder's fee for that idea?

RB: If she's out there, I'd be delighted to give her one. But it was very fortunate, because we've gone into so many different sectors, so many different businesses, we've been a virgin in all of these different sectors. And Slipped Disc Airlines would not have been that good.

DR: Probably wouldn't have worked. So you start a record company. Initially it's a record retailer?

RB: Initially it was a mail-order, selling records much cheaper than any-body else had done. We were the first people to sell records at a discount. Then there was a mail-order strike for six weeks, so we went looking for a very, very cheap music store in Oxford Street in London.

DR: Then you start building Virgin megastores in the U.K. and other places. How many did you have?

RB: We had about three hundred megastores around the world in all the main places, like Times Square, the Champs-Élysées, Oxford Street, at the heyday of when music was really all that young people did—before video games, before mobile phones, before all the other things that young people do today.

DR: Was the success because of the Virgin name and your self-promotion of it, or you selling things cheaper than other people?

RB: Virgin was synonymous with music credibility. We had a very cred-ible brand.

One day a young artist came to me with a fantastic tape. I took it to a number of record companies. None of them would put it out. I thought, "Screw that. We'll start our own record company." And we put it out. It was called *Tubular Bells*, by Mike Oldfield, and it became a great suc-cess.

DR: Then you decided, "I need to start an airline." Where did the idea come from?

RB: I was trying to get from Puerto Rico to the Virgin Islands. I was twenty-eight years old, and I had a lovely lady waiting for me.

DR: You went to the Virgin Islands because you like the name Virgin?

RB: Actually, that's true. Anyway, American Airlines bumped us. I had been away from this lady for three weeks, so I went to the back of the airport and hired a plane. I hoped my credit card wouldn't bounce. I got a blackboard. I wrote: "Virgin Airlines One-Way $39 to BVI." I went to all the other people who were bumped, and I filled up my first plane.

When we landed in the BVIs, the passenger next to me said, "Sharpen up the service a bit and you could be in the airline business!"

And I thought, okay. The next day I rang up Boeing and said, "Do you have any secondhand 747s for sale?"

We started with one secondhand 747 against British Airways' three hundred planes and Pan Am and TWA's three hundred planes. British Airways launched a dirty-tricks campaign against us, and they did everything they could to drive us out of business. We took them to court. We won the biggest libel damages in British history. It was Christmastime. We distributed it to all our staff equally. So I think every year they hope British Airways will launch a dirty-tricks campaign against us.

DR: People liked the fact that you were against the establishment airline. One time I read you focused on what's now called the Eye—the big Ferris wheel in London. British Airways was sponsoring it, and they couldn't put it up and you rented a blimp?

RB: We actually had a little blimp company just outside London. We scrambled the blimp and we flew over the Eye, which was still lying flat on the ground. All the world's press were there to watch this Eye being erected. All we said was "BA can't get it up" on the side of the airship. And we stole their thunder!

DR: So it turned out pretty well. Then you began building other companies. Did you always think that the name Virgin and your creativity could get them off the ground?

RB: The only reason we would go into a new sector is if we felt it was being badly run by other people. The reason we went into trains was that the government were running trains. British Rail had dilapidated trains, miserable service, and we felt we could go in, get fantastic new rail stock, motivate the staff, and we could make a big difference.

I think that transformed the experience for people. In every new sector we've gone into, we've seen a gaping gap in the market where the big guys have not been doing it very well and we can come in and shake up an industry.

DR: How many companies have you started with the name Virgin?

RB: It's in excess of three hundred.

DR: Presumably not every one has worked. When you start them and they don't work, you end them after a year or so? None have ever been filed for bankruptcy.

RB: We've been fortunate we've never had a bankrupt company. If something doesn't work out, we'll make sure we settle all the debts and then move on to the next company.

DR: Is there something in your life you haven't achieved that you'd like to achieve?

RB: We've spent fourteen years working on our space program. It's been tough. Space is tough. It is rocket science. I think we are on the verge of finally fulfilling the dream. Before the end of the year [2018], I hope to be sitting in a Virgin Galactic spaceship going to space.

DR: You've had about two hundred thousand people, maybe more now, who signed up. Are they still there ready to go?

RB: Actually, signed up and paid up, it's about eight hundred.

DR: What does it cost?

RB: It's $250,000. About 50 percent of the people reading this would love to go to space. About 50 percent will think these people are mad: "What on earth do they want to go to space for?" But the market of people who want to go to space is gigantic.

DR: You think you can make a profit on this in the end? Or is it really just a love of doing this?

RB: I never go into a venture with the idea of making a profit. If you can create the best in its field, generally speaking you'll find that you'll pay the bills and you'll make a profit.

DR: Will you be on the first flight?

RB: I'll be on the first official flight. We've got very brave astronauts, effectively test pilots, who are testing the craft time and time again and ironing out anything that can go wrong before myself and members of the public go up. This year five of those test pilots became astronauts on the spaceship *Unity*.

DR: I'm sure it will be safe. But one time, when you were doing hot-air ballooning, you weren't sure whether you would survive. [Branson's 1987 attempt to make the first transatlantic crossing in a hot-air balloon ended in a fiery crash.]

RB: With the ballooning adventures, I was doing something nobody had done before. I was trying to fly across the Atlantic, or the Pacific, or go around the world in a balloon.

I was flying at forty thousand feet in the jet stream with one other person, Per Lindstrand, and the technology was completely unproven. We were the test pilots. Things could go wrong, and they did go wrong.

DR: But you set a number of Guinness World Records for that. In hindsight, do you have any regrets about taking those risks on the hot-air balloon?

RB: I think as a family we live life to the full. Quite often, when you're actually completely focused on an adventure, it's less likely in some way that you're going to die, because you're ready and sharp and know how to deal with it.

DR: You're well recognized for all the things you've done around the world, but your hair and your goatee are also really well recognized.

Have you had a goatee most of your adult life? Your hair is always this length?

RB: I've been a hippie, yeah, ever since I was fifteen years old. I've had a beard ever since I was fifteen or sixteen years old. I shaved it off once when we launched a company called Virgin Brides. I put a bridal dress on and gave people a good laugh.

DR: Now you're a "Sir." Did you ever expect to be knighted?

RB: We once put out a record called "God Save the Queen" by the Sex Pistols on the Queen's Silver Jubilee. Then I found myself twenty-five years later being knighted. I was slightly nervous that if she had remembered the words on the record, it would have been a slice of the head rather than a tap on the shoulder. But she forgave us anyway.

DR: In the late 1970s, there was an opportunity to buy an island in the British Virgin Islands.

RB: They wanted $5 million for this beautiful island. I thought I could scrape together about $100,000, so I offered $100,000. Nobody else, fortunately, came to see the island, so a year later they said if I make it $120,000, we'd have an island. I went everywhere to borrow and beg to get that $120,000, and we ended up with the most beautiful island in the world in the Virgin Islands.

DR: You've built a house there, and there's also a resort.

RB: Necker has become our home. It's a magical place. We have fantastic get-togethers with people, sometimes conferences there where we try to sort out the problems of the world. Or people come on holiday and book the whole island.

DR: Barack Obama and Michelle Obama managed to go to Necker Island.

RB: He was good enough to invite me to the Oval Office for lunch about three months before he stepped down. We had a lovely lunch. We basically agree with each other on most aspects of life.

DR: I guess he was a nice houseguest.

RB: Both of them are absolutely delightful. We had a fun competition, and he beat me. He learned to kite before I could foilboard. It was a great privilege to spend time with them.

DR: You've met a lot of great leaders. You've brought a lot of them together in something called the Elders—people like Nelson Mandela and others who were great leaders in their time. You were very close to Mandela.

RB: Very close. I was very, very lucky that for ten years we knew each other very well. So we set up the Elders, twelve incredible men and women who go into conflicts and try to resolve them. Conflicts are maybe the most important thing to focus on, because if you have a conflict, everything else breaks down.

DR: What is it that makes great leadership, in your view?

RB: Being a really good listener is one of the most key things. When I sit around listening to the Elders talk in meetings, I realize they've become Elders because they spent their lifetimes listening and absorbing and then only speaking by choosing their words carefully.

Another key thing is loving people—a genuine love of everybody, and looking for the best in people. Even if they're being a pain, you can normally find the best in pretty well anybody.

DR: If you're a business leader who wants to be Sir Richard Branson, what is the key ingredient?

RB: Surrounding yourself with great people. Learning to delegate early on—not trying to do everything yourself. Making sure you've got the kind of people who are praising the team around them, not criticizing them. And having people who are willing to really innovate, be bold, and create something that everybody who works for the company can be really proud of.

DR: One of the great things about your life is you've had a terrific family life. You've been married for more than forty years. Where did you meet your wife?

RB: I met her in a recording studio called the Manor, which is a studio we had in the U.K.

DR: Was it love at first sight?

RB: It was from my point of view. She was making a cup of tea. I looked across the room and I was absolutely smitten. She was with somebody else. I had to, I'm afraid, chase her.

My nickname became Tagalong because a friend who worked at Virgin knew her, and I would ask her if I could tag along when they were going out to dinner.

DR: Well, it worked out. And you have two children, whom you're very close to. I always think it's important if somebody successful can do this while their parents are alive. Your father died a few years ago, but he lived to be—

RB: Ninety-three.

DR: Ninety-three. Your mother is still alive. What was it like having your parents see your success?

RB: It was wonderful to be able to share it with them. My first $200 that I got to start my business—my mum found a necklace and went to the police station and handed it in, and nobody claimed it. She managed to sell it for $200. That was the critical money that helped me start.

We managed to share with them this wonderful life that I've been lucky enough to lead, and with my mother we still do.

DR: Did you ever think when you were growing up that you'd be wealthy enough to give away staggering sums of money?

RB: I certainly never dreamed that the incredible dream of my life would actually happen, and that I would one day be in a position to hopefully make a difference.

DR: Many times, people who become financially successful and are otherwise well known seem to be unhappy for some reason. But you seem to be a very happy person, very content. Is that a fair assessment?

RB: I'd be a very sad person if I wasn't a very happy person. I've been blessed to have an absolutely lovely lady. We're complete opposites, but we get on great. Blessed to have been together most of our lives. Blessed to have wonderful children, wonderful grandchildren.

And every day I'm learning. I see life as the one long university education I never had. I'm learning something new from getting out there, listening to people; I scribble everything down. I feel like I am a perpetual student.

DR: Let me ask you a question I've asked Bill Gates. Do you think you could have been more successful in life if you had a university degree? Obviously, you couldn't be more successful.

RB: No. At age forty, I turned to my wife and said, "I think I might give everything up and go to university." And she turned to me and said, "You just want to go and chat up those young ladies at the university. You go straight back to work." And it was good advice.

OPRAH WINFREY

CEO, Oprah Winfrey Network (OWN);
Actress and Producer

"Your legacy is every life that you've touched. We like to
think that these great, philanthropic moments are the ones
that leave the impact, or will make the huge difference in
the world, but it's really what you do every day. It's how
you use your life to be a light to somebody else's."

F ew American success and leadership stories rival that of Oprah
Winfrey's. Raised in absolute poverty by her grandmother, hired in
Nashville for her first job in television at nineteen years old, and demoted
from anchor to field reporter while working in Baltimore at the local
broadcasting station, she then moved to Chicago, where she became the
most admired, most watched television personality in the United States
for nearly three decades. By the time Oprah ended her show on May 25,
2011, she was a multiple Emmy Award–winning host with her show

available in 150 countries around the world, and had a reach into America's homes unmatched by any U.S. television performer ever.

In the process, Oprah also became a major force in American public life and dialogue, the wealthiest African American woman in the U.S., and a leading philanthropist, raising more than $51 million through her Angel Network. Hollywood could not have created a more unbelievable rags-to-riches story.

Beyond her daily talk show, Oprah helms a magazine; leads an eponymous cable network; and continues to foster reading through her world-renowned book club, which has supported the sale of more than fifty-five million books. In 2007, she publicly supported Barack Obama in his presidential campaign. Following her widely popular acceptance speech at the 2018 Golden Globes, #Oprah2020 trended on social media. (She has continued to decline running for public office.)

How did she manage to do all of this? How did Oprah become such an important and visible part of American life?

She was obviously determined to rise from humble roots. Many others have had similar dreams. But no one else became Oprah. (She really does not need a last name at this point. She is like Elvis, Cher, Madonna, Bono—one word says it all.)

I tried to get Oprah's perspective on her extraordinary career and life when I interviewed her at a Bloomberg studio in front of a live audience in New York City in December 2016. It is not easy interviewing a master interviewer, but I felt somewhat comfortable doing so. I have known Oprah since 2009, my initial year as chairman of the board of the John F. Kennedy Center for the Performing Arts in Washington, D.C. That year, she received one of the Kennedy Center Honors—an award highly deserved. No other daytime TV host or TV interviewer had ever received one.

In talking about her at that time, I related the story of my mother telling me, while I was away at college, that a new local TV personality in Baltimore was truly extraordinary and would no doubt soon be leaving town for a larger stage. I told my mother that was certainly not going to happen. Baltimore newscasters were never that great. I should have listened to my mother and invested in Oprah's future.

Oprah said that her critical skill as an interviewer was listening to what the interviewee was actually saying, and trying to understand the impact of what was being said. I have tried that approach to the best of my own ability. But Oprah has always had a unique way of showing

empathy for her interviewees and audience, and it's that ability to connect so viscerally with those watching that has made her so appealing, so
unique, and so influential.

In truth, Oprah does not need an interviewer to draw her out.

The interview is Oprah's format, and she was giving a master class
during this interview. I told her I thought she really had a future in
television if she ever wanted one. And I told her she might also have a
future as a presidential aspirant—she had all the requisite skills to be a
compelling candidate—but I realized later, as she instinctively knew,
that being Oprah was better than being president.

DAVID RUBENSTEIN (DR): The live audience doesn't intimidate you, right?

OPRAH WINFREY (OW): I feel right at home, actually. It's the one thing I miss from the daily show.

Every now and then, somebody will say, "Do you miss the show?" I don't miss the show. What I miss is the people, the camaraderie.

What I did every day was have my own aftershow with the audience. I would talk to the audience probably half an hour to forty minutes after every show, starting ten years in.

At first I did autographs every day. I'd stand there by row and I'd do all the autographs and never look up, trying to get through 350. One day I decided, "I don't want to do that anymore. But what do I really want to do? I want to talk to this audience. I want to find out who they are, where they come from." That became my favorite part of the day.

DR: Wow.

OW: It was my own personal focus group. It's the reason why we were number one for twenty-five years.

I used the information that I gathered every day from people who were the greatest resource. They were the people who were viewers, who had taken the time to come with their aunts and daughters and cousins and a few husbands who would be like, "Well, I came to *Oprah*. That's going to be good for at least two months."

DR: The show was on for twenty-five years in Chicago. You won almost fifty Emmy Awards, and it was voted one of the best shows in the history of TV. You ended it, though, after twenty-five years to do other things. No regrets about ending that show?

OW: No regrets whatsoever. I didn't want to be punch-drunk in the ring, still trying to come up with "What is the next thing, what is the next thing?" Over the years, we became our own greatest competition. When I first went national in 1986, every time there'd be another talk show, it'd be, "What are we going to do?"

I realized a couple of years in that you run your own race better than anybody. If you take the time to see what everybody else is doing, you lose your ground. I could be a better me than I could be anybody else. No need to try to compare myself to other people.

Once I got that, we hit our own rhythm. I discovered that it wasn't just a show, but that it was a platform on which to speak to the world. That was about 1989 when I thought, "Okay, what do you want to say to the world? How do you want to be used and not have the TV use you? How do I want to use it?"

DR: What drives you to keep working so hard? Why have you decided to work even harder than you did before?

OW: The thing that worked for me all these years—whether it was the magazine, which I still have, or whether it was the show—is that I understood there's a common denominator in the human experience. I want the same thing you want, which is the same thing you want and you want.

What we all want is to be able to live out the truest, highest expression of ourselves as a human being. That doesn't end until you take your last breath. What is the truest, highest vision that you hold for yourself? No matter where you are in your life, there's always the next level. There's always a next level, to the last breath.

I always knew that I would be done with the show when I felt like, "Oh, I've said as much as I could say here on this platform. And then, how will I be used?"

DR: Today, as you look back on what you've achieved already—and let's suppose you've got a long way to go before you're finished achieving everything—what would you say you're most proud of?

OW: I have a school in South Africa for girls. Just celebrated a tenth anniversary. I've got girls from Brown to Stanford to Elon, all over the United States, going to school.

Helping girls, because I was a poor girl and I know what that feels like, it resonates in my spirit. I know that when you change a girl's life, you not only change hers, you change her entire community, because girls give back to the family, give back to the community.

There's a moment that happened to me, just about a year after I went national. There was a woman in Ann Arbor, Michigan, who wrote me a letter that will go in my will. I'm not going to have a tombstone. But if I had a tombstone and wasn't cremated, it would go there. She said, "Oprah, watching you be yourself every day makes me want to be more myself." I just don't know of anything better than that.

Your legacy is every life that you've touched. We like to think that these great, philanthropic moments are the ones that leave the impact, or will make the huge difference in the world, but it's really what you do every day.

It's how you use your life to be a light to somebody else's. And it's how you use your work as an expression of your own art, whatever that is.

DR: You come from very modest circumstances. You didn't come from a wealthy family.

OW: *Modest* is not the word. I was poor. A lot of the girls at my school— actually, all the girls from my school—are poor. I was saying to them just recently—I was just in South Africa for a graduation—"You all come from the same circumstances. You are poor."

One of the girls raised her hand and said, "I don't like using that word." I go, "Well, if you're not poor, then you should excuse yourself, because that's why I'm paying for you to be in this school."

I don't have a problem with the word. I don't have any shame about it. Earlier in my life or career, the word would have bothered me. But I *was* poor. No running water, David, or electricity, living with an outhouse— that's poor.

DR: You were also shuttled between your mother, your father, your grandmother. That's very disconcerting, to be shuttled back and forth. At what point did you realize that you had some skills that were maybe going to enable you to rise up?

OW: I think in kindergarten I kind of felt it. I was raised on this little acre. I used to call it a farm. Then I went back and saw it. It wasn't a farm. It was an acre. I remember my grandmother taught me how to read. I grew up learning to read. We read Bible verses. That's how I grew up reading.

By the time I was six and got shuttled to Milwaukee, and because my birthday came at the wrong time, the grace for me is that I didn't spend a day in a segregated school. I did not have one moment of ever being conditioned to believe that I was less than anybody. When I walked into my first kindergarten class, it was the first time I'd ever seen little white children that my grandmother didn't work for.

Everybody was doing their ABCs. I was like, "Why are the children doing the ABCs?" I wrote my kindergarten teacher, Miss Knew, a letter, and I said, "Dear Miss Knew, I do not belong here, because I know a lot of big words." Then I proceeded to write every big word I knew. Anybody who reads the Bible here—it was Shadrach, Meshach, Abednego, Nehemiah, Jeremiah. Then I put in *elephant* and *hippopotamus* just because they were some more big words. I saw the impression that made on Miss Knew.

DR: Speaking of big words and the Bible, your first name came from a biblical source. But it was supposed to be—

OW: Orpah.

DR: How did it get to be Oprah?

OW: Misspelled the first day I went to school and it stayed that way. It's on my birth certificate as Orpah.

DR: But it's very famous. Very few people in the world are known by one name. There's Oprah. There's Elvis. There's Jesus. Very few people. Suppose your name was just Mary or Jane?

OW: It wouldn't have worked. I remember I had a news director who, when I first came to work in Baltimore, said to me, "We're going to have to do something about that name. Nobody's going to remember it or know how to pronounce it."

Up until that time, David, I always wanted to have a name like everybody else's. It was only when my bosses told me that I needed to think about changing it that I thought, "No, I'm going to keep my name." When I started in Baltimore, they started me with a campaign called "What Is an Oprah?" trying to explain to people how to pronounce the name.

DR: For those who may not know your background, you went to college in Tennessee, then you worked briefly in a Tennessee broadcasting operation. Then you were recruited to go to Baltimore, my hometown. My mother used to watch you. She would call me up and say, "There's a terrific person on a show here. She's going national." I said, "Come on, people in Baltimore don't usually go national." But she was right.

OW: Your mother knew.

DR: She was smart. You should listen to your mother. So, when you went to Baltimore, you went initially to be—

OW: An anchorwoman.

DR: It didn't quite work out.

OW: I got fired. Well, demoted.

DR: You got demoted. You had a contract, so they didn't say good-bye. How did you work it out to be on an afternoon show where you actually got to be an interviewer?

OW: This is what I now know with age and perspective—that many times, getting demoted or getting fired is an opportunity for something else to show up. Lots of people I've interviewed over the years have these stories about it being the best thing that ever happened. It puts you in the next best place. I was not a good television reporter. I was too emotional. I would go out on stories and then try to take blankets back to the people.

DR: You were also very young. You were twenty-one, twenty-two.

OW: Yes, but I was also very empathetic. I was always getting written up for getting myself involved in other people's business. I was making

$22,000 a year, and my best friend, Gayle King, she was also working there. She said, "Oh my God. You're twenty-two making $22,000. Imagine when you're twenty-five, then you're thirty." I'd be making $60,000 about now. It'd be good, $62,000.

I'm glad that didn't work out. Once I got demoted, they didn't want to pay out my contract. I was making $25,000 a year. They didn't want to pay me the $25,000. So they kept me on and said, "We'll put you on this talk show just to run out your contract."

DR: You did this afternoon show. Part of it was called "Dialing for Dollars." You were supposed to call people up?

OW: You have done your homework. Wow.

DR: I'm from Baltimore, so I know about this show.

OW: You'd be in the middle of a conversation, like right now. I'd get up and I'd say, "Gotta go do 'Dialing for Dollars.'" I'd move over to a little set and I would call someone. You'd go to the yellow pages, you'd dial, say, "I'm dialing for dollars. Do you know the count and amount if you are watching right now?" It was crazy.

DR: The show worked very well. All of a sudden, somebody comes along and says, "Why don't you do a show in Chicago?" And you decided to leave. Is that right?

OW: I decided to leave. My contract really wasn't up at the time. But I think everybody knows I've moved my whole life on instinct. When I've grown as much as I can grow in a space, that's my instinct to move.

I started to feel like I needed to move someplace else. New York felt too crowded, too hard to get around. It was the number-one market. Everybody wanted to come here.

I had an agent at the time, and I said to the agent, "I just want to be a substitute for Joan Lunden." Remember Joan Lunden? I said, "Could you just get me a job as the substitute for Joan Lunden when she goes on vacation and maybe she wants to take a break?" That agent said to me, "That's never going to happen, because they've already got one black person. Bryant Gumbel."

I said, "It's the wrong station. He's on another station. So maybe they would take one more over." But he said, "No, that's not going to work out." I let that agent go.

I ended up going to Chicago because I was on somebody else's audition tape. One of my producers had gone there. She called me up and said, "Dennis Swanson just saw you on my tape." She had been hired as a producer. "He wants to know, would you be interested in doing a job here called *A.M. Chicago*?" That's how it happened.

DR: It was an existing show. You got there and took it over and it became pretty popular. In fact, they changed the name to *The Oprah Winfrey Show*.

OW: People started calling it the "Oprah Show." You'd say, "Did you see the 'Oprah Show' today?" They weren't calling it *A.M. Chicago*.

And this is the thing: every single person other than my friend Gayle, who was still in Baltimore, had said to me, "You're going to fail in Chicago." Because I was going to be going up against Phil Donahue.

It didn't matter to me. I did not think that he was beatable. I actually said that to my boss, Dennis Swanson, who has gone on to do great things in television. He said, "We know you can't beat him. So don't worry about it, just be yourself."

That saved me. Because imagine little chubby me with a Jheri curl being told, "Now you've got to go and beat Phil Donahue." Dennis said, "We're just a local show here. If you can get a number, we'll take it." So I had no pressure. I just went on the air and I was myself.

DR: Phil Donahue ultimately left Chicago and moved to New York because of the competition, I guess.

OW: I have always said that had there not been a Phil Donahue, there couldn't have been an "Oprah Show." He paved the way for that kind of audience—smart women at home, many of them stay-at-home mothers taking care of their kids, some of them going back into the workforce in the mid-'80s when I started, who were interested in talking about purposeful things, meaningful things. He opened that door.

DR: When did you realize that you had a skill as an interviewer that was better than anybody else's?

OW: I never thought it was better than anybody else's. What I do think I have that is really uniquely my own is my ability to connect to the audience. My skill comes not from my interviewing ability. My skill comes from my listening ability. And my skill comes from me knowing fundamentally inside myself that I am no different than the audience.

What gave me the power in the seat and the power with the microphone was I always saw myself as the surrogate for the audience. I would ask people questions that I would not normally ask.

I asked a really embarrassing question once, not because I wanted to know the answer, but because I thought the audience did. I asked Sally Field, when she was dating Burt Reynolds, did Burt sleep with his toupee on?

DR: What was the answer to the question?

OW: I was thinking I was doing it on behalf of the audience. She shut down. I could see that it embarrassed her, and I never got another thing from her. So I thought, "Okay, that was wrong."

I learned from that. I would never do that today. I was doing it because I was getting pushed by the producers—"People want to know. People want to know."

DR: While you were there doing the show, you got an opportunity to be an actress in *The Color Purple*.

OW: Not just an opportunity. Oh Lord. I don't even have time for this story. Because I never wanted anything more in my life, David, and I haven't wanted anything since as much as I wanted *The Color Purple*.

I'd seen a review in the *New York Times*. I went and bought the book. I read it that afternoon. I went back and bought eight more books. This is before I had a book club, of course. It was, like, 1983, '84.

And I would pass it out. I've always been the kind of person that, if I find something that's interesting or sharable, I want everybody to have it. I went back to the bookstore, bought every copy that was there. I took it to work the next day and said, "You've got to read this book."

I started hearing that they were going to do a movie. Long story short, I auditioned for the movie, and only because Quincy Jones happened to see me on TV. He was going through Chicago, and my little show, *A.M. Chicago*, was on.

They were looking for an actress to play this part. I did not know Quincy Jones.

He's there in Chicago. He's coming out of the shower. The TV set is on. And he sees me on *A.M. Chicago*, and he thinks, "That girl could be in the movie." So he tells his people, who call me.

I had been praying and hoping to be in this movie. One day I'm just in my office, and I get a call. The casting agent says, "I'm calling about a movie we're doing. Would you be interested in coming to audition? The movie's called *Moon Song*."

I said, "Well, I wasn't praying for a movie called *Moon Song*. I was praying for a movie called *The Color Purple*. Could this be *The Color Purple*?" He said, "No, the movie's called *Moon Song*." At the time, that's what they were all calling it, because the director didn't want people to know he was doing it. I went and auditioned for it. I knew, of course, it was *The Color Purple*. And Steven Spielberg was the director.

DR: You got the part?

OW: I got the part.

DR: You were nominated for an Academy Award. You should have won but didn't win that year.

OW: But it's okay. The dress didn't fit, and I wouldn't have been able to get out of the chair anyway.

DR: Barack Obama was the first African American to be elected president. Now we've had somebody elected president who was a media figure, you might argue. We've never had a woman elected president of the United States. Have you ever thought, given the popularity you have and that we haven't broken the glass ceiling yet for women, that you could actually run for president and be elected?

OW: I never considered the question even a possibility until this year.

DR: It's clear that you don't need government experience to be elected president.

OW: Up until this year, I thought, "I don't have the experience. I don't know enough." Now I'm thinking, "Oh."

But no, that won't be happening.

DR: Today, as I look at what you're doing, your highest priorities are developing OWN and acting and also executive producing?

OW: I'm going to continue acting. I'm going to continue developing shows that speak to the humanity of people in a way that makes them want to live better and do better and that exalts their victories and lets them know they are important and meaningful in the world.

Every day, David, that show was like therapy for me. Every day of the show I paid attention. I've never been to a therapist. But I paid attention all those days on the show. And I made therapy acceptable for a lot of people who thought, "Not me, no."

One of the things I started to get in the mid- to late '90s was that everybody I had on the show would say something to me like, "Was that okay? How was that?" at the end of the interview.

I started to track it. I was interviewing a father who was in jail for life for murdering his twin daughters. At the end of the interview, even behind bars, he said to me, "Was that okay? How'd I do?"

Barack Obama said it when he sat in the chair the first time. George Bush said it. Beyoncé said it. She taught me how to twerk and then said, "Is that okay?"

DR: That's an acquired skill, right?

OW: Yes, the twerking thing. But this is what I learned sitting in that chair for twenty-five years. At the end of the day, whether you are interviewing me or I get to interview you, whatever your profession is, wherever you are in your life, in your relationships, every person that you encounter, after every experience, wants to know, "Was that okay?"

What people are really saying is, "Did you hear me? And did what I say mean anything to you?" I started to listen with that in mind, with that intention of validating that your being here, your speaking to me, your taking the time to do this with me is important because you matter. That's true for everybody who's watching or listening, that every argument that you ever have, every encounter, the person just wants to know, "Did you hear me? Did you see me? And did I say anything that mattered?"

WARREN BUFFETT
Founder and CEO, Berkshire Hathaway

"Look for the job that you would want to hold if you
didn't need a job. You're probably only going to
live once. You don't want to go sleepwalking through life . . .
Look for the job that turns you on. Find a passion."

Warren Buffett is widely if not universally recognized as the world's greatest investor. During his nearly seventy-year career, Warren has made more for investors (including himself) than any other financial manager in history. Now, at ninety, he is still going strong, with his principal investment vehicle, Berkshire Hathaway, enjoying a market value in excess of half a trillion dollars.

From the time that he was a youth, Warren was obsessively interested in business and investing. For a few years after Columbia Business School—he was rejected by Harvard Business School—he worked in

New York for his financial idol, Benjamin Graham (the coauthor of Warren's bible, *Security Analysis*).

He then returned to his hometown of Omaha and not only built the world's greatest, most admired investment track record, but did so in a unique way: with a small staff, no office computer, and no use of investment banking advisors; making quick decisions on transactions, with no competitive bidding or price negotiation, no unfriendly transactions; and with a focus on core industries at value (i.e., low) investment prices. He favors homespun aphorisms, has no interest in the trappings of wealth—he still lives in the house he bought in 1958—and invariably demonstrates low ego and self-deprecating humor alongside seemingly unhealthy food tastes, with no apparent impact on his sharp-as-a-tack brain in his ninth decade. Most recently, he's become one of the world's largest philanthropists, agreeing to give the bulk of his $75 billion fortune to the Bill & Melinda Gates Foundation.

Among investors who have admirers eager to learn their secrets, none has ever had a following to rival Warren Buffett's. Tens of thousands flock to the Berkshire Hathaway annual meeting to hear, for six hours or more, his latest observations. (In 2020, this was done virtually.) Scores of books and other analyses discussing his investment activities have been written, and these are avidly read by his enormous number of followers around the world.

I first met Warren a fair number of years ago, before he was quite so famous, and have come to know him better through Giving Pledge meetings and various investment and philanthropic gatherings. I have interviewed him on numerous occasions, and have always found doing so to be a complete pleasure and a learning experience.

In this interview, which took place in 2016, at his favorite Omaha restaurant, Gorat's, Warren discusses his rise from modest financial circumstances to global investment leader. He attributes his success and leadership to his passion for what he has been doing his whole life—looking at opportunities to invest in companies at prices that seem likely to increase and thereby create attractive returns.

Warren has stayed true to that initial passion—buying stocks or companies at a far lower price than their intrinsic and likely future value, and then, with few exceptions, never selling, thereby avoiding transaction costs and capital gains taxes. Warren does enjoy spending time playing bridge, giving away his money, and supporting the philanthropic goals of his family, but nothing seems to get him as excited as reading annual reports, finding an inexpensive investment, and then adding that investment to Berkshire Hathaway, the world's largest accumulation of disparate assets, all held together by Warren's insights and capabilities and dedication. Despite Warren's age, his investors are more than content that he is still leading Berkshire Hathaway. An investor who bought shares in the company in 1965 will have seen shares multiply in value 20,000 times by 2019.

There is only one Warren Buffett. We are not likely to see anytime soon someone remotely able to do all that he does and has done, all the while saying he "tap-dances to work every day."

DAVID RUBENSTEIN (DR): You grew up in Omaha, then moved to Washington, D.C., when your father became a congressman. Did you really want to move to Washington or did your father kind of force you? You were too young to be able to resist.

WARREN BUFFETT (WB): I did not want to move. I was having a great time. I was in eighth grade and had lots of friends. Everything was going wonderfully in the world, and now I had to move to this strange environment.

We moved first to Fredericksburg, Virginia, because my dad thought that Washington was probably a den of iniquity of some sort, and that if he could keep us geographically separated it might not taint us. I lived there for six weeks and I got very unhappy.

I developed this strange malady where I told my parents, "I can't breathe at night, but don't worry about it. I'll just stand up all night. You get a good night's sleep and don't worry about me."

That message got back to my grandfather, and my grandfather says, "Come back." So I went back and lived for a while with him. Then, when we moved to Washington itself, my family decided they'd heard enough of that.

DR: And then you went to Woodrow Wilson Senior High School. When you were there, you were doing jobs on the side. How did you start your business career in Washington?

WB: The best business we had was the pinball machine business, the Wilson Coin Operated Machine Company. That was named after the high school my partner and I went to.

We had our machines in barbershops, and the barbers always wanted us to put in machines with flippers, which were just coming in. But those machines cost 350 bucks, whereas an old obsolete machine cost 25 bucks. We always told them we'd take it up with Mr. Wilson. This mythical Mr. Wilson, he was one tough guy, I've got to tell you.

DR: When you graduated from high school, you graduated, I think, six-teenth in your class. You could have been first, I guess, if you'd spent all your time on academics. But you weren't as interested in academics at that time?

WB: I was not interested.

DR: Your high school yearbook said, "He's likely to be a stockbroker." You went to Wharton. Why did you go to Wharton, and why did you only stay two years there?

WB: I didn't want to go to college, but my dad wanted me to go. We didn't have SATs then, but he practically would have done the SATs for me. I always wanted to please my dad. He was a hero to me and still is.

He kept kind of drawing me along and said, "Why don't we just fill out an application for the hell of it?" He suggested Wharton, and I applied there. And they let me in.

After the first year, I wanted to quit and go into business. My dad said, "Give it one more year." So I went the second year, then I said, "I still want to quit." He said, "Well, you've got almost enough credits. If you go to Nebraska"—which I was quite willing to do for one year—"you can get out in three years." So that's what I did.

DR: Has Wharton ever called you up and said, "You were a half gradu-ate, you should give us some money"? Or they never bother you?

WB: So far they haven't tried that line.

DR: After that, what did you want to do? You wanted to go to business school?

WB: I'd won some minor scholarship at Nebraska to go to any graduate school I wanted to and they'd give me 500 bucks. My dad suggested Harvard.

DR: And you didn't get in?

WB: I didn't get in. The guy near Chicago who interviewed me took ten minutes. I spent about ten hours on the train to see him. He looked at me and he said, "Forget it."

DR: Have you ever run into that guy again?

WB: No, but he needs protection now.

DR: Why did you go to Columbia Business School?

WB: I was at the University of Omaha's library, leafing through catalogues, and I just happened to see that Columbia had Benjamin Graham and David Dodd as teachers. [In 1934, Graham and Dodd had written *Security Analysis*, the seminal book about what came to be known as value investing.] I'd read their book but I had no idea that they were teaching.

Dodd was an associate dean. Graham just came up once a week to teach. I wrote Dean Dodd and I said, "Dear Dean Dodd, I thought you guys were dead, but now that I found out that you're alive, I'd really like to come to Columbia if you could get me in."

DR: And you got in. Sometimes when people meet their heroes, they are a little disappointed. You met Mr. Graham. Was he as good as you thought?

WB: Absolutely. And Dean Dodd turned out to be a wonderful, wonderful friend the rest of his life.

DR: You did, I assume, pretty well at Columbia Business School. After you graduated, you wanted to go work for Mr. Graham in his partnership. How did that work out?

WB: It was terrific in the sense I was working for my hero. But Ben was going to retire in a couple of years, so I was only there about a year and a half. But every day I was excited about being able to work for him.

DR: What you were good at was picking stocks according to his formula, which was to look for companies that were undervalued. Now we call it value investing. Did you realize that he had some principles that were unique?

WB: By the time I went to work for him, I probably could have recited the words of his book better than he could have. I read his books multiple times. It was more a question of being inspired by him than it was of learning something new from him.

DR: Ultimately he decides to retire, and there's no more Graham partnership. Did you consider starting your own partnership, staying in New York City, the city I assume you liked living in? Why did you come back to Omaha?

WB: I wanted to come back to Omaha. I had made many friends in New York, but we had two kids by that time and I lived in White Plains. I'd take the train in, I'd take the train back. It didn't strike me as much of a life compared to being here in Omaha. Both sets of grandparents were alive at that time, and uncles and aunts. Omaha was a more pleasant place to live.

DR: You move back here. You're married to Susie. And you have two children, Howie and Susie. You buy a house here?

WB: I rented a house for $175 a month.

DR: When did you buy your house that you're still in?

WB: In 1958. My third child was on the way.

DR: You started a partnership here. How did you raise money? Did people know of you, or they knew of your father? How did you get the money to do your first partnership?

WB: When I came back, I had about $175,000. I thought that was all I would need to live the rest of my life. I could take care of everything. I really planned to go to school. I thought about going to law school.

I went out and took some courses at the University of Omaha. I had no idea of starting a partnership. But after I came back, a few months later, a few members of my family said, "Lookit. How do we invest? What should we do?"

I said, "I'm not going to go back in the stock brokerage business, but I worked for a partnership in New York called Newman and Graham. I'll start a similar partnership if you'd like to do so."

But I had no intention, when I came back, of doing that. That was in May of '56, and I came back at the end of January.

DR: Think how successful you could have been as a lawyer.

WB: That's true. I've regretted it ever since.

DR: Your first partnership, how much money did you actually cobble together?

WB: We met one night early in May of 1956. There were seven people there aside from myself, and they put in $105,000. I put $100. So we started with $105,100, and I gave them a little piece of paper called the ground rules.

I said, "If you feel we're in sync, if we're on the same page and you read these and you agree with it, join the partnership. You don't have to read the partnership agreement, but you do have to agree on the ground rules."

DR: Those people who put in that $105,000, today they would be worth—

WB: A lot.

DR: A lot. So that was your partnership. You did some buying of stocks. Ultimately you ended that partnership because you couldn't find any more companies to buy or stocks to buy that were cheap?

WB: What happened was that between May of '56 and January 1 of '62, I started ten more partnerships. I made a mistake. Somebody else, a friend of mine, read in the paper the notice on the first partnership and said, "What's this?" And he joined. And another fellow came from Vermont.

So I kept starting all these separate partnerships. I had no secretary, no accountant or anything. Every time I'd buy a stock, I'd break it into eleven tickets. I'd write eleven checks. I kept eleven sets of books, filed eleven tax returns.

DR: Oh, wow.

WB: And I did it all myself. I took delivery of all those stocks because I was worried it was other people's money. So I'd go down to the bank and have these things delivered right after. Then finally I got wise and on January 1, 1962, I put all eleven of the previous partnerships together in something called the Buffett Partnership. I ran that till the end of 1969, at which time I dissolved it.

DR: You dissolved that one, but then in 1969 you started a new partnership?

WB: No, by that time we had about $105 million in the partnership. About $70 million or so of that was in cash to be distributed. The balance was in three stocks, mostly Berkshire Hathaway, that I distributed, prorated, to everybody.

DR: Then you started buying more stocks through the vehicle of Berkshire Hathaway?

WB: Stocks and businesses.

DR: Berkshire Hathaway was a textile mill in New England.

WB: In New Bedford.

DR: It was a company that is now very famous because that's the name of your company. But it was one of your worst investments. Is that not right?

WB: A terrible, terrible decision.

DR: Why did you use a failed textile company name as the name for your company? Why did you not change it after a while?

WB: Because I made a dumb decision. I backed into buying a fair amount of stock in Berkshire Hathaway. They had a record of closing mills, and they were using the money to buy in stock. It was what I call a cigar-butt investment that you get one free puff on.

I bought a fair number of shares, close to 10 percent. They sold some mills. The CEO said, "What price will you tender your stock at?" I said, "Eleven and a half." And he said, "Fine." And then he sent out the tender offer, and it came out at eleven and three-eighths. That got me very irritated. So I went on to buy control of the company, which was a terrible decision.

DR: That was some fifty years ago. If somebody had been an investor with you when you bought Berkshire Hathaway, over the last fifty or fifty-one years, they would have compounded 19 percent or 20 percent a year?

WB: Yeah, about.

DR: Nobody else in the history of investments has ever done that over that long a period of time.

WB: Plenty of people have done better, though.

DR: Not better than that over that long a period of time?

WB: Oh, it's a long period of time.

DR: What would you say is the reason for your ability to do this? Is it that you studied the companies more than anybody else? You stuck to your principles? You're smarter than other people? You didn't get caught up with fads? What would you say is the reason for this success?

WB: We bought businesses that we thought were decent businesses at sensible prices, and we had good people to run them. But we also bought marketable securities in Berkshire. Over time, the emphasis shifted from marketable securities to buying businesses. At first we bought some stocks. Then in 1967 I bought a local insurance company for $8.7 million.

DR: Was that National Indemnity?

WB: National Indemnity. There were two sister companies. National Indemnity was the main one. That was a terrific deal, but it was very stupid to put that in with the textile mill. I should have just formed a separate company.

DR: You say "we." It's really you making the decisions, but you say "we" because you have a partner. It's Charlie Munger?

WB: Well, I had a partner. I had a lot of other people who were limited partners, in effect, and some of them are still around.

DR: How did you go into business with Charlie Munger? He's from Omaha, is he not?

WB: Charlie was from Omaha. I love him. He worked in my grandfather's grocery store, as did I. He lived about a half a block from where I now live, went to the same grammar school as my children, went to the same high school as my children. But I'd never met him.

In 1957, when I was twenty-six, I was forming a partnership with a Dr. Davis and his family. I said to Dr. Davis, "How come you decided to give me a hundred thousand dollars?" Which was a lot of money. "Well," he says, "you remind me of Charlie Munger." I said, "I don't know who Charlie Munger is, but I like him." Then Dr. Davis, a couple years later, got us together physically.

DR: Over the years, you've bought a number of companies and had stakes in companies. One of the ones that I know very well is the *Washington Post*. You bought a stake in the *Post* many, many years ago. I know that because I live in Washington and my wife had worked at the *Washington Post*. How did that investment come about?

WB: The Washington Post Company had gone public in 1971, right about the Pentagon Papers time. But in '73 the Nixon administration was challenging the licenses of two of the Florida television stations the company owned.

The stock went from $37 down to $16. At $16, there were about five million shares outstanding. The whole Washington Post Company was selling for $80 million. That included the newspaper, four big TV stations, *Newsweek*, and some other assets, and no debt to speak of.

So the Washington Post Company, which was intrinsically worth $400 or $500 million, was selling for about $80 million in the market. We bought most of our stock at about the equivalent of $100 million in the market. It was ridiculous. You had a business that unquestionably was worth four or five times what it was selling for. And Nixon wasn't going to put them out of business.

DR: So you bought a stake in it. Was Kay Graham upset initially?

WB: She was apprehensive. I wrote her a letter. She called it the "Dear Mrs. Graham" letter. I said, "I own Berkshire Hathaway, and it owns a little less than ten percent of your stock. We recognize that the company is Graham-owned, Graham-controlled, and we welcome that. I have been an admirer of the *Post* over the years, and here I am."

DR: You obviously admire the name Graham.

WB: Absolutely, absolutely.

DR: When you're doing these analyses, then and now, do you have computers that help you? Did you just get printed materials? How did you, in those days, get the materials to read about the *Washington Post*, and how do you do it today?

WB: Pretty much the same way, except there's fewer opportunities now. I met Bob Woodward back then, and he had just come out with *All the President's Men*. When the book came out, all of a sudden—he was below thirty years of age—he was getting quite wealthy.

We had breakfast or lunch over at the Madison hotel [in Washington, D.C.]. He said, "What do I do with this money?" I said, "Investing is just about assigning yourself the right story." I said, "Imagine Ben Bradlee [then the executive editor of the *Post*] this morning said to you, 'What is the Washington Post Company worth?' What would you do? You have to write the story in a month. You'd go out and interview TV brokers and newspaper brokers and the owners and you'd try to value each asset."

I said, "That's what I do. I assign myself the right story. It's nothing more than that." Now, there are some stories I can't write. If you asked me to write a story on what some glamorous but non–profit-making business is worth, I don't know how to write that story. But if you ask me to write a story on what is Potomac Electric Power worth, or something like that, I can write the story. And that's what I'm doing every day. I'm assigning myself a story, and then I go out and report it.

DR: So you get the annual reports, then you read them. Just like other people might read novels, you read annual reports.

WB: That's right.

DR: Then do you do the calculations of what things are worth in your head?

WB: Sure.

DR: Do you have computers that help you?

WB: No. If you need to carry something out to four decimal places, forget it.

DR: Do you use a computer today?

WB: I use it to play bridge, and I use it to search. I don't have one in the office, but I have one at home.

DR: If somebody wants to get hold of you, can they get hold of you on a smartphone or mobile telephone?

WB: No, a smartphone is too smart for me. [In 2020, Warren Buffett announced that this was no longer the case. He now has an iPhone.]

DR: And a computer you use rarely?

WB: One of the trick questions Bill Gates and I give when we're talking to an audience is, "Who's on the computer more, excluding e-mail?" The answer is, I probably am, because I play twelve hours a week of bridge on it, and then I use it a lot for search.

DR: Who do you play bridge with?

WB: My name is T-Bone, and I play with a woman in San Francisco who goes by the name of Sirloin. She's a two-time world champ. I'm a two-time world chump. So we're a good team. We've been playing together for decades.

DR: Are you at a world-class level after all these years?

WB: No, no. You couldn't have a better teacher than she is, but the student had limitations.

DR: You mentioned Bill Gates. How did you actually come to know him? It wasn't obvious that you would be a partner or a friend of his, because he was a computer person and you were not a computer person. He's interested in technology. He's twenty-five years younger than you, or something like that.

WB: Meg Greenfield, who was the editor of the editorial page of the *Post*, called me in the late 1980s, and she said, "Warren, I've always loved the Pacific Northwest." She'd grown up there. She said, "I want to know whether I have enough money to be able to afford to buy a vacation-type house on Bainbridge Island near Seattle."

I said, "Meg, anybody that calls and asks me whether they've got enough money does have enough money. If you don't call, then you don't have it." So she bought the house, and in July of 1991 she said, "I want you so much to see this house that you enabled me to buy by saying yes."

She invited me and Kay Graham and a few people out to the house. She knew the elder Gateses, so she called Mary Gates and said, "We're in town." Mary graciously said, "Well, let's meet at our home on Hood Canal." Then Mary went to work on Bill to try to get him to come, and Bill said, "I'm not going to go down there to meet some stockbroker."

Mary was a very firm type and said, "You're coming." He said, "I'm not coming." They started negotiating hours. She said, "Four hours." He said, "One hour." This went back and forth, and he came down. When we met, we talked for about eleven hours straight without being interrupted. We hit it off.

DR: But you never bought any of his shares?

WB: I bought a hundred shares just to keep track of what this young kid was doing.

DR: You've had a lot of highlights and some lowlights.

WB: You bet.

DR: One of the lowlights might be an investment you made in Salomon Brothers.

WB: That was a lowlight.

DR: You made an investment there, and later there was a crisis or a scandal. As a result of some things they'd done in the treasury bill market, you had to replace the CEO of that company. What was that like? You didn't want to be the CEO of Salomon, did you?

WB: No. Matter of fact, I got a call on a Friday morning. It was 7 a.m., roughly. It woke me up on a Friday, in August of 1991. On the other end was John Gutfreund, who was the CEO, and Tommy Strauss, who was the president of Salomon.

They said they had been told the previous night by Gerry Corrigan, who was president of the New York Fed, that they were unacceptable and would have to resign. They were going to stop trading in the stock. They were not going to be redeeming any commercial paper. How did I feel?

I said, "Let me get my thoughts together." They said, "You can read our obituary on the front of the *New York Times*." So I went down to the office and read the *New York Times*.

I achieved every politician's dream. I won unopposed. There wasn't anybody else to take the job. I, fortunately, had a job I could leave. I knew something about the business. I was untainted in any way by what had happened in the past. I actually flew back there that day, and on Sunday the board officially voted to make me the CEO. [Buffett ran the firm for nine months.]

DR: Many people would say you saved Salomon Brothers at the time because of your credibility and so forth. But that was really a low point in your business career because you had to do something you didn't really want to do.

WB: It wasn't fun. But I did it. To be fair, I couldn't have done it without Deryck Maughan, who was operating Salomon. I couldn't have done it without the help of a lot of people.

DR: What would you say are some of the highlights, the deals that you're most proud of? Let's take one that you did recently. The biggest deal you've ever done was Precision Castparts, about $37 billion in purchase price?

WB: It was between $32 and $33 billion in cash. Then we assumed about $4 billion of debt.

DR: To spend $37 billion, you spent a year studying the company?

WB: No.

DR: How much time did you spend with the CEO?

WB: I met the CEO, I think, on July 1 of last year. He happened to be calling on certain shareholders, and one of the fellows in our office had had a position in the stock for some time. It was an accident I met him. If I'd been out playing golf or something, it never would have happened.

But I went in, and I liked him. I heard him talk for thirty minutes, and I then said to the fellow in our office, "Call him tomorrow, and say if he would like to receive a cash bid from Berkshire Hathaway, we would supply one. And if he wouldn't like to receive one, forget we ever called."

DR: That was it. Did you hire any investment bankers to help with the analysis?

WB: No.

DR: Do you ever hire investment bankers to help you analyze a company?

WB: Not to help analyze a company. Sometimes they're involved in the deal. We're perfectly willing to pay a fat commission.

DR: One time you told me a story about how an investment banker was hired by somebody you were going to try to buy, and the banker came out and spent a week trying to get you to increase your price. Finally you increased it by a very modest amount.

WB: What happened on that was I said we'd pay $35 a share for an American energy company. They hired an investment banker, who came out and spent about a week, and they kept, you know, trying to get a high price. They said, "You've got to increase your price to make us look good." I said, "I'm not really worried about whether you look good." They hung around for about a week. Finally they called up and sort of pleaded and said, "Can't you increase your price somewhat so that we can send a bill and get paid appropriately for our nonservices?" I said, "Okay. You can tell them we'll pay $35.05 and you can say you got the last nickel out of me." So that's what we paid, $35.05.

DR: Normally you name a price and you don't depart from that. Do you ever do any unfriendly deals?

WB: No, no, no.

DR: Why is that?

WB: Although you could say Berkshire Hathaway originally was an unfriendly deal. We're just not interested. Not that unfriendly deals are necessarily bad. There are managements that should be replaced.

DR: People must call you every day and say, "I have a deal for you." How often do any of these deals ever pan out?

WB: They don't call every day. We've made our criteria fairly clear, so there's relatively few that call. When somebody calls, I can usually tell within two or three minutes whether a deal's likely to happen or not. There's just half a dozen filters, and it either makes it through the filters or it doesn't.

DR: One time I was told that you got a letter from somebody from Israel saying, "I'd like you to look at my company." What's the likelihood that somebody from Israel sends a company prospectus to you over the transom and you say you're going to buy it? And you did buy it.

WB: Yes, we did buy it. We bought 80 percent of it at that time for $4 billion. And then we later bought the remaining 20 percent.

DR: Before you bought it, did you go to Israel to look at the company?

WB: No, I did not go to Israel. I hope it's there.

DR: But you've since looked at the company.

WB: I promised the family that sold it to me that if we bought the company, I would go to Israel.

DR: You were happy with what you bought?

WB: Absolutely.

DR: You also bought one of the biggest railroads in the world. That's worked out okay recently?

WB: That's worked out okay.

DR: What was the theory behind buying a railroad? People thought they were kind of fossils as businesses.

WB: There are only four big railroads in the United States. Then there's two that are Canadian-based that come in. The railroad business had a bad century. They're kind of like the Chicago Cubs. Everybody has a bad century now and then.

The railroad industry got rationalized to quite an extent, and modernized, and the railroad business is a good business. It's not a great business, but it's a good business.

In the fall of 2009, we already owned a fair amount of BNSF, Burlington Northern Santa Fe. We scheduled a directors' meeting in Fort

Worth and I dropped in on Matt Rose. [Rose was CEO of BNSF.] He was giving his third-quarter 2009 earnings report that day. If you remember, the third quarter was the bottom of the recession. I knew it was a good railroad, and I knew the map was terrific.

It looked like we could do it at a sensible price. That was a Thursday. On Friday I said we would pay $100 per share if the directors were interested. He checked with them over the weekend, and the following Sunday we had a contract signed.

DR: If somebody comes and outbids you, do you ever increase your bid? Or you don't usually get into bidding wars?

WB: I don't think that's ever happened. There may be something way in the past.

DR: During the Great Recession, many people were in trouble financially. A number of them came to you for money—Goldman Sachs, Bank of America, General Electric, among others. Every time you worked out a deal, those deals all worked out for you?

WB: We said no to some others too. But they worked out. Those companies weren't in trouble independently of what was happening in the world. They were in a line of dominoes that, all of a sudden, people thought, "Those dominoes are very close to each other." The dominoes were toppling fast, and everybody was in line.

DR: So today we are not in a recession. We haven't had a recession for seven years or so, and we average one every seven years or so. But we don't have to have one every seven years. Do you think the economic prospects for growth the next couple years are pretty good? What is your assessment of the economy? [This interview took place four years before the novel coronavirus pandemic of 2020 and its economic fallout.]

WB: I think no one's been luckier than the baby being born in the United States today. The United States has a terrific economic future, and the world has a good economic future. I don't know what's going to happen tomorrow or next month or a year from now. I do know that people will be living a lot better in the United States ten and twenty and thirty years from now.

DR: You've often said, if you were born somewhere else, you might not have been as fortunate. Your view, still, is that the best place in the world to invest is the United States?

WB: It's the best I know of. And it's been wonderful. Nobody has sold America short since 1776 and enjoyed what happened subsequently.

DR: We were having roughly 2 percent or lower growth in the last couple years. You think that it's possible to grow 3 percent and 4 percent and 5 percent again in this economy?

WB: There will be some years. But 2 percent growth, if you have a little less than 1 percent population growth, means in one generation—twenty-five years, call it—that we will add maybe $18,000 or $19,000 of GDP per capita. Family of four, $75,000. So we're just beginning.

If you have an already prosperous economy—and we've got the most prosperous economy the world's ever seen—and you keep compounding it over time, people will be living far better twenty years from now than they are now.

DR: In recent years, presidents of the United States have called upon you for advice. Whoever the next president is will likely call upon you for advice. What would you tell the next president about how we might jump-start or get our growth to be slightly better than it is now? Is there something you would recommend?

WB: It would depend on circumstances at the time I'm called, and I probably wouldn't get the call. But I would tell them two things.

I would tell them that we've got the greatest golden goose the world's ever seen. We have a system that unleashes human potential in a way that allows people in my neighborhood to live better than John D. Rockefeller Sr., the richest man in the world when I was born. Something is working. And we don't want to mess that up, to start with.

The second part of it is that, in a country this rich, anybody willing to work forty hours a week should have a decent life. I would say that doesn't mean they have to equalize everything. We want to keep the golden goose producing more and more eggs, and we want to make sure that they get distributed in such a manner that anybody willing to work forty hours a week has a decent life for themselves and their family.

DR: Your secretary has become one of the most famous secretaries in the world, I suspect, because you have said your secretary pays a higher tax rate than you do.

WB: Counting payroll taxes, yes. Still does.

DR: So you're in favor of changing that.

WB: Yes. Some years ago, somebody from the White House—not the president—called and said they'd read my views on taxation. They said, "Would you mind having a tax named after you?" I said, "Well, if all the diseases have been taken, I'll take a tax."

But I really do feel that anybody that's making millions of dollars a year should have a combined payroll-and-income tax that is at least 30 percent. In my office, everybody in the office does have that except me.

DR: Wow. Your father was a conservative Republican congressman.

WB: Very conservative.

DR: And you're a liberal Democrat?

WB: I'm probably liberal on social issues. I would not be on the liberal side of the Democrats, but I would not be some conservative.

DR: How do you think you became a Democrat when your father was a big Republican, and you live in a very conservative state?

WB: Civil rights more than anything else. I didn't think about it when I was twelve years old or fourteen years old and I went to Alice Deal [Junior High School] and there was a school for blacks just a few hundred yards away. It just never dawned on me how different life was for other people. As I got to see more of the world, I decided there were a lot of things that were unfair, and the Democrats seemed to be doing a little bit more about it.

DR: Today you're admired by virtually everybody who cares about business because of your investment track record, the company you built, your integrity, and your sense of humor. What would you like to have as your legacy?

WB: I'd like to be the oldest man that ever lived, actually. I like teaching. I've been a decent teacher, and I have a lot of university students come out every year. I enjoy teaching. And that's what the annual report is. It's a teaching mechanism.

DR: Is there anything on your bucket list that you would like to do that you haven't done? Any place you would like to go that you haven't been?

WB: I'd have done it. You know, if there's anything I want to do, I do it. Money has no utility to me. Time has utility to me. But money, in terms of making trips or owning more houses or having a boat or something, it has no utility to me whatsoever. It has a lot of utility to other people, which is the reason for the Giving Pledge.

DR: What motivates you to still run a company when most people your age are playing shuffleboard or relaxing?

WB: They spend all week planning their haircut, usually. I get to do every day what I love, with people I love. It doesn't get any better than that.

DR: So you expect to keep doing this forever?

WB: As long as I keep my marbles.

DR: Your successor here is likely to be somebody who is identified after you're not doing this anymore. Have you figured out who it might be yet?

WB: The successor is identified to all members of the board of directors at Berkshire. The board at all times knows what they would do the next morning if I died that night.

DR: Right. And so the greatest pleasure in your life, other than doing interviews like this, is what, looking at new companies, making investments, giving away the money? What gives you the most pleasure? Your grandchildren?

WB: It's all of the above. But the truth is that I regard Berkshire Hathaway sort of like a painter regards a painting, the difference being that the canvas is unlimited. There's no finish line at Berkshire. It's a game that you can continue to play.

If I was a pro golfer, which nobody's ever suggested, or a football player or something, you know there's physical limitations on it. It's really not the case with what I do. Over time, I've assembled this wonderful group of people, many of whom are personal friends. They make my life easy.

DR: So you're a very happy person with what you're doing and you couldn't be happier and you still tap-dance to work every day?

WB: Absolutely. Absolutely.

DR: Is there any final word of advice you'd give to a young investor who would like to emulate you?

WB: Look for the job that you would want to hold if you didn't need a job. You're probably only going to live once. You don't want to go sleep-walking through life.

Whether you make x or 120 percent of x isn't remotely as important, in most cases, as whether you marry the right person and you also find something that you would do if you didn't need the money. I've had that job for fifty or more years. I was lucky in that I found early on what turned me on that way.

But don't settle for something if you can [avoid it], don't worry about making the most money this week or next month. When I offered to work for Ben Graham, I said, "I'll work for nothing." Look for the job that turns you on. Find a passion.

BUILDERS

Phil Knight

Ken Griffin

Robert F. Smith

Jamie Dimon

Marillyn Hewson

PHIL KNIGHT

Cofounder and Chairman Emeritus, Nike Inc.

"Hollywood will portray a leader as tall and handsome
and strong-jawed. A lot of times, the real good leaders
are just the opposite. First of all, they've got to want it.
But they come in all shapes and sizes."

In 1964, pursuing the idea he had earlier proposed in a paper at the
Stanford Graduate School of Business, Phil Knight began to import
running shoes made in Japan. That undertaking, thinly financed and
staffed, ultimately led to the creation of Nike, the world's largest, most
profitable, and best-known athletic-shoe company.

A few years ago, Phil, quite reserved and even shy by normal company founder/CEO standards, wrote a book, *Shoe Dog*, about his early
days at Nike. Given his personality and demeanor, it is not surprising
that in the book he attributes much of Nike's success to good luck and
timing, and to the help and leadership of others. But Phil Knight was

the leader who had the vision, drive, and discipline to take Nike to its dominant position in the sports-apparel world.

He retired as Nike's CEO in November 2004 and as board chair in June 2016, but he remains the company's chairman emeritus, largest shareholder, and inspiration. I came to know him as a fellow board member of the Brookings Institution, and as a fellow history buff.

Phil has regularly attended the Brookings board meetings for many years, invariably wearing Nike shoes and dark sunglasses—it is difficult to know at times if he is focusing on what is being said or catching a few winks. But I suspect he is mostly thinking about how to make his life's passion, Nike, into a company whose products are bought by every person on earth.

Phil does not generally give extended interviews, but I convinced him to do this one, held in March 2017 in Washington, D.C., in part by assuring him that I would wear my Nike shoes during the interview. I did in fact wear my Michael Jordan–branded Nikes, having bought them many years ago in the view that they would enable me to be a better basketball player. That has not happened yet, but hope springs eternal.

Although Phil is reluctant to attribute Nike's success to his own efforts, he does make clear that leaders are individuals who, whatever their background, education, looks, or intellect, really are committed to doing the hard work it takes to make a venture succeed. And this is an important point about Phil. He clearly was not only able to have the vision of a global athletic-shoe and apparel company, but was also willing to put in the long hours—and to suffer the occasional failures and crises—to make this vision a reality, and in recent years to turn the operation over to experienced managers who could further build the company.

DAVID RUBENSTEIN (DR): When you first started Nike, you knew nothing about shoe design, you didn't know a lot about management, and you didn't have any money. Today the company is worth a market capitalization of about $100 billion, with revenues of about $40 billion and seventy-four thousand employees. Did you ever imagine, when you started Nike in the early '60s, that it could ever be what it became?

PHIL KNIGHT (PK): Sometimes when I get that question, I say, "We're exactly on plan." But with you I can't be a smartass. It's been a ride that really nobody could foresee.

When we started out, the total branded athletic-shoe sales in the United States were about $2 billion. Last year we did $9 billion. Based on the original year, we're at 450 percent market share. We took advantage of the running boom, which became a jogging boom, which became a fitness boom, and we've benefited from all of that.

DR: Would you say the company benefited more from being a good marketing company or a good technology company? In other words, having a better product or having better marketing, or a combination of both?

PK: We're a marketing company, and the product is our most important marketing tool.

DR: What skill set would you say you brought to it? Was it great intellect, great drive, great leadership?

PK: All of that. No, if there's one thing, I've been pretty good at evaluating people. One of the things that I wanted to get through—and I hope did come through—in the book [Knight's memoir, *Shoe Dog*] was how valuable those early partners were—my fellow employees, my teammates. They were terrific.

DR: I must confess that before I read the book, I didn't know what a shoe dog was. What is it?

PK: In twenty-five words or less, a shoe dog is somebody that really loves shoes. That was me. I was a runner. There's no such thing as a ball in the mile, all you really care about are the shoes. That became important to me, and it's been with me ever since.

DR: You're from Oregon. Your father was a newspaper editor. When you wanted a summer job once, he told you he wouldn't hire you. Why?

PK: Well, he knew me pretty well. There were two major newspapers in Portland at the time. He was the publisher of the *Journal*, and he wouldn't hire me. So I went across the street to the *Oregonian* and applied for a job and got it. I worked there for three summers.

DR: In high school, you were an athlete. You ran. Were you a superstar or were you an average athlete?

PK: I was a little better than average, but I was certainly not a superstar.

DR: But you got a scholarship to go to the University of Oregon?

PK: No, I did not. I was a walk-on.

DR: Your best time, as I remember it, was four minutes, ten seconds, for a mile.

PK: [It was] 4.13, but that's close enough, yeah.

DR: Oh, 4.13. I gave you three seconds.

PK: That's right. I should have taken it.

DR: Suppose I tell you today that you had these choices: you could either have built Nike or run a 3.56 mile. Which would you have preferred?

PK: A 3.56 mile or build Nike? I'll take Nike. But I did pause.

DR: After a year in the army, you served in the reserves for a number of years, then went to business school at Stanford. How did you happen to pick Stanford?

PK: Well, it was and is a good school, and I got admitted.

DR: You got admitted. And there was a class on entrepreneurship.

PK: The professor was really a dynamic professor, an inspirational professor. He had you write a term paper, which was mostly what your grade would be. You were supposed to attach yourself to a small business in the Bay Area, or make up a small business. He said, "Make sure you write about something you know."

Most of my classmates wrote about some electronics project, which was beyond me. But I remembered my old track coach playing with shoes, and I was one of the guinea pigs for the shoes he played with, so I was quite aware of the process.

It just didn't make sense to me at the time that running shoes should be made in Germany, which was dominating the world's markets. I said, "They should be made in Japan, and maybe Japan can do to German shoes what Japan did to German cameras." That was the premise. I worked pretty hard on the paper, and the professor liked it.

DR: Did you get an A on it?

PK: I did, yes.

DR: Then you graduated. Despite this great paper, no shoe company hired you. You didn't then have the big Silicon Valley venture-capital world, so you didn't get a job there. You went back home and became an accountant. Was that exciting for you to be an accountant?

PK: I didn't ever plan to be an accountant for fifty years. I talked to a lot of people about what I should do. I was kind of a finance major at Stanford, and they said, "There really is no such thing. You should get your CPA certificate and it'll be a great education, put a floor under your earnings." So that's what I did.

DR: But before you did that, you went by yourself on a trip around the world.

PK: I started out with another guy, and he got waylaid by a girl in Hawaii. I didn't have that problem, so I went on alone.

DR: When you were in Japan, did you not stop in to see a shoe manufacturer?

PK: That was part of the idea inspired by the paper that I wrote—that I would call on Japanese shoe manufacturers to see about importing the shoes into the United States. I only called on one, and they were enthusiastic, and so it began.

DR: You came back, and they started shipping you shoes, to a company that you had named Blue Ribbon. Where did the name come from?

PK: They asked me, "What's the name of your company?" I had to come up with something.

DR: So you called it Blue Ribbon. They started shipping you the shoes, and your job was to then sell these shoes. As I understand, you had a green Valiant, and you would put the shoes in the trunk, and you'd go around to track meets and sell them.

PK: That's what I did.

DR: At that time, you had no vision of building a great global company?

PK: I thought it was the start and we could be bigger. Nobody expected it to be as big as it is.

DR: At some point they [the Japanese company] began to be competitive with you, so you began to build your own company called Nike. You needed a symbol, and somebody came up with this swoosh. You paid thirty-five dollars for that?

PK: It was a graphic-arts student at Portland State who needed money. We said, "We'll pay you two dollars an hour to practice it to get some designs." She spent seventeen and a half hours on that.

DR: Wow, thirty-five dollars. That's pretty good.

PK: It did have a happy ending.

DR: You gave her some stock.

PK: When we went public, we gave her five hundred shares of stock. She has not sold a single share, and it's over $1 million now.

DR: Wow, that's pretty good. So you began your own company after you parted ways with the Japanese company, Tiger. Did you actually design the shoes yourself, or were you the person who figured out what the shoes were going to look like?

PK: It reminds me of when they asked John Kennedy how he became a hero, and he said, "It's easy, they sank my boat." Tiger basically gave us an ultimatum that said: "Either sell us fifty-one percent of your company at book value, or we're going to set up other distributors, no matter what this piece of paper says." That gave us an idea that we maybe better change manufacturers. We were in a hurry, and I did the first shoes, yes, in an office in Tokyo over the course of a weekend.

DR: If you actually have better shoes, can you run faster? Or it really doesn't make that much difference?

PK: I think the shoes are key. We still believe that in the mile run, lighter is better and makes a difference. If you try to run a mile in a pair of dress shoes, as an example, you're not going to run as fast as you are in a pair of four-ounce cleats.

In the old days, when I was running at the University of Oregon, we had a lot of canvas training shoes. You'd go for a six-mile run and you'd come back and your feet were bloody. So it matters.

DR: When you started your company, the dominant companies were German—Adidas and Puma. Were they happy with you coming along? Did they try to get you out of business?

PK: They didn't worry too much about us until it was too late. We kind of snuck up on them.

DR: There was a University of Oregon runner, Steve Prefontaine, who was a legendary track star. You became close to him. How did you get him to wear your shoes?

PK: We worked at it, and worked at it, and worked at it. He had worn Adidas his whole life, but he was right there in Eugene. We had a small office in Eugene, and the guy that ran the office became his brother, practically, and ultimately convinced him to switch to Nike. He was our first really prominent track-and-field athlete.

DR: You went after others. How hard is it? You have to pay them to use your shoes, or they just like them so much they just wear the shoes?

PK: They all just like it so much they wear them.

DR: Really?

PK: No. Obviously, if they're good enough, they demand an endorsement fee from us or whoever they're going to wear. Other than Pre [Steve Prefontaine], the one that comes immediately to mind is Michael Johnson at the '96 Olympics in Atlanta. He wore the gold shoes, which lifted us significantly.

DR: A man named Tiger Woods came along, and you signed him up relatively early in his professional career. Was it hard to convince him to do this?

PK: Tiger Woods, you could see him coming from way back. He had won three U.S. Juniors, and then went on to win three U.S. Amateurs, in a six-year span from the time he was, like, fifteen till twenty. He would play occasionally in the Portland area, and we'd always invite him and his father out to lunch. We were working on that for about probably three years before we actually signed him.

DR: And when you sign him up, he then wears your shoes exclusively.

You began to make golf equipment as well, but now you're out of that business. Is that because you just want to focus on shoes?

PK: It's a fairly simple equation. We lost money for twenty years on equipment and balls, and we realized next year wasn't going to be any different.

DR: For a while you were doing casual wear as well. There was the aerobics effort, and there was casual wear. You decided to try to make athletic shoes into a casual kind of shoe. Did that work as well?

PK: Yeah, sportswear and casual shoes and clothes are still a fairly significant part of our business.

DR: In other words, it's not just for athletes. You try to now design shoes, and you have been for some time, for people who are just wearing them casually. You like it when people are wearing suits and wearing your shoes as well. [*Shows he's wearing Nike shoes with his suit*]

PK: You look great.

DR: Do you ever wear anything other than Nike shoes?

PK: No.

DR: So, when you wear a tuxedo or something, you wear Nike shoes as well?

PK: I wear black Nike shoes.

DR: So let me ask about basketball. You had somebody named Michael Jordan. That's a basketball player you've heard of, right?

PK: I've heard of him.

DR: Was it hard to sign him up? Why was his shoe so successful? It became the most successful shoe ever in the athletic world.

PK: It was hard to sign him up, because everybody wanted him. We won that bid; we won that war.

DR: Was it on your personality?

PK: Clearly.

DR: It's not money, it's just personality.

PK: No, we offered pretty good money. We had a lot of good players, but we didn't have really great players. We thought he had the chance to be that. He was obviously way better than we ever could have imagined, but, yeah, when he started wearing the shoes, we made them really dramatic. They were red and black and white. They had three main colors, and of course he was a very exciting player. He jumped, and he was quick, and he shot, he did everything well, and he was handsome, and he spoke well. And the shoe was distinctive-looking.

Then NBA commissioner David Stern did us a huge favor. He banned it in the NBA. We ran a big ad that said, "Banned in the NBA." Every kid wanted the shoe then.

DR: Michael Jordan hasn't played in the NBA for more than two decades, and yet the shoe is still maybe your best-selling basketball shoe. Why is that?

PK: When Michael Jordan retired from the game of basketball, we were selling about $700 million worth of Jordan product. It's now become a brand, and we're selling over $3 billion worth of Jordan product. There are some kids who really know who he was and that he's an all-time great, but some kids don't even know who he was. It just became a brand. It went from an endorsement to a brand.

DR: When you wear his shoes, can you jump higher? If I wore those shoes, I wouldn't be jumping higher, right?

PK: I think you might.

DR: The high point of your career, you would say, was when Nike went public, or when Nike came to the success it currently has? What would you say is the high point or the most favorable memory you have?

PK: I just look at Nike as my work of art, if you will. The whole painting is what matters.

DR: Let's talk about leadership: whether you're born with it, or you inherit it, or you become a leader by education. What do you think makes a great leader?

PK: Hollywood will portray a leader as tall and handsome and strong-jawed. A lot of times, the real good leaders are just the opposite. First of all, they've got to want it. But they come in all shapes and sizes, and I don't know that there's any one lesson.

DR: You are famous for wearing sunglasses. I appreciate your not wearing them at this interview. Do you wear them because you're shy by nature? You just don't want people to see you?

PK: I wear contact lenses and it makes the sun bright. And the future's so bright I wear them all the time.

KEN GRIFFIN

Founder and CEO, Citadel; Founder,
Citadel Services

"The market is rarely dead wrong. The history books are
littered with people who are 'smarter than the market'
who have lost all their money. When you're in an investment
and it's not working out, you really need to take a step back:
'What don't I understand in this situation?' If you really
think you've resolved all the unknowns that you can possibly
get your head around, you stay with your position.
But in the history of finance, the failure stories are
people who do not respect the market."

Fulfilling an early interest in and fascination with the stock market,
Ken Griffin started trading options, from his Harvard dorm room,
at a time when his classmates were no doubt focused on more traditional
student concerns. Had Ken not been successful, he might have gone into
another profession.

But he did quite well—by any standard. The result was that he went directly from Harvard into starting his own investment company, and ultimately built Citadel from its Chicago base into one of the world's most successful hedge funds and Citadel Services into one of the largest securities-trading firms.

The firm's success has given him legendary status in the investing and securities-trading world. It has also enabled him to become one of the U.S.'s most generous philanthropists, with a particular focus on education, and one of the country's leading art collectors and supporters of visual arts.

I have known Ken over the years—we both serve on the University of Chicago board of trustees—but have not been involved with him or his firm in any particular business. Ken is not someone who gives many lengthy interviews, and I was pleased he agreed to do *Peer to Peer* with me before a live audience at the Bloomberg studios in New York in March 2019.

In the interview, Ken's razor-sharp, brilliant mind becomes readily apparent as he discusses, among other things, how he admires and likes to hire those who have real passion for what they do. In his view, these are likely to be the ones who become leaders in their area of focus.

That is not surprising, for Ken is clearly passionate about his company. He's equally passionate about the importance of education and freedom. In time, his leadership in these areas may well exceed his leadership in the investing and securities world—and his leadership there is already legendary, perhaps because he came back from an existential threat to his business during the Great Recession.

I wish that I had known Ken many years ago and had invested in him. Those fortunate enough to do so have also been able to afford to be art collectors and philanthropists.

DAVID RUBENSTEIN (DR): The legend is that you began trading convertible bonds out of your dorm room. Is that true or not?

KEN GRIFFIN (KG): That is true. My freshman year at Harvard, there was an article in *Forbes* on how Home Shopping Network was overpriced. Having read this article, I went and bought two put contracts on Home Shopping Network. Lo and behold, the stock cratered, like, 30 or 40 percent shortly after I bought these puts. When you make a few thousand dollars as a freshman, you've made it—this is the moment you have dreamed of! That was what really started my interest in trading.

DR: You had never been involved in it before?

KG: I never traded a financial asset before that.

DR: Your classmates at Harvard were presumably doing other things, not worried about convertible bond arbitrage. What did they think of you?

KG: I was a bit of an anomaly. My classmates and I, we'd talk politics rabidly. We would have fun playing soccer in the yard at sunset and hoping not to run into a tree. You'd have your Friday-night fun. So, it was a college experience, but I spent a lot of time at Baker Library just trying to understand and to learn about finance.

DR: The story is that you installed a receiver in your room so you could receive stock-market data. Is that true or is that a legend?

KG: It's true. In those days, Harvard had a policy against any form of business on campus. The supervisor of the building gave me permission to put a satellite dish on top of the building so that I could have real-time stock quotes. Because, remember, this was before the days of the Internet. There was no way to get quotes other than, for example, a satellite dish.

I put the dish on the roof, threw the cable over the side of the building, and pulled it in through the window and down the hallway into my dorm room. With that, I had access to real-time prices to facilitate my trading.

DR: Did you have a roommate who said, "This isn't a good thing to do"?

KG: I purposefully chose a single so I would not have a roommate I would annoy every day.

DR: You presumably did reasonably well. By the time you graduated, did you say, "I'm now going to do this full-time"?

KG: You're going to love this. Timing is so important in one's career. When I started to engage in convertible bond arbitrage in 1987—I literally launched in September of '87—I was very confident as to how this portfolio would behave in a bull market and very uncertain as to how it would behave in a bear market. The mathematics on the way down are just much more nebulous than on the way up. I was short more stock than my back-of-the-envelope math would tell me to be short. And what happened a month later? It was the crash of '87.

So at that moment I became a "boy genius." Now, I knew I was "boy lucky" because I was short in the market intentionally, but outside investors went, "Look, this person's a genius. He made money in the crash." The crash of '87 was a defining moment in my career, and being net short gave me a track record early on that was attractive to investors.

DR: So you made money for this group of investors. You had investors when you were in college. Some people gave you money?

KG: I had a friend who was a retail broker, and this gentleman, Saul Galkin, came in to chat with my friend and me. My friend said, "Tell Saul what you're thinking about doing in the convertible bond market." I laid out my idea, and Saul goes, "I've got to run to lunch, but I'm in for fifty." I had no idea, but my friend was like, "You just got your first fifty thousand dollars to manage." That was really what gave rise to the start of my trading career.

DR: You graduate and you say, "I'm going to set up my own company." Your family says, "You're a little young to set up your own company," or they said this was a good idea?

KG: I was incredibly fortunate. My father was the first generation in his family to go to college. He was one of seven. My grandfather worked on the railroads. My parents always placed great importance on education. On my mother's side, my grandfather was an entrepreneur. He literally borrowed money from my grandmother's mother to start a small business and ended up in the fuel oil distribution business back in the 1950s and '60s. So that entrepreneurial bug was part of my mom's entire life. She grew up in a family that was defined by my grandfather, who was a bit of a maverick. The idea that I'd go off and try to pursue this dream to my parents was very much just "Go for it."

DR: You decided not to go to New York where many people do these kinds of trading operations. You decided to go to Chicago. Why Chicago?

KG: It was a tough choice. Obviously, from an East Coast school, most of my friends were going to New York. The firm that backed me out of college, Glenwood Partners, had two partners, Frank Meyer in Chicago and a gentleman in New York. The gentleman in New York was central casting from Wall Street. Extraordinarily polished. Understood financial markets.

But Frank . . . Frank was like my high school physics teacher. I just had a sense of trust in Frank, of comradery. As somebody who just graduated from college thinking, "This is how I'm going to make my career bet," I wanted to be close to Frank. That brought me to Chicago, which is where Frank lived. Lo and behold, you find yourself two years out of school and Chicago's home.

DR: How many employees did you have when you first started? And what year did you start?

KG: The official launch of our first hedge fund was 1990. It was probably myself and four or five employees at that point in time.

DR: In the early days, did you have to go out and raise a lot of money by meeting with investors, or the money poured in and you just had to worry about the trading operation?

KG: You and I have run into each other at places like the Beijing airport. Right? The joy of owning our own firm is we get to work for hundreds of people around the world, and we've got to be on the road to raise capital. In the early days, Frank Meyer was a fantastic partner helping me to raise capital. His reputation was pristine. His vouching for me was incredibly important to my success. And I was on the road.

DR: Who actually made the trading decisions?

KG: We had, in the early days, a series of models and analytics that would help to guide our trading decisions. I was very fortunate to have hired a handful of colleagues who understood the products and who had very good judgment.

What was most important, in many respects, in my life's journey is that we traded twenty-four hours a day from almost day one. We traded convertible bonds in the United States. We traded Japanese equity warrants in Tokyo. Then we'd trade the convert market in Europe. Why was this so important? Because I can only be at work thirteen, fourteen, fifteen hours a day. I had to learn to delegate. If I look at our success over the last thirty years, it really comes down to having learned to trust people, to trust their judgment, and to delegate to skilled people.

DR: Sometimes when you're a trader—which I'm not—when the market moves against you, you say, "The market isn't smart enough to know that I've made a better decision than it has for the time being, so surely it'll come back." Sometimes people wait for a long time and it doesn't come back. And sometimes people say, "Look, I made a mistake and I'll get out of it quickly." Which are you? Someone to hold on until the market comes around to your knowledge and wisdom, or to get out when it's going against you?

KG: The market is rarely dead wrong. The history books are littered with people who are smarter than the market who have lost all their money. When you're in an investment and it's not working out, you really need to take a step back: "What don't I understand in this situation?" If you really think you've resolved all the unknowns that you can possibly get your head around, you stay with your position. But in the history of finance, the failure stories are people who do not respect the market.

DR: Before we went through the Great Recession, how big was your company in terms of employees or assets under management?

KG: From 1990 to 2008, we grew from effectively 3 people to around 1,400 people. Assets under management, ballpark $25 billion.

DR: The Great Recession comes. How did you survive it, and how close did you come to not surviving it?

KG: *Survival* is the right choice of words. It was the only moment in the history of Citadel that our actual existence was in question. I did not foresee the intensity of the collapse that we were going to experience in the banking system. Being a levered money manager put us in a very precarious position as access to financing disappeared and a portfolio of financed assets cheapened in value because no one could engage in the arbitrage to keep the prices at equilibrium. We'd never lost 10 percent, and in sixteen weeks we lost half our capital.

DR: Did you think you might not survive?

KG: I'll make it very clear. I would go home on a Friday. If Morgan Stanley did not open for business on Monday, I would be done by Wednesday. If you remember, with Morgan Stanley, the question was would the Japanese follow through on their financing commitment. Their very existence was in question.

So you quickly come to terms with the fact that we may not survive, and it may be an exogenous event in some sense that causes us to fail. I had to accept that reality. Once I had accepted that reality, what were the best decisions we could make to survive?

That was the playbook we came to work with every day: We are going to fight to survive, knowing we might fail. But we are not going to give up.

DR: You've built up your business in the hedge fund world to what size now?

KG: We're at $30 billion today. We've been there roughly the last three or four years.

DR: Do you make the investment decisions, or do you delegate that to your various investment professionals?

KG: We've been here now [in the interview] for about thirty or forty minutes, and in our hedge fund today we'll trade about 3 or 4 percent of the entire U.S. equity turnover. There's no BlackBerry. There's no iPhone.

Ninety-nine-point-nine percent of the decisions that we make, my colleagues are making. I want the individual closest to the information who has good judgment to make the call. There's no way from my seat that I'm going to be able, generally speaking, to make a better decision than my analyst who has covered Xerox for five years or has covered Amgen for a decade. There's no way I'll make a better call than they will.

DR: It is said that you spend a fair amount of time recruiting very good investment professionals. Is that a big part of your job, recruiting others to come to Citadel?

KG: I have interviewed, ballpark, ten thousand people in my career. I will do two interviews today. I will do two interviews tomorrow. I am always, always looking for talent.

DR: If somebody is watching this and they say, "I'm going to be interviewed by Ken Griffin," what should they do in the interview to make you like them?

KG: "Make you like them" is a cognitive bias we have in interviewing people. You actually want to avoid being caught in that trap. I'm looking for two key drivers in a candidate. I'm looking for their passion. Do they actually love what they do?

There was a young woman who worked for us fifteen years ago, a year or two out of an Ivy League school, I forget which one. Her boss came into my office and he says, "She's going to leave. She's incredibly talented. She wants to go to medical school, and you need to convince her to stay."

I said, "With all due respect, the minute she walks in my office, I will offer to write her a letter of recommendation." If she wants to be a doctor, the world needs another great doctor, and I'm going to help her make that happen. I'm really looking for what's the passion of the individual in this field, because that passion's what drives so much of our success.

The second driver is I'm looking for clear accomplishment. I'm looking for individuals who have a demonstrated track record of having made good decisions and having accomplished things in their lives.

DR: Do you look for people who went to very good schools and did well there, or you don't really care what school they went to?

KG: I signed off on a hire this week for somebody who never went to college. He is an extraordinarily good software engineer. A number of extraordinarily good software engineers, they find so much opportunity early in life they never go to college. It's helpful in the recruiting process to have gone to a great school. But there are some exceptional people who never finish college. Bill Gates. Mark Zuckerberg. If you're exceptional, I don't really care what your background was. I care that you're exceptional.

DR: Anybody watching this will see you're obviously a smart person and might say, "I'd like to invest with this person." How does somebody invest with Citadel? Is there a minimum, and is there a certain rate of return that that person should reasonably expect? How long should they hold the money with you?

KG: I'm going to be the bearer of bad news. Our funds have been closed for a long time. We're not actively soliciting new investment.

DR: Your wealth has created opportunities for many other things, including philanthropy. How do you decide what your philanthropic gifts are going to be?

KG: Look, nothing is more important to American progress than education. There is nothing more important. Literally it starts at preschool and goes through our greatest universities.

I've done a lot of work in K–12 education. The numbers involved are staggering. If you look at a city like Chicago, we'll spend about $5 billion in K–12 education. Here's what's incredibly regrettable. We know how to educate youth in America. We just choose not to do it.

It's heartbreaking. In that arena, I spend much more time on the political front, because it's our body politic that is letting our kids down. It's simply inexcusable. It creates so many of the problems that we face today.

On the issue of higher education, America leads the world. This is not a given. It is not a given that we have the greatest universities in the world.

But I want to support excellence in American education. When Harvard or the University of Chicago is at the forefront of new ideas, new concepts, whether it's behavioral finance at Chicago or other work being done at Harvard, that impacts all of higher education in the U.S.

So Harvard is near and dear to my heart because of what it represents. It represents really the greatest body of ideas that we create in our country in academia. And the University of Chicago has a place very important to my heart for two reasons. A number of my colleagues at Citadel are U of C graduates. They've helped me build one of the great financial-services firms in the world. And then Bob Zimmer is at the university.

DR: He's the president.

KG: He's the president. Yes. He fights every day for free speech. Free speech is what makes our country free. It's unbelievable we have to fight this fight on college campuses for free speech. But we need to. The University of Chicago principles—which you and I both are aware of and which include a mandate for free speech on college campuses—I just believe in so passionately.

DR: You're obviously a successful businessman, philanthropist, art collector. Your parents must be very proud of you. Do they call you to tell you how great you are? Do they still give you advice?

KG: I'm certain Mom's proud of me, just as I'm proud of my children. We're all proud of our children. We don't talk about it much. I saw my mom yesterday. I was at a conference in Boca Raton. My mom's down there for the winter. We went out and had a quick drink together, and I got parenting advice—like how to be a better parent. We talked about raising children because that's near and dear to my heart. I have three little kids, and Mom's going through, you know, "In high school, here's how I thought about trying to encourage your interests," and so on and so forth. Parenting advice.

DR: Does she ever say, "Where do you think the markets are going? Where should I invest?" Does she invest with Citadel or she does her own thing?

KG: Mom's all set. Mom is going to be just fine.

DR: You have been somewhat involved in the political world, as a donor to Republican causes and conservative causes. What's your view on political matters?

KG: I've supported, over the years, candidates on both sides of the aisle. I do live in Illinois, which means that in our mayor's race, for example, I get to back who I think as a Democrat will be the most business-friendly, education-friendly candidate I can find.

You probably know this: I was an early supporter of President Obama because he came to me as the education president. You want my vote? You want my support? That's the issue. You come to me and you say, "I'm going to fight for education in America"? I've got your back. So that's number one.

Number two is freedom. In our country, a government that can take care of all of our needs also takes care of having left us with no freedom. It's very important that we as a country embrace freedom of speech, freedom of opportunity, freedom that our Founding Fathers put their lives on the line for. That's important to me. Candidates that really support personal rights, personal liberty on all causes, are important to me.

DR: You've obviously got many years ahead of you, but do you ever think what you'd like your legacy to be as you get older?

KG: David, I'm fifty, for God's sake.

DR: I know. It's very young. But Bill Gates pretty much retired at fifty from running the company. John D. Rockefeller retired in his late forties. So you haven't thought of retiring at fifty?

KG: Rockefeller grew up in a different era. Knock on wood, we will live much longer, much healthier lives. I really hope to contribute to society for decades to come, whether it's in the business realm or in the philanthropic realm. I want to be relevant to society.

I'm very fortunate to know how to build teams, to know how to make things happen. That wasn't a gift given to me. That's a lot of trial and error. A lot of learning.

If you look at the success of Citadel, we are far more than the sum of the parts. When you can put together the right team with the right mission, you can accomplish great things.

What I'm most proud of is how we've reshaped financial markets around the world with Citadel Securities. If you look at interest rate swaps, for example, we've helped to create a competitive dynamic that has brought bid-ask spreads down by roughly 80 percent in the last ten years. That's money that goes right into the bottom line: pension plans, corporate treasuries, and other parts of society, not into the Wall Street value chain. By bringing competition into the securities markets, we have caused a huge creation of value for the end users of these products.

ROBERT F. SMITH

Founder and CEO, Vista Equity
Partners; Philanthropist

"When I look back at those days and the formative
elements of who we were in our communities, I see parents
who gave generously of their time, energy, effort, and
intellectual capacity. That led me to always think
about striving for excellence."

Robert F. Smith is the wealthiest African American (now and ever), a completely self-made business leader who built one of the world's most successful and admired private equity firms, Vista Equity Partners, specializing in enterprise software companies. And he did this in a little more than two decades.

Robert Smith's innovation was in developing and implementing a rigorous series of intensive steps to dramatically change the way the software companies he was acquiring would be operated in the future. The formula he developed seemed to work without any visible failures, giving Vista an unusually high rate of return for its rapidly growing group of global investors.

Trained as an engineer, Robert initially took his engineering skills into tech investment banking at Goldman Sachs, and later into the private equity world. As his firm became increasingly successful, and profitable, he ventured into philanthropy, following the lead his parents had shown him as civic leaders in the largely segregated area of Denver in which he was raised.

His commitment to philanthropy has made him by far the most significant African American philanthropist. His passion is for helping less fortunate African Americans get a better education, and for letting all Americans know more about the contributions to this country made by African Americans.

In 2019, Robert received global attention for his commencement speech at Morehouse College, a historically black college in Atlanta. During his speech, he announced his intention to pay off all of the student loan debt of the graduates, and the debt their parents took on to send them to college—ultimately amounting to about $34 million.

Through his involvement in the Smithsonian Institution, the National Park Service, and the Giving Pledge, I have come to know him as a truly visionary business leader and an obviously passionate philanthropist. I talked to him for *Peer to Peer* in March 2018, at the Smithsonian's National Museum of African American History and Culture, an institution with which both of us have been involved.

Robert Smith is a clear role model not just for African Americans but for all Americans. He has built a world-class business, and has used that success to pursue world-class philanthropy.

Unlike many such successful individuals for whom clothes are not a high priority, he is a stickler for appearance. He's a throwback to an age when successful business leaders always wore three-piece suits. Robert always has one on. I used to have some, but the vests must have shrunk over the years, and they no longer fit.

DAVID RUBENSTEIN (DR): When you were growing up in Denver, the son of schoolteachers, did you ever think you would become the wealthiest African American in the United States?

ROBERT F. SMITH (RS): I was raised in a family of achievers. My mother and my father both had doctorate degrees in education. They emphasized the importance of a) becoming educated, b) working really hard, and c) trying to become the pinnacle of success in one's community.

When I look back at those days and the formative elements of who we were in our communities, I see parents who gave generously of their time, energy, effort, and intellectual capacity. That led me to always think about striving for excellence.

DR: When you grew up in Denver, was there a lot of discrimination against African Americans?

RS: I grew up in a predominantly African American community. We all lived there, for the most part, because you still had redlining. You still had the inaccessibility to capital to buy homes that created, in essence, the basis of a lot of the wealth in America.

Growing up, I really understood the importance of community. It was pretty much a segregated community that I grew up in until we started busing. Forced busing created desegregation, at least in the school systems.

DR: And your grandparents, what did they do?

RS: My grandfather was the postmaster for three post offices here in the D.C. area. Before that, when he was in high school, he worked in the [Russell] Senate Building, in the Senate lounge. He served coffee and tea, and took hats and coats from various senators as they came in.

When President Obama was first inaugurated, I brought my grandfather, who was ninety-three at the time. While we were sitting there in our seats, and feeling the majesty of the moment, he said, "See? Grandson, you look up there in that Senate building." He pointed to a window above one of the flags. He said, "I used to work in that room. I remember looking out that window when FDR was being inaugurated. I remember there wasn't a black face in the crowd."

And here we are. I'm sitting with my grandfather seeing the first black president being inaugurated. He said, "America's a great place so long as you're willing to work hard, and drive forward on a set of principles and ideals that are important and authentic." That sticks with me to this day.

DR: In the three jobs you had before you went to business school, did you feel any discrimination against you because you're African American?

RS: Oh, yes. In America I have and still do.

I remember a time when I was at Air Products and I was invited to give a talk in San Francisco at one of the big conventions. This man comes over and asks, "How does this work in the extension of the shelf life of rice?" I'm explaining the dynamics, the biology, and the organoleptic issues you have to think about in addition to the microbiological issues. The guy says, "You're a very smart guy. You just have your heritage to overcome in order to be successful in business."

That stuck with me—that after all of this wonderful work I was doing, he still viewed me through that lens instead of judging me on the work I had done.

DR: You went to Columbia Business School. I assume you did pretty well there, because you went to Goldman Sachs afterward. Did you go from working in the engineering departments of various companies to the financial engineering world of Goldman Sachs?

RS: It's quite an interesting story. I had done very well. I was the top student for our first year in business school. I had to come back for the summer graduation to get this award. There was a gentleman by the name of John Utendahl, who ran his own investment bank at the time, who was the keynote speaker.

He comes over to me after they gave me my award. He said, "You have a really interesting background. Have you ever thought about a

career in investment banking?" I said, "There's a bunch of former investment bankers in my class. I don't like any of them. They think they know
everything, and they're pretty arrogant." I said, "I'm an engineer. We *do*
know everything. It bothers us."

And he chuckled. I was happy that he didn't take offense at my joke.
I said, "Honestly, I don't understand what investment bankers do." I was
a scientist. I was a technologist. I thought about the world through that
lens.

This is another case where someone extended themselves for me,
which is why it's important that I continue to pay that forward. He says,
"Why don't you come to my office, and let's talk about it." He invites me
down. We sit down and we have lunch. And he picks up the phone and
calls people like Stan O'Neal, who at that time was the CFO of Merrill
Lynch and ultimately ran it, and Ken Chenault, later the CEO of American Express.

DR: These are all prominent African American business leaders.

RS: All of them took the meetings, and they introduced me to other
people to take meetings.

I literally had over a hundred interviews in the fall of my second
year in business school. I figured out that mergers and acquisitions was
the only business I wanted to be in in investment banking, because, with
the exception of warfare, it's how assets get transferred on this planet.
It's a CEO-level discussion. It's a board-level discussion. It's a strategic
discussion. That was quite interesting to me. I thought I could add particular value and insights to that particular business.

DR: What year did you join Goldman?

RS: In 1994.

DR: You worked there for a while. How did you decide you wanted to go
into technology banking?

RS: Like all things, in the land of the blind, the one-eyed man is king.
At the time, technology for us was defense contractors. We had another

company we took public called Microsoft. We had this other company called IBM. That was the world of technology as far as Goldman was concerned.

I was our first mergers and acquisitions banker on the ground in San Francisco focused on tech. Then we decided to form a tech group. That created another nexus and dynamic of opportunity.

DR: So you're doing very well out there, living in the San Francisco area, making a big success. By investment banking standards, I presume you're highly compensated. What propelled you to say, "I'm going to give all this up and go start my own company"?

RS: As an engineer I realized, way back in my Goodyear Tire and Rubber days, the impact that software really had on businesses. I noticed that very few software companies were efficiently run. Well, why? The big part was most executives who started software companies wrote code, or they knew a market opportunity and they sold code. There was never anyone who taught them how to run software companies.

Then I run across this small company in Houston, Texas, that is the most efficient software company I've ever seen. They had some very basic things they just did extremely well. I said, "Wow. If you took those basic things and applied them to other enterprise software companies, you could run those businesses very similar to the way they ran theirs. And it would create tremendous value in those companies." That was the idea. That was the conceit.

DR: And Goldman said, "That's a good idea. Why don't you do it?"

RS: Yes, in essence. I said, "If you actually thought about taking some of these practices, and buying enterprise software companies, and driving them forward, you could do pretty well." They said, "That's a great idea. Would you do that?" They gave me one of those offers that looked quite interesting. I remember my lawyer said, "This is a bad deal, Robert, but you should take it."

DR: How old were you when you took the offer?

RS: I was thirty-nine. Of course I started doing research. It was the same age that others left what they were doing to go start their businesses, so I said, "Well, let's go give it a run."

DR: You actually put a system together to make sure every one of your companies was going to follow the system. Can you explain that?

RS: Sure. We took these kernels of best practices and, in essence, have now developed a whole systemic approach: "Here's how you use this best practice to improve the efficacy of whatever that functional area is within that company."

The way I like to think about it, we install the best practices in those businesses that actually crack the Rubik's Cube of profitable growth. Not only are we increasing the profit margins, we actually can accelerate the growth of those businesses at the same time.

DR: When you became very wealthy in the last few years, you became very involved in philanthropy. Was this something that your parents instilled in you? Why did you decide to become such an active philanthropist in just a few years?

RS: Growing up, I saw my mother write a twenty-five-dollar check to the United Negro College Fund every month. Even when I wanted a new pair of Converse All Stars, she said, "Go earn the money to get them yourself." I said, "You wrote that check for twenty-five dollars, which I could have bought two pairs with." She instilled in me the importance of giving to the community.

My father was on the board and ran the local YMCA, the East Denver YMCA. He contributed time and energy and intellectual capacity to raising funds, so the kids in our neighborhood could go to summer camp and enjoy the outdoors and understand the importance of the outdoors in building one's sense of spirit and one's soul.

So all through my growing up, philanthropic endeavors were a part of my family and my family dynamic.

DR: You signed the Giving Pledge, which says you're going to give away half your wealth. Was that a hard thing to do?

RS: It wasn't hard. It's wonderful that Bill Gates and Warren Buffett and folks like you are out there being evangelists for what this is.

One thing we have to do is ensure that our society is a just society, that our society has the ability to cure its own problems. While we accumulate wealth on the one hand, we need to also solve the problems that are facing us today while we are alive.

I know today the problems that are facing the communities I care about. If I have the capacity to do something about them, frankly, it's on me to do something about them. The Giving Pledge is a good way to put a signal out there that says, "Listen. This is the right thing for anyone who accumulates wealth of any size, irrespective of whether you sign the pledge, to actually care about the community in very meaningful ways."

DR: The National Museum of African American History and Culture, where we are now—what attracted you to that cause?

RS: There are two elements. We have been stained by the history of slavery, and are still stained by racism. What we need to do is make sure we have a monument to the people who have actually put their blood into the soil that created what is the best country in the world.

That's point number one. Point number two, I think it's important that African American people have a place to come to feel a sense of pride of who we are, and where we're going, and also to contribute their story.

The majority of my gift is actually the digitization of the African American experience. Any family can now digitize their photographs, their narrative, their videography, whatever it might be, and it's now a part of this museum. People will be able to learn about their family histories in ways that come alive.

DR: You have another very interesting philanthropic project. You have a ranch in Colorado that you have converted.

RS: It's called Lincoln Hills. It's actually the oldest resort community founded by African Americans, a place where they could buy a plot of land for twenty-five dollars and build a cabin. That's where they would come in summer, and spend their vacations.

I went up there the first time when I was just six months old. It goes way back in history. Everyone from Duke Ellington to Zora Neale

Hurston to Langston Hughes and Count Basie all came and stayed there, because they could not stay in the hotels in Denver during that period of history.

Over time, after desegregation, the ranch, like a lot of the African American institutions, fell into disrepair and got sold off in different parts. Now we've developed a wonderful program that serves our community in so many different ways. Six thousand inner-city kids every summer come to the ranch. We also get two hundred to three hundred wounded veterans every year.

In the winter, though, when the ranch is pretty much shut down, one of the things that we identified—my wife identified this—was that there are programs, one's called Together We Rise, which we partner with, that handle placing out foster kids. We have built at the ranch a sixteen-bedroom ranch house, and we can host up to thirty kids during the holidays. We host them and do all sorts of fun activities with them during the Christmas holidays.

DR: Now, your parents are alive?

RS: My mother still is.

DR: She must be extremely proud of what you've achieved. Does she call you all the time to tell you how great you are?

RS: She usually calls me to tell me what I need to do a little better. Her thoughtfulness about what our community needs is still very relevant and valid. She identifies areas that she says, "You know, Robert, you need to think about this. How can you help this one kid, or these hundreds of kids, in certain ways?"

DR: What would you like to have people say is your legacy? Eventually you might slow down. You might do something else. Would you ever go into government?

RS: I don't know. Like all things, you look for areas that you can bring a unique solution to and solve a problem. The problems I want to solve now are an equalization of opportunity for African Americans, to help them on board into the commercial enterprise that is America.

How do we create sustainable career opportunities for people—not just a job, or not just a place to go work? I think it's through education. It's through internships. I hope that I'm able to establish and build a sustainable fabric to identify these folks, get them educated in a series of schools, get them the right internships, and put them on a path to be not only creative business leaders but also creative engineers and technologists who contribute to the fabric of America.

DR: Robert Smith, it's a great story, a great American story.

JAMIE DIMON

Chairman and CEO, JPMorgan Chase & Co.

"My contribution to making it a better world is running
a good JPMorgan Chase. I tell people, 'If I don't do a good
job at JPMorgan Chase, I hurt the opportunities for our people.
I hurt the opportunities for the two thousand hamlets we do
business in. We can be philanthropic. We can help people
grow. If I do a good job, we can do all those things.' I'm
not an artist. I'm not a tennis player. I'm not a musician.
I'm not a politician. This is my contribution."

J amie Dimon has been the world's best-known, most respected, and most successful commercial banker since he became CEO and president of JPMorgan Chase in 2005. During his tenure, its market value has increased from $132 billion to $429 billion, its assets under management from $828 billion to $2.2 trillion, and its stock price from $38.57 to $111.23 as of early June 2020.

This level of banking-industry achievement might not have been predicted when Jamie, fresh out of Harvard Business School, passed on offers from Goldman Sachs and Morgan Stanley to work for a family friend, Sandy Weill, then at American Express. That path seemed to work for a while, but Jamie was eventually and very publicly fired as the president of Citigroup, a company that he helped create—and fired by his onetime mentor and friend, Sandy Weill.

I tried around that time to recruit Jamie to Carlyle, but he was resolute in waiting for the right opportunity for his skill set—running a large bank. When the right opportunity came—to lead Bank One—Jamie took it, grew the bank, and sold it to JPMorgan.

The rest became banking history, as he built that bank into the world's strongest. How did Jamie overcome his big career setback, and how did he simultaneously come to symbolize banking, business, and leadership for so many around the world?

His skills are obvious to all who know him: a first-rate intellect, a passion for knowing all the details and surrounding himself with talented individuals, a willingness to take risks and be outspoken, a commitment to long working hours, and an infectious enthusiasm for building and leading a successful global bank. That is a rare combination.

Any one of those qualities can produce an outstanding business leader. All of them in one leader can produce, as with Jamie, a once-in-a-generation phenomenon.

Someone else with this track record might say: Why not leave at the top? Or why not serve in a senior U.S. government position?

Jamie has stayed at JPMorgan because he loves what he does, and relishes building an even stronger bank. While he has said he would love to be U.S. president, he recognizes as a Democrat that his party is unlikely to nominate the CEO of the nation's leading commercial bank. All of this is to the good fortune of JPMorgan's shareholders, customers, clients, and employees.

I have known Jamie since his early days in the financial world, and have interviewed him on several occasions. He is always an exciting, colorful, insightful, and frank interviewee—also a rare combination.

This interview, done at the Economic Club of Washington, D.C., in September 2016, is one that Warren Buffett subsequently told a number of his friends to watch. He really admired what Jamie had to say, especially about the strengths of the United States.

Since the interview, Jamie had heart surgery in March of 2020. He was able to return to work remotely in early April, to the delight of his many friends, colleagues, and admirers. It is hard to imagine anyone but Jamie leading the bank—no doubt Mr. J. P. Morgan himself would agree that he never had a better successor.

DAVID RUBENSTEIN (DR): Your father was a stockbroker and you started out with some background in this area, but did you ever consider going into banking?

JAMIE DIMON (JD): No. I knew more what I didn't want to do. I didn't want to be a lawyer and I didn't want to be a doctor. I wanted to be part of building something.

I grew up around stockbrokers and Wall Street. I was always in the financial world, but to me it's just building something. So I went to business school. I didn't have to go into the financial world, but it was fascinating. Everything you read in the paper matters. They're global and you get involved in so many policy issues. It was just a fun place to build, but I would have had just as much fun building something else, to tell you the truth.

DR: Normally, if someone is a Baker Scholar at Harvard Business School—in the top 5 percent of the graduating class—they can pick almost any job they want. You could have gone to Goldman Sachs, which is a great firm. You chose to go work for Sandy Weill. Why did you do that?

JD: Sandy had a small brokerage that he sold to American Express. I found him to be down-to-earth. He had offered me a chance to go to Shearson, their investment bank. I said no, because I had offers from Goldman Sachs, Morgan Stanley, and Lehman. I thought I would learn a lot more at these other places than at Shearson.

They eventually called me up. I was a Baker Scholar, which was important to Sandy, and he said, "Why don't you just come here and be my assistant? You'll learn a lot. I don't know what's going to happen."

He lasted at American Express about three more years. But I did learn a lot.

DR: When he left, he was eased out.

JD: He left, and I left with him. I was offered a bunch of jobs to stay, but he said, "We're going to find something and build something great." He took over this little company called Commercial Credit in Baltimore. One of my babies was born in Sinai Hospital in Baltimore.

I moved down here and we took this little company. It had a consumer finance thing and other little companies, including a leasing company in Israel, a small international bank—which ultimately went bankrupt—that made something called lesser-developed-country loans, a property casualty company, a small life-insurance company. That company is the same company that became Citi.

Over those twelve years we bought Primerica, Smith Barney, Shearson, Salomon Brothers, Aetna Property-Casualty, Travelers Life, Travelers Property Casualty. We did a good job running them. We did a good job for shareholders and merged the conglomerate with Citi. It was a hell of a run, and then he fired me.

A year later I called him up—I called him, he didn't call me, just so you know—and I said, "Sandy, it's time to break bread." I wanted to do it privately. He said, "No, we'll meet at the Four Seasons restaurant." It was on the front page of the *Financial Times*: "Dimon, Weill Have Lunch."

He was a little nervous. I said, "Sandy, we're not going to spend any time on the past. All I want to say is you did the wrong thing for the company. I made a lot of mistakes too, and here are some of the mistakes I made." After I gave him the mistakes I made, he said, "Thank you for sharing that with me." We had a very nice lunch, and life goes on.

DR: When you were fired and you were looking for something to do, you had a lot of job offers. You were offered the job of CEO of Home Depot—

JD: I was offered Home Depot and a couple of big international investment banks—not to run their parent company but to run the investment bank.

Hank Greenberg, who ran AIG, said, "Why don't you come over here?" All I could think to myself was, "To go from Sandy Weill to Hank Greenberg—can you imagine?!"

A bunch of private equity folks called. Jeff Bezos called me up. He was looking for a president. I love the guy, and we have been friends ever since. I was thinking, "I would never have to wear a suit again. I'm going to get one of those houseboats in Seattle." I spent my whole life in financial services, so I told him working for him would be like playing tennis your whole life and then going to play golf.

I went down to have dinner with Bernie Marcus and Arthur Blank and Ken Langone, and I said to them, "I have to confess to you guys, until you called me up, I had never been in a Home Depot." The only reason I went is because a guy who worked for me said, "Jamie, you've got to go to one before you go to that dinner."

They didn't care. They said, "We want you, the person. We're looking for the heart, the mind, the spirit. We're not interested in what you know about merchants and stuff like that."

A couple of Internet companies called. With a lot of them, it was about money: "Oh, you'll make a billion dollars." With Bank One [earlier First Chicago], I figured, "This is my chance." How many major financial companies are there? Thirty? How many have changed their CEO in a three- or four- or five-year period? Four or five? How many of those are going to go outside? One? It's probably going to be a troubled one. So I said, "This is my Commercial Credit. It will be what we make it."

I put a lot of my money into it, not because I thought the stock was cheap. I look at business like "I wear the jersey every day. I'm not a hired gun. I'm going to bleed for the company and give it everything I've got and then hand it off to someone else." I don't like people who work at a company and talk about it like it's a third party. It's not a third party to me. This is what I do.

I don't do what I do for the compensation.

DR: When you went to Bank One, you moved to Chicago. Did you ever expect you'd move back to New York? Or you thought you were going to Chicago and that was your career there?

JD: I had no idea. I love Chicago, by the way. It's a great city. And I really didn't know, though there's a cartoon of me sitting at an airport and someone is saying to me, "Mr. Dimon, there are no scheduled flights to New York."

When I went to Chicago, they didn't believe it. "Are you moving here? Are your kids going to school here?" I said, "Yes, I'm really here. I'm staying here." I used to say that if I stayed my whole life and died in

Chicago and they shipped my ashes back to New York, they would say, "We told you."

The banking industry was consolidating. It's still kind of consolidating. I knew that if I did a good job I'd probably be part of that, but I didn't know whether I'd be an acquirer, building up a bigger regional bank, or be an acquire.

But remember, it's not up to me. It's also up to a board of directors. To me the thing is to make the company as good as you can, and it actually creates all the opportunities you have.

DR: You come to Washington from time to time to meet regulators and legislators. What kind of experience is that for you?

JD: It's important that businesses get involved in Washington. I'm not a person who says you never go there.

Policy is set here. There are a lot of people here who really do care about making it a better country. If you don't get involved, that means policy will be set by other people. So it's necessary.

I travel the United States of America, and when I go to groups like this, in any city, I get an earful about regulations, completely unrelated to banks. This is a serious issue—diminishing the regulatory burden that's being put on the economy.

When you come down to Washington as a businessperson, the interest of the country should be put before the interest of your industry or your company. Businesses are constantly coming down here asking for that one little thing that helps them. I hear these horror stories. Just do what's right for the damn country. Your business is going to be fine. In fact, your business will be better off if the country's strong.

So business has to be careful not to be too self-serving. That does not appeal to the American public. It doesn't help politicians get things done.

That's why I'm saying to expand earned income tax credits—taxing your carried interest a little bit—those would be good things for America. We should do that and help those at the lower end with education, income assistance, all those things we need, but have corporate tax reform.

DR: You have data from all over the world that JPMorgan gets. Would you say right now the U.S. economy is in reasonable shape? Do you fear a recession? We haven't had one in seven years, and we usually have them every seven years.

JD: I don't think there's an automatic rule that it's seven years. When you look at the economy, you always look for the potholes. We did see potholes in 2007, in 2008, in leverage and mortgage.

There are no real potholes there now. Fifteen million more people are working. Wages are going up. Stock prices are much higher than where they were. We need to build more homes. People are spending their money. Markets are wide open. Companies are flush with cash.

The potholes are not systemic. Auto loans might be a little bit stretched. There's too much bad student lending. But they're not going to sink the American economy.

You hear the politics of today about all the serious problems we have. But I give it the other way around. America has the best hand ever dealt to any country on this planet, today or ever. We have peaceful, wonderful neighbors in Canada and Mexico. We have all the food, water, and energy we will ever need. We have the best military on the planet, and we will for as long as we have the best economy. We have the best universities on the planet. There are great ones elsewhere, but these are the best. We still educate most of the kids who start businesses around the world. We have a rule of law which is exceptional.

We have a magnificent work ethic. We have innovation from the core of our bones. You can ask anyone in this room what you can do to be more productive. Ask your assistants, factory floors, we do it. It's not just the Steve Jobses. It's the broad depth. We have the widest and deepest financial markets the world's ever seen. I just made a list of these things, and maybe I missed something. It's extraordinary. And we have it today.

DR: You would never consider running for office, would you?

JD: I would love to be president of the United States of America, okay? Until Donald Trump got to where he was, they said you'll never have a rich businessman who's never been in politics be president. I clearly was wrong about that.

It's just too hard. For most people, you have to be senator, governor, run for years, be part of a party. It's why a lot of you probably haven't done it.

What you hear today is "Get the experts out of the room." We've heard that before. We need policy set by thoughtful people. We need analytics. We need it done right. We need to do it together.

A hundred and forty-five million people work in America; 125 million work for private enterprise. Government can't fix all these things itself. When they act like government is the only solution, I remind them of the Post Office, Veterans Affairs, the Department of Motor Vehicles. The only thing the government does really well is the United States military.

If you go around the country, you see that collaboration works in all these cities, all these states. For some reason, we just get bogged down. It's maybe just too complicated for mankind.

DR: You've been now running a bank as CEO—at Bank One and JPMorgan—for about sixteen years. What's the greatest pleasure of running a bank?

JD: My contribution to making it a better world is running a good JPMorgan Chase. I tell people, "If I don't do a good job at JPMorgan Chase, I hurt the opportunities for our people. I hurt the opportunities for the two thousand hamlets we do business in. We can be philanthropic. We can help people grow. If I do a good job, we can do all those things."

I'm not an artist. I'm not a tennis player. I'm not a musician. I'm not a politician. This is my contribution.

DR: I assume your shareholders would be happy for you to stay forever. Do you have any plans about how long you might stay in this position?

JD: You know, I love what I do, and I still have the energy to do it. It does take a lot of energy.

MARILLYN HEWSON

Executive Chairman and Former Chairman, President, and CEO, Lockheed Martin

---

"I didn't have a scholarship. I worked nights, on what was called the graveyard shift, from eleven at night to seven in the morning, and then I went to class from eight to one or two, and then I'd sleep. Unless I had a date—then I'd go right back to work, without sleeping, because you can do that when you're eighteen or nineteen years old. I worked full-time, paid my own way through school. Finished in three and a half years. You do what you have to do."

In 2013, Marillyn Hewson became president and CEO of Lockheed Martin Corporation. One year later, Marillyn became the company's chairman. In taking on these positions, she became the first woman to lead the nation's largest defense contractor.

Such a result would probably not have seemed likely when Marillyn first joined Lockheed in 1983. (At the time, there were few female senior executives at Lockheed or at any of the companies in the defense industry.) Or when Marillyn's father died in her youth, leaving her mother to raise five children alone. Or when she worked full-time on the night shift to afford the costs of attending the University of Alabama.

Throughout her career at what would eventually become Lockheed Martin Corporation, Marillyn was given leadership roles of increasing responsibility, frequently moving around the country to run many of the company's key divisions before becoming chief operating officer and board member. She was seen by her colleagues and customers as an always prepared, efficient, and results-oriented executive. She knew how to get things done in a large corporate bureaucracy, and she knew how to work well with the company's dominant customer: the Pentagon.

I did not know Marillyn that well, though one of my Carlyle partners was on her board, and Lockheed Martin is based in the Washington, D.C., area. She was always focused on customers, shareholders, and employees, and therefore not interested in her own publicity. But after a few tries, I eventually convinced her to let me interview her at one of the Economic Club of Washington, D.C.'s luncheons in March 2018.

It was clear from the start of the interview that she was quite adept in this format. I had a sense that while her rise might have seemed unlikely, given the male-dominated executive suite in the company and other defense companies, Marillyn had readily mastered the various skills needed to be a successful CEO.

One of her areas of focus has been developing other women—at Lockheed Martin, and the young girls and students in the talent pipeline—for senior leadership positions. She recognizes that she had support in climbing the ranks: her husband agreed to be the stay-at-home parent, enabling Marillyn to do more of the kinds of travel and long office hours often required of senior executives. That option might not be available to every woman in her position, but it has certainly worked well, in her view, for her family—and for Lockheed Martin's shareholders. The stock quadrupled under her leadership.

Marillyn stepped down as CEO in June of 2020, and will no doubt soon be taking her considerable talents into other pursuits that can utilize her well-honed leadership skills.

DAVID RUBENSTEIN (DR): Since you've been the CEO, Lockheed Martin stock has gone up roughly 330 percent. The market capitalization is up roughly 280 percent. Another company that you compete with, General Dynamics, has a female CEO as well, Phebe Novakovic, and their stock is up about 250 percent since she became the CEO. Do you think that women can run defense companies better than men, or they can run all companies better than men?

MARILLYN HEWSON (MH): I'm just looking at the audience—how many women are out there clapping. But, David, I just say it's a team sport. It isn't all about me on the performance of our company. I'm really proud of what our team has been able to accomplish over the last five or six years. I'm in my sixth year as CEO.

DR: When you walk into the shareholders' meetings, do they give you a standing ovation? They must be pretty happy.

MH: We have some happy shareholders, yes. But they always keep a bead on us to make sure we're constantly creating value. It's "What have you done for me lately?"

DR: During the presidential transition, Donald Trump sent out a tweet saying that your biggest product, the F-35, was too expensive. You were out of the country at the time?

MH: I was in Israel, where we were delivering their first two F-35s.

DR: What was your reaction to the president of the United States tweeting that you were charging the U.S. government too much?

MH: We needed to get those aircraft delivered. Prime Minister Netanyahu was at that event, and he asked me about the fact that our new president was going to get a better price on those aircraft, and that maybe *he* should get a rebate on the ones that we were delivering. That presented a bit of a challenge.

It's important to recognize what our president-elect was communicating. He was trying to communicate to the American people that he was going to get good deals on the equipment he purchased, and that he was going to increase defense spending but he was going to make sure he spent the taxpayers' dollar wisely. I personally engaged my team to have a dialogue with him.

DR: You did give him a little discount?

MH: We drove the price down. We got the deal done, and we did it in an accelerated fashion. He definitely had an influence on that.

DR: You grew up in Kansas. Your father died when you were nine years old, and you had four siblings. How did your mother support five children?

MH: It was tough, frankly. My father was with a department in the army. My mother was the at-home mom with five children. We were an average family. It set us back a lot.

I give great credit to my mother, who raised five children on her own. She just passed away a couple years ago at ninety-seven. It was an incredible life that she had.

DR: She was from Alabama.

MH: She was from Alabama. She taught us the value of a dollar. We had to learn how to economize at a very young age. She'd send us in to pay the electric bill. She just got her kids out and said, "You've got to learn how to do these things." It taught me to be very self-reliant.

DR: I was told that she used to say to you, "Go to the grocery store. Here's five dollars. Bring back seven dollars of groceries."

MH: That's true. I learned early how to economize, yes.

DR: You went to the University of Alabama. Did you get a scholarship and not have to work?

MH: I didn't have a scholarship. I worked nights, on what was called the graveyard shift, from eleven at night to seven in the morning, and then I went to class from eight to one or two. Then I'd sleep. Unless I had a date—then I'd go right back to work, without sleeping, because you can do that when you're eighteen or nineteen years old. I worked full-time, paid my own way through school. Finished in three and a half years. You do what you have to do.

DR: After you graduated, did you say, "I want to be the CEO of Lockheed Martin"?

MH: No. I started looking for a job. I took a job out of college as an economist here in Washington with the Bureau of Labor Statistics. They were in the midst of redoing the producer price index. It was a good job for a recent graduate. So I actually started my career here. Four years later, I interviewed with several companies, one of which was Lockheed, in Marietta, Georgia, and started there as a senior industrial engineer.

DR: When you went to Marietta, you worked your way up. You had, I think, twenty-two different leadership positions. You must have been moving around a lot.

MH: I was in Marietta for about thirteen years. Eighteen months in, I was promoted to supervisor in industrial engineering, and then, at about the two-year mark, I was put on a general management development program—great credit to my sponsor that he put me forward for the program—so I spent two years rotating around the company. At the end of the two years, I was a manager over all of our production estimating and budgets.

DR: At one point your husband was unemployed, and he got a job interview with a company. What company was that?

MH: His company went out of business, and he was out looking for a job. We had a five-month-old baby, so we were very much hoping he'd find a job. It was a tough labor market at the time, but he came home one day and he said, "Okay, I got a job." I said, "Where?" And he said, "At Lockheed." And I said, "You're at Lockheed? Why my company?"

It turned out he went to work in the finance department. We didn't really cross paths. I was running industrial engineering by that time. He retired from Lockheed after five years.

DR: You have given him a lot of credit for what you've been able to achieve. You might describe how, after he retired, he took on the role that many people would say a wife might have normally taken on.

MH: Yes. I say he "retired." Our boys were three and six. We moved from Marietta to Fort Worth, Texas, because my job moved us. You know how stressful it is to have a couple of young children at home. I said, "Why don't we try you working from home for a year?"

And we just never changed the model. He became the at-home dad. He was the coach. He was the Scout leader. He went on the field trips. He managed that, because I travel a lot in my job. We were maybe a new-age family back then, in the way we worked, but it worked for us.

Today our kids are in their twenties, and they're off doing their thing. When I said he retired, he basically hit that five-year mark. He got a retirement check from Lockheed Martin not long ago.

DR: So I guess he's happy with shareholder performance as well.

MH: Yes, he is.

DR: Let's talk a moment about the product I mentioned earlier—fighter jets. There's an F-14, F-15, F-18. There was an F-22. Then you'd come up with something called the F-35. What happened between 22 and 35?

MH: Aircraft are not numbered by Lockheed Martin. The U.S. government determines what the number is. *F* stands for fighter, and *B* for bomber. The terminology is kind of general, and usually it is sequential.

We won the contract with our X-35. You named them with an *X* or a *Y* if they were experimental or a prototype. Lockheed was the winner of this competition, and the secretary of the air force said, "The F-35." We were all shocked, because we thought it was going to be the F-23. Once he named it, that's what it became.

DR: You didn't want to tell him he made a mistake, I guess, since he just awarded you the contract.

In the history of our country, this is the biggest defense contract ever. Tens of billions of dollars, I assume. Why does it cost that much to make these planes? What's so great about the F-35?

MH: The F-35A, which is your conventional variant of aircraft, was priced at $94.3 million. We're on a path to drive that down to $80 million by 2020. Think about that. Maybe you fly a Gulfstream.

DR: Occasionally.

MH: Think about what you pay for that. Then think about the most sophisticated jet fighter in the world that might cost $80 million. That's pretty remarkable, in my mind.

It is the most advanced fighter in the world. It has stealth. It has sensor fusion. Not only is it a game changer in terms of providing air superiority, it can communicate with all assets on the battlefield. It is basically a force multiplier. I don't have to tell you that. Talk to some of the pilots who fly it.

DR: What's it like to be the CEO of our nation's largest defense contractor? You get about 70 percent of your revenue from the U.S. government. How much of your time do you have to spend with the government? How do you spend your time in a typical week?

MH: Between 60 and 70 percent of my time is spent on the strategy of the business, the customers, and engagement—traveling around the world on the customer side of the business. It's important, in my role, to be out meeting with not only our congressional leaders and our government leaders to make sure we're aligned with what their needs are, and their priorities. I also travel a lot outside the country. Thirty percent of our business is outside of the United States, with governments around the world.

DR: You were recently voted the twenty-second most powerful woman in the entire world—not just in business. When you saw that, did you say, "I should be higher"? How does it feel to be the twenty-second most powerful female on the entire planet of 3.6 billion women?

MH: I don't focus on it that much, David. I got a note from my brother that said, "Why was Oprah higher than you?" That's not something I'm focused on. There are a lot of lists. It really comes down to having the privilege of leading a national asset, a company that's doing some of the most important and interesting work in the world.

DR: When you started out, were you often the only woman in the room at Lockheed?

MH: I was, yes.

DR: Was that intimidating, or was it the kind of thing where you said, "I can show them that I'm better than them"?

MH: It's like any team you come into: you have to establish your credibility. Recognizing that I was a different gender, maybe the first moment I was different in that sense. Once you're contributing and you're part of the team, it was no longer a factor—for me, at least—through my career.

What is really positive is that today, 22 percent of our leaders are women; 24 to 25 percent of our workforce are women. There's a pipeline of women. There's no longer only one woman in the room. We have many women leaders in the room.

Thirty-five years ago, there weren't as many women coming out of engineering and other fields into the workforce. But you look at our customers today, look at our military services, women are in uniform and in leadership positions. It's just a pipeline issue. We're always working to get more women into that pipeline.

DR: What do you do for relaxation? Are you an exercise person? A traveler? Do you play sports?

MH: My husband and I like to get out and play some golf as relaxation. Our family gets together and travels. I travel a lot for the job; probably 40 to 50 percent of my time I'm on business travel, but one of the things we really enjoy is traveling together as a family. I always try to create some travel that our kids will find fun. As long as Mom and Dad pay for it and it's fun, they'll come.

TRANSFORMERS

Melinda Gates

Eric Schmidt

Tim Cook

Ginni Rometty

Indra Nooyi

MELINDA GATES
Cochair, the Bill & Melinda Gates Foundation

"One of the things I've learned about data and the data
we collect is we think data is objective. Data is actually
sexist. We don't actually know why women have dropped
out of computer science, but there's some theories looking at
the data we do have. . . . When I played home video
games, it was Pong, Pac-Man. Then, with the advent of
computers, they were promoted to boys, and so
more boys' games were made, became shoot-'em-up
games, and women and girls said, 'I'm out.' Then
it became this self-referential circle."

"I thought about leaving. Then I thought, 'I'll try being
myself in this culture and just see if it works, and if not,
I'll go take some other job.' I started to be myself, and I started
to build teams that were collaborative and that worked
together more and were less abrasive. It turned out
I could recruit people from all over the company, to
my surprise, to work on these teams."

I n recent years, Melinda Gates has become one of the world's leading advocates for women, particularly those in the less developed countries in the world. Her passion for and commitment to correcting the challenges that she sees have made her one of the most powerful, visible, and admired women in the world.

She has also become a role model to women all around the globe—but not because she is married to one of the world's business icons (and the world's richest man for most of the past quarter century). To be sure, being married to such a legendary person, someone in the public eye for decades, cannot be an easy situation. Raising three well-adjusted children in this environment presented a whole other set of challenges.

Family matters aside, Melinda has become a role model for so many men and women because of her passionate commitment as cochair of the Bill & Melinda Gates Foundation—the world's largest private philanthropic organization. Melinda has been an equal partner with her husband in creating the foundation, formulating its goals, and traveling the world to see how its grants are meeting those goals. The impact has been global and transformative, particularly in addressing health problems in the less developed economies in the world.

Melinda has also taken the lead in organizing the activities of the Giving Pledge. Beyond these efforts, though, in recent years she has become a global leader in addressing the problems faced by women in so many parts of the world: lack of the basic means to raise their children; the pain and suffering inflicted by abusive partners; insufficient access to and knowledge about contraception; and the difficulty of pursuing the education needed to secure wage-paying jobs. Melinda addressed many of these issues in her 2019 book *The Moment of Lift*.

Although Melinda is a graduate of Duke and former member of the Duke Board of Trustees, I preceded her at the university by about fifteen years, and did not join the board myself until shortly after she completed her term. I came to know her over the years because of my involvement as an original signer of the Giving Pledge. But I had not interviewed her before the *Peer to Peer* session conducted at the Bloomberg studios in Washington, D.C., in April 2019.

In the interview, Melinda describes how her high school interest in computers led her to Duke and then to Microsoft, and ultimately into a marriage with Bill Gates and a commitment to tackling, through philanthropic leadership, some of the world's most vexing challenges. But her greatest commitment today, other than her family, comes through very clearly in the interview—helping women, especially in the least developed parts of the world, fulfill their potential for a satisfying, healthy, and meaningful life.

To meet that commitment, Melinda is tirelessly traveling to some of the least accessible places in the world, consulting with the most knowledgeable experts about how programs can be made, speaking to world leaders about the challenges that she is trying to address, and motivating other individuals with the necessary resources to address these challenges as well.

This is not the life that the wife of one of the world's wealthiest individuals had to choose. But it is a life she feels an obligation to pursue, even when her leadership causes problems for others (such as her advocacy in the area of contraceptives—an undertaking not supported by the hierarchy of her Catholic faith).

DAVID RUBENSTEIN (DR): Let's talk about the foundation for a moment. It's the largest foundation in the world. It has assets of how much now?

MELINDA GATES (MG): About $50 billion.

DR: Since it was created, how much has it given away?

MG: Forty-five billion dollars.

DR: Nobody's given away anything close to that in the foundation world. You created the foundation from the wealth created by Microsoft. Then one day Warren Buffett called you and Bill and said, "Guess what? I don't know what to do with my wealth, but I want to give it to you because I like what you're doing."

MG: That's essentially it. Warren's wife, Susie, was very involved in philanthropy, and his plan had been to give it away through the foundation that he and she had, but she passed away early, unexpectedly. He came and surprised Bill and me, and said that the vast majority of the money would go through our foundation, along with three that his children had and the Susan T. Buffett Foundation.

DR: When he called you and said, "I'm giving you fifty or sixty billion dollars," what did you say?

MG: Bill and I took a walk after that discussion, and we were alone, and we both cried. To know Warren's generosity, and that we would be able to do even so much more than we were already doing for people around the world—it was just an unbelievably touching moment, and a touching moment of friendship.

It's been fabulous to have Warren as a trustee, because he thinks long-term, just like we do, but he also is the wind at our backs at times.

Even when I've taken on something hard, he will often say to me back-stage, "You're doing the right thing." He said to his three kids, and to us, "Swing for the fences. You are taking on the things that society has left behind. To do that, you are going to have to take risks, and I expect you to take risks."

DR: When was the foundation created?

MG: We had two foundations that we started right after we got married. We merged them in 2000 and made them the Bill & Melinda Gates Foundation.

DR: Patty Stonesifer, who had been a Microsoft employee for ten years or so, ran the foundation. When Bill retired as the CEO, he went over to the foundation. Then both of you, together, decided what you wanted to do with its resources. You said, "There are two issues we want to tackle: global health, principally in sub-Saharan Africa and Southeast Asia, and K–12 education in the United States."

How did you decide on those two issues? There are so many you could have tackled.

MG: We felt that in countries around the world, low-income countries, the thing holding people back the most was health—a bout of malaria, HIV/AIDS, tuberculosis, children dying needless deaths. We thought there was something that philanthropy could do to work on health. If you start with health, then you can go on to get a great education.

In the United States, we believe that all lives have equal value but not equal opportunity, and the piece that's holding the U.S. back is a great K–12 public education system.

DR: Some people would say, "Why are you taking so much money from a U.S. company's profits and putting them in sub-Saharan Africa or Southeast Asia?"

MG: For just a few dollars in the developing world—$50, $100—you can save so many more lives. When you do save those lives and then you help people lift themselves up, you get peaceful and prosperous societies all over the world. We care about everybody, not just U.S. citizens.

DR: You decided, when your children came, that you wanted to spend more time with them, and you left Microsoft. What was Bill's reaction?

MG: "Really?" He knew I loved working, and I loved working at Microsoft. He also knew I had that piece of my brain that loved to be on the working side, so he was quite surprised when I told him I was going to leave.

My whole issue about how much I was going to work at the foundation is I had it timed for when our kids would get older. I knew that until our last daughter went off to preschool, I was not going to be full-time. Once she was in preschool, my plan always was to work full-time then.

DR: Doing the work of the foundation, you went to sub-Saharan Africa, among other places, and eventually you decided that you wanted to focus more on women's issues.

MG: What I've seen in twenty years of work with the foundation is that if we can help lift up all women, we will change the world. There are a lot of forces pushing women down today. I've seen it in country after country, all over the world. If you lift up women, they lift up everybody else around them. That ultimately lifts up a community and a country.

DR: One of the first issues you thought about was contraception. You are a committed Catholic. Was it difficult for you to say, "We should focus more of the foundation's efforts on contraception"?

MG: It was a difficult decision for me because of my Catholic roots. I am still Catholic. But I met so many women around the world and they would discuss with me that this was literally a life-or-death crisis for them as a mom. They would say, "If I have another baby too soon, I'll die in childbirth," or "I have five children. It's not fair to my last child or the others to have another one when I can't feed them."

So I had to wrestle with my Catholic faith and say, "What do I believe in? I believe in saving lives." This was the right thing to do.

DR: Did you find sometimes a woman would say, "Take my child because I can't raise this child"?

MG: More than once. I learned from Warren's wife, Susie, that if you can, go in anonymously. I'll go into many rural settings in a pair of khaki pants and a T-shirt, and I will talk to women. Susie said, "If you talk to the men and women in the villages, you will learn so much."

I'll give you an example. I was in northern India and I had visited a health clinic. We and the government were working on this health clinic for pregnant women to go in and deliver. It saves their lives and their babies' lives.

I went into a village to talk to a woman. She had her little son next to her, and her husband, and a newborn in her arms. She had had a great experience in the health clinic. I was there to talk to her about that. By the time I was finished speaking with her, I had one last question. I said, "What hope do you have?" Her name was Mina.

She looked down for a long time. She cast her eyes down, and I thought, "I've asked something inappropriate." She finally looked up at me and she said, "The truth is I have no hope. I have no hope for feeding this child or that one, or educating them. Please, take them home with you."

When that happens, it is heartbreaking. To see a woman who loves her sons that much, but knows they would be better off going home with a stranger, that's heartbreaking. And that's the story of many, many women and families around the world.

DR: Did you decide to make contraception available to women in these areas?

MG: We and our partners built a global coalition in 2012 and raised $2.6 billion to provide access to all types of contraceptives around the world, in the sixty-nine poorest nations where women do not have good access to them. We are systematically working to educate women about them. You'd be amazed how much women know already, but it is important to educate them about their bodies and then to make sure they have access to the tools they want to have.

DR: Let's talk about the beginning of your life, before we go back to some of the specific women's issues you address. You grew up in Dallas, and your father was an engineer?

MG: He was an aerospace engineer, working on the Apollo missions early on.

DR: We're about to celebrate the fiftieth anniversary of the Apollo moon landing. Your father was involved in that?

MG: He just got an award from Georgia Tech, where he got his engineering degree, because of that work.

DR: Your mother was not college-educated, but she helped start a real-estate business that enabled your family to pay for private schooling?

MG: There were four kids in our family. My parents had this goal that all four of us would be college-going. We could go anywhere in the country we wanted to go, and they were going to figure out how to pay for it. So my parents founded a small real-estate investment business, and my mom ran it full-time during the day, raising four kids. Then my parents and we worked on it at night and on the weekends.

DR: You went to an all-girl Catholic school, then to Duke. Where else did you think of going?

MG: The first place I thought I wanted to go was Notre Dame, because many of my high school girlfriends' dads had gone there. But when my dad and I went to visit Notre Dame, they were phasing out computer science. They thought it was a fad, and they were putting it back into the departments. I wanted to study computer science, because my math teacher in high school had gone to the head nun and advocated to bring computers into the school when almost nobody had computers.

So I knew I wanted to study computer science in college, and I was kind of devastated because my dream had been to go to Notre Dame. Then I saw Duke. They just had a big grant from IBM, two great computer labs, and I said, "This is where I'm going."

DR: Interestingly, women were more involved in computer science years ago than maybe today. Why was that?

MG: At the time I was in college, the late 1980s, about 37 percent of college undergrads in computer science were women. We were on our way up, we thought, like in law and medicine. That has since dropped to about 17 or 18 percent. Now it's on a slight uptick to 19 percent.

One of the things I've learned about data and the data we collect is we think data is objective. Data is actually sexist. We don't actually know why women have dropped out of computer science, but there's some theories looking at the data we do have.

Personal computers were really promoted to boys as a home gaming device. When I played home video games, it was Pong, Pac-Man. Then, with the advent of computers, they were promoted to boys, and so more boys' games were made, became shoot-'em-up games, and women and girls said, "I'm out." It became this self-referential circle.

DR: You also point out in your book that computers were often thought to be for women because accounting and other back-office tasks were done by computers and those were, quote, "women's jobs." When they became sexier, because you could do a start-up company in the technology area, men drifted into that area.

MG: That is definitely a factor. It becomes a self-reinforcing mechanism. We have to create more pathways in for women. The best colleges in the nation, which are getting far more minorities and women in, they're making that first computer-science class more welcoming, with more real-world problems.

DR: You went to an all-girl Catholic school. You went to Duke University, which is coed. What was it like having classes with boys?

MG: In my high school, if you wanted to take physics and calculus, which I did senior year, you went to the boys' school down the road. It was rambunctious.

When I got to Duke, and the professor would throw out a question in my political science or my economics class, I thought I was supposed to raise my hand like a good Catholic girl. But the boys would shout out the answer. I was pretty taken aback. I had to learn to play that game if I wanted to have my voice and my thoughts heard in the classroom, which I did.

DR: You went into a special five-year program at Duke, where you get an undergraduate degree and an MBA. After five years, you were about to get your degree and were interviewing at computer companies, and the company you wanted to work for was IBM.

MG: Because I had several internships with them in the summers. It was a standing offer from IBM coming out of college, and that was really nice.

DR: There was a small company interviewing at Duke as well called Microsoft. They said they would interview you. Why did you think about going there when you had an offer from IBM, the leading computer company?

MG: Microsoft's products were just starting to become popularized. To my surprise, when I went and interviewed at Microsoft, just the energy and the pace—I could see they were about to change the world. I just thought, "I want to be around that kind of energy and that talent."

Everybody on my interview schedule, except one person, was a man, but I was used to working in a male environment, because in computer science there were so few women my sophomore and junior years. I was part of the first hiring class of MBAs at Microsoft. There were nine men and me.

DR: You went to Microsoft. Was it as good as you thought it would be?

MG: We were changing the world. I loved that. I loved the innovative nature. I loved creating products. As somebody at IBM had told me, "If you get a job offer there, your chance for advancement as a woman will be meteoric." I found that, and I loved that.

I did consider leaving Microsoft, though, within about two years, because the culture was abrasive, quite honestly. I could play that game. I knew how to stand up for my ideas, stand up for my team's ideas, but I didn't like myself, and I didn't like how I was treating other people when I'd go to the grocery store or go out in the world and interact with other people.

So I thought about leaving. Then I thought, "I'll try being myself in this culture and just see if it works, and if not, I'll go take some other job."

I started to be myself, and I started to build teams that were collaborative and that worked together more and were less abrasive. It turned out I could recruit people from all over the company, to my surprise, to work on these teams.

DR: The IBM recruiter said that if you got an offer from Microsoft, you should take it.

MG: She did. She was going to be my hiring manager at IBM. I said, "I have one last place I'm going to go interview, and then I'll probably take this job." She asked me where, and when I said, "This little company called Microsoft," she looked me in the eyes and she said, "Can I give you a piece of advice? If you get an offer, you should take it." And I said, "What?"

She said, "I think you would do very well at IBM, but you'll have to go through each level of management. Whereas working for a young start-up like that, if you're as good as I think you will be, you will have this meteoric rise." And she was right.

DR: Have you ever thought how your life would be different had you taken the IBM offer?

MG: It's hard to imagine, because I wouldn't have my three beautiful children with Bill. I probably would have lived in Dallas, Texas. I know I wouldn't have traveled the world the way I've gotten to with the foundation.

DR: Was it hard to work at the company while people knew that you were dating the CEO-founder?

MG: The first date with Bill, I thought I would go out with him once, maybe twice. I just thought, "Well, he'll be interesting—he's running this company that's doing all these amazing things in the world." When I realized we were going to start dating more after the first two dates, I thought, "This is tricky and I'm not sure I want to do this," because I had worked really hard. I studied computer science, to get my MBA I studied economics. I thought, "I'm not sure this is going to go well for me."

I decided that I would date him, but I didn't try to hide it. I made it clear to the teams I was managing that I had these very bright lines, and that I did not go home from Microsoft and talk to Bill about work. I'm preparing teams to go into meetings with senior leadership, including Bill, and they're nervous, right? I'm having to prepare them, prepare myself. The last thing I could do was go home and talk to him. They had to know I had their backs in the meeting.

DR: Well, it worked out.

MG: It did work out.

DR: You point out in your book—and it must have been difficult to write about this—that you had an abusive relationship before you were married. What can your foundation do to reduce abusive relationships?

MG: The reason I write in the book about having been in an abusive relationship is that I want people to know it can happen to anyone. It silences your voice. It is a way of silencing a woman's voice in a marriage or in her workplace or her community.

For me, I lost my self-confidence. As I would be traveling out in the world, talking to women about vaccines or talking to them about venture capital—you know, even in the United States, you get venture capital, I would hear about harassment and abuse at different levels—but it was coming up over and over and over again.

Millions of women are being either harassed or abused in all kinds of places. Again, it silences women. Even in the United States, 80 percent of women harassed in their workplaces leave their jobs within two years.

We have to talk about this barrier and we have to lift it up. What we can do is collect data about it. The world doesn't actually collect data on abuse. Then we can go in and name it and recognize it and all commit to changing it everywhere in the world.

DR: A few years ago, you, Bill, and Warren decided to launch the Giving Pledge. What was the purpose of the pledge, and how many people have now signed it?

MG: The purpose—this was Warren's big idea—was to say, "If you have great wealth, if you are a billionaire in our country or anywhere in the world, you can afford to give half away, and that is the right thing to do for society."

Bill and Warren are really clear that they could not have founded their businesses if it had been, say, in Malawi or Mozambique. We benefit from what society gives us, the infrastructure, so at least half should go back to society. You've been a big help to us in this, David. We now have 190 families who have committed to the Giving Pledge, in twenty-two different countries around the world. [The number was 207 as of March 2020.]

DR: There's been a reaction against wealthy people saying, "Let's put our money here, put our money there." How do you respond to that?

MG: What I know to be true is that Bill and Warren and I believe that we should not have this inequity that exists in the United States. We need to do something about that. I meet so many people around the world who would like to live in our country, who would like to live in our democracy and our capitalistic system.

But we do have gaps in it and we need to do things to fix those gaps. The thing that Bill and I try to be most cognizant of is the role of philanthropy. All philanthropy can be is that catalytic wedge. We can try things, we can experiment with our own money where you wouldn't want a government to experiment with taxpayer money.

We have to prove it out, and then it's up to government to scale up. We feel that philanthropy with government, with a private sector, with a nongovernmental organization, that that set of partnerships and that ecosystem can do the best for the world.

ERIC SCHMIDT
Former Chairman, Google/Alphabet

"That stereotype of a general manager is not really how
the world works today. Now the managers are uniquely
good at something and then they learn other things. I
don't think it matters where you start, but you need to
be incredibly good at that one thing and then you
broaden your skills. Discipline, hard work, and
loving what you do will get you very far."

E ric Schmidt was educated and trained as an engineer, became the
CEO of a tech company, Novell, and seemed destined, given his
intellect and knowledge of the Silicon Valley tech world, to be a longtime tech industry leader—though perhaps at a less visible level than
ultimately occurred after his meeting with Sergey Brin and Larry Page,
who were being pushed by their venture investors to find an "adult" to
serve as CEO of a young search-engine company, Google.

The explosive growth of Google (now Alphabet) and its revolutionary search-engine algorithm is well known to anyone not sleeping under a rock for the last two decades. The company now has a market value in excess of $1 trillion; had an annual revenue of almost $161 billion for fiscal year 2019; employed more than 123,000 individuals as of early 2020; and processes an estimated 1.2 trillion searches a year in its core search business. What may not be quite as well known is that Schmidt, in his role as Google CEO (for nine-plus years), brought seasoned management, finance, and operations experience to the venture that the two founders of Google were widely seen as needing by their Silicon Valley venture-capitalist backers.

Google's success—indeed omnipresence—was not inevitable. There were already many search-engine companies when Google came along. Its search mousetrap may have been better than others, but that does not guarantee success in Silicon Valley.

A good deal of Google's early success, its public listing, and its almost unprecedented market-value growth as a public company can be attributed to the experienced leadership Eric provided Sergey and Larry and the other young technologists and engineers in the company's early days.

Although now retired from his CEO and board positions at Google and Alphabet, Eric has become one of the country's most respected public commentators and experts on the rapidly changing technology world, advising the U.S. government, state governments, universities, and a host of nonprofit organizations. He is both a well-known venture investor and a committed philanthropist, with a particular focus on the oceans and education.

I first met Eric when he was CEO of Google, and have worked with him on a number of nonprofit and philanthropic matters. I have often sought his advice on technology-related issues.

Over the years, I have interviewed him at a variety of forums—no easy task, for Eric himself is a skilled and experienced interviewer. This particular exchange for *Peer to Peer* took place at the Google offices in Washington, D.C., in October 2016.

In discussing what makes a leader, Eric emphasizes the importance of mastering one skill or area before branching out to other areas. I echo that advice. At the outset of a career, it is essential to become an expert in something, so that others will come to you for help and guidance. Once you establish your knowledge of and competence in one area, the skills learned and the credibility established there make it possible to expand your reach and expertise to a second or third area.

Eric has shown that very well as he took his management and engineering expertise and expanded his reach and experience into investing, public policy, and philanthropy.

DAVID RUBENSTEIN (DR): When you joined Google, it was a very small company. Did you in your wildest dreams ever imagine it would become one of the most valuable companies in the entire world?

ERIC SCHMIDT (ES): I don't think any of us did. I certainly did not. When I met Larry and Sergey, they just seemed incredibly intelligent. They had this huge argument over something technical, and I hadn't had that good an argument in a long time. I thought, "I've got to work with these people." I wanted to join a company that was going to stay in one building. Today, of course, we are in many buildings.

DR: You were the CEO of Novell at the time you were getting ready to go to Google. You had many opportunities. What propelled you to pick Google?

ES: I actually didn't interview anywhere else. [Venture-capitalist investor] John Doerr asked me to visit Google. I said, "Who cares about a search engine? It won't matter very much. Who uses search engines?" But he said, "Nevertheless, go visit with Larry and Sergey." What they were doing was so interesting, and the quality of the people they had recruited was so compelling, I just had to be there.

DR: There were plenty of search-engine companies. Why did you think Google had a search engine that was going to change the world?

ES: I didn't particularly think Google was going to be that successful, but I thought the technology was unusually special. Alphabet had invented a different way of doing ranking. All of the previous search engines used a ranking easily manipulated by business forces. But Larry Page had invented something now known as PageRank, which is a different algorithm, a different way of doing search. It had spread virally, first at Stanford and then throughout the Bay Area, all by word of mouth. But I thought, "What a great project."

DR: You had two people who were, quote, "the founders," Larry and Sergey. But they wanted a CEO who had more experience—or at least the venture investors did. Was it awkward to come in and be the CEO when you were dealing with founders who didn't have the CEO title?

ES: They had been searching for sixteen months for somebody they could work with. They would have each candidate do something with them for the weekend. So they'd go skiing with one of them, and they'd play sports with another one to see if they were compatible.

When I met them, we all had similar backgrounds, in the sense that we're corporate scientists. But it was [*snaps*] an immediate click. I always knew, based on what had happened with John Sculley and Steve Jobs in the 1980s, that it was their company and my job was to make their company successful.

DR: Was it a normal interview?

ES: I walked into their office—a tiny office in this incredibly crowded building, which Google still has—and they had my biography up on the wall. They proceeded to ask each and every question possible based on the biography. I had never been so thoroughly questioned.

They came to a product I was building at Novell and they said, "This is the stupidest product ever made." Which I, of course, had to respond to.

DR: You didn't think you were going to get the job after they said that?

ES: I didn't realize it was a job interview. I just came to visit. But as I left the building—which was, curiously, a building I had been in when I worked at Sun [Microsystems] years earlier, which shows you how history repeats itself—I knew I would be back.

DR: You did come back. It was a small company—a hundred employees, two hundred employees—when you joined. Did you realize that advertising would be the medium through which you would actually make the company grow?

ES: No. I was convinced the advertising approach they had taken did not work at all. When I became CEO, I was very concerned that there was something wrong. I actually asked them to audit the cash accounts to make sure people were selling these ads.

What we learned was that these targeted ads worked incredibly well, even though they were these little text ads. That discovery—and then the subsequent algorithmic improvements that allowed for auctions and so forth, which were done by impossibly young and creative engineers whom I viewed as sort of experimenting with things—created what is today Google.

DR: The culture at Google was very unusual at the time. Others have emulated it. But it's a culture of "Do what you want, wear what you want, sleep in the office if you want"?

ES: We do have a dress code: you have to wear something. We had problems where engineers would move in and put cots on the floor. We would explain that you can do anything you want to at Google, but you can't live here. You have to have a bed somewhere else.

We famously encouraged people to bring pets. We had lots of rules about the pets. We didn't have any rules about the people. But if your pet was over here, you had to keep your pet over here.

DR: What about the food? You had free food for everybody. What was the purpose behind that?

ES: The comment was that the free food really changed everything. Many of these things were marketed as great fun, but there was a serious business behind them. In the case of the food, this was Sergey's idea. Families eat dinner together, and he wanted the company to be a family. If you made sure people had proper, good food—breakfast, lunch, and dinner—they would literally work as teams.

They would work in whatever way made the most sense. Larry and Sergey invented something called 20 percent time. The idea is that if the employees, especially the engineers, are interested in something, they can spend 20 percent of their time on whatever they're interested in.

Oh my God, how could you run a company that way? Well, it allowed the engineers who were sitting there at dinner to have conversations: "What do you think, what do you think, what do you think?"

I'll give you another example. Larry Page was looking at our ads as they came out. He studied them. He put a big sign on the wall: "These ads suck." I was looking at this and I said, "This is another stupid Google thing, right? Nothing's going to happen." We have an ads team, we have a manager, we have a plan.

This was Friday afternoon. I came in Monday morning, and a completely different set of teams had seen the sign and had invented, over the weekend, what today is the underlying ad system of Google and delivered it on Monday morning. That could not have occurred without such a culture.

DR: You told me on a previous occasion that one time you were out of the office, then you came back and somebody had occupied your office.

ES: At the time, Google's culture was seen as very unusual. I knew this, and I was always careful not to commit a faux pas, if you will. One morning I walk in and my assistant has this look on her face like something bad has happened. I walk into my office, which is eight feet by twelve feet, and here is my new roommate.

He has moved himself in. He's working. I didn't know that I had a new roommate. After all, I am the CEO. Someone should tell me these things, right?

So I said, "Hello, who are you?" He says, "Hello, I'm Amit. Nice to meet you." I said, "Why are you here?" And he goes, "You're never here and I was in a six-person office. It was too loud."

I thought, "What to say to this?" because this is a career-limiting moment. If I say, "Get out of my office," they're going to fire me or something. I said, "Okay. Did you ask permission?" He goes, "I asked my boss and he said it was a great idea." I said, "Okay." So we sat next to each other, and he would program and I would do my work, literally next to each other, for a year. And we became best friends.

DR: You grew up in Virginia?

ES: Rural Virginia.

DR: What made you think you wanted to be an engineer?

ES: I was a normal science-interested boy. This was at the time of the space program, and everyone wanted to be an astronaut. In my high school, they had a terminal. These were the old ASR-33 teletypes. My father had the good thought to get one for our house, which was highly unusual at the time. I would spend every evening working and reprogramming. Today, of course, if I were a fifteen-year-old at home, I'd have five personal computers and a supernetwork and sound blaring out of the speakers.

DR: You went to high school in Virginia. You must have done pretty well to get into Princeton.

ES: Yes, although it was easier back then.

DR: You knew you wanted to be an engineer?

ES: I actually applied to Princeton as an architect. When I got there, I discovered that I wasn't a very good architect, but I was a much better programmer. Princeton, again, was kind in that I was advanced enough that I was able to skip the introductory courses and go straight into the advanced courses and then the graduate courses.

DR: You must have done pretty well, because you then got a scholarship to go to Berkeley and get your PhD. Was it hard to move across the country?

ES: No. To give an example of how naïve people were back then, I decided I wanted to move out to California because I heard that it was nice and had sunny beaches. Of course, I went to the wrong part. This was before Google Maps.

I worked at Bell Labs, where Unix, which is the basis of much of computing today, was invented. I was a junior programmer there. And I worked as a young programmer at Xerox Palo Alto Research Center, where the workstation, and the screens, and many of the editors, and many of the networking things that we use today were invented. I was unusually fortunate to be an assistant to the people doing that kind of research. From there I went to Sun Microsystems, where I was an executive for many years.

DR: And from there you were recruited to Novell?

ES: Yes. I was at Sun for fourteen years, Novell for four, and now Google for sixteen-plus years.

DR: As the company became bigger and bigger, it dominated the search business. It has 90 percent of the search world, more or less. Why did Google say, "We don't want to just be in the search business"?

ES: Google's motto was not only "Search the web." It was "All the world's information." Information is broadly consumed. The company set out, with all of the hiring that we were able to do and the talent, to begin to solve some new problems.

We became very interested in maps, then we developed our own maps—a hugely successful product line. We bought a company called YouTube, which today is incredibly successful in video and other forms of information. We built an enterprise business that has done incredibly well. I can go on. In some cases, we've bought little companies that we grew, like Google Earth. In other cases, these were technologies that we grew ourselves.

The whole idea was to integrate around information. At some point four or five years ago, we became interested in solving problems—not just information problems but problems where digital technology could make a material difference, the most obvious one being self-driving cars. We've been working on that as a research project.

More than thirty-two thousand will die from car-related accidents this year in America; we just don't know who they are. That's how bad this is. Imagine if we could reduce that by half, or a third, or a quarter. Most of the accidents are driver-induced. We may ultimately be able to make driving accidents a very, very rare event.

DR: You're obviously a leader in the science and technology world and in the corporate world. Do you think leaders are born? Are they made or educated?

ES: Leadership is a little bit of both. You have to have some innate skills, but it can certainly be learned. I also believe that as a leader you need to do something very well.

That stereotype of a general manager is not really how the world works today. Now the managers are uniquely good at something, and then they learn other things. I don't think it matters where you start, but you need to be incredibly good at that one thing and then you broaden your skills. Discipline, hard work, and loving what you do will get you very far.

TIM COOK
CEO, Apple

"As I look at the world, many of the problems come down
to the lack of equality. It's the fact that the kid who is born
in one zip code doesn't have a good education because
they happen to be born in that zip code. It's someone in the
LGBTQ community who is fired because of that. It's
someone who has a different religion than the majority and
therefore is ostracized in some way. Very simply, I think if
you could wave a wand and everybody in the world would
treat each other with dignity and respect, there are
many problems that would go away."

Tim Cook succeeded one of the most legendary leaders in American business history, Steve Jobs. Not an enviable task. Succeeding legendary business figures does not always begin or end well. The expectations are often too high, and the scrutiny can be even more intense. When Cook, an IBM-trained operations expert, joined Apple from

Compaq, shortly after Jobs returned to Apple as CEO, there was no reason to think it would become one of the world's most valuable companies, or that Cook would be chosen by Jobs as his successor. But that is
what happened when Steve Jobs stepped down as CEO on August 24,
2011, due to an illness that shortly thereafter caused his death.

Many analysts had relatively low expectations for Tim Cook. Steve
was the larger-than-life genius behind the Apple personal computer, the
iPhone, the iPad, iTunes, and the Apple retail stores, among other creative and transformative products and services. Tim, by contrast, was a
mild-mannered manufacturing and supply-chain expert. How could
someone with that personality and background lead Apple into the future?

The results speak for themselves. Under Tim's leadership, Apple's
market value has increased from $359 billion to $1.4 trillion in the nine-
plus years since he became CEO. Apple became the first company to
have a trillion-dollar market value, and today remains the most valuable
non–government-related company in the world.

Why did so many observers get so much wrong?

To begin with, Apple was in good shape because of Steve's leadership, which included assembling many top executives throughout the
company. But just as important, Tim Cook proved to be a leader who
led in a particularly effective way—by methodical attention to detail,
collaborative teamwork, and the quiet and consistent manner that had
always been his trademark. The results at Apple since his accession have
been so breathtaking that Tim has emerged as one of the world's most
respected and influential CEOs.

To some extent, the respect and influence come from his decision
not to try to replicate the role of Steve Jobs—the creative force, the brilliant innovator, the designer, the master of surprise, the center of all that
Apple does. Instead, recognizing that no one could really be a new Steve
Jobs, Tim chose to focus on what he knows best: organization, teamwork,
efficiency, predictability, low-key leadership. This has worked to such an
extent that Apple's value has tripled under Tim Cook's direction.

I first met Tim, a graduate of Duke's Fuqua School of Business, when
I was serving as Duke's board chair and interviewed him at a Duke event
in Silicon Valley. I came to know him better when we served as members of the advisory board of China's Tsinghua School of Economics and
Management.

This interview was done for *Peer to Peer* at Duke in May 2018, following Tim's commencement address that year. The audience was mostly Duke students, parents, and faculty, but also included Laurene Powell Jobs, Steve Jobs's widow and a strong supporter of Tim's.

Tim's modest demeanor comes through in the interview. He would be the last person to attribute Apple's success in recent years to his unique skills and leadership talents. But he clearly understands the type of leadership needed for Apple's unique place in the global business world—a focus on Apple's products and services and customers rather than himself.

DAVID RUBENSTEIN (DR): You've now been the CEO of Apple since August of 2011. Earnings are up about 80 percent. Have you ever thought you can't do better than this? Maybe you should just say, "I've done a great job, and now I'm going to do something else with my life"?

TIM COOK (TC): We view the stock price and revenues and profits as a result of doing things right on the innovation side, on the creativity side, focusing on the right products. Treating customers like they're jewels and focusing on the user experience. I didn't even know the numbers that you just quoted. This is not something that's even in my orbit, to be honest.

DR: When you announce your quarterly earnings, analysts always say, "Well, they didn't sell as much of this product as we thought they would." Does that bother you?

TC: It did at one time. It doesn't anymore. We run Apple for the long term. It's always struck me as bizarre that there's a fixation on how many units are sold in a ninety-day period, because we're making decisions that are multiyear decisions. We try to be very clear that we do not run a company for people who want to make a quick buck. We run the company for the long term.

DR: One of the shareholders who recently surfaced as having bought seventy-five million additional shares is Warren Buffett. Are you pleased to have him as your shareholder?

TC: I'm overjoyed. I'm thrilled. Because Warren is focused on the long term. And so we're in sync. It's the way we run the company. It's the way he invests.

DR: Have you thought about this? Warren still uses an old flip phone.

TC: I know.

DR: He has no smartphone. Have you thought how much more your stock could go up if he actually used the product?

TC: I am working on him. And I told him that I'll personally come to Omaha to do tech support for him. [In 2020, this effort must have succeeded, because Warren Buffett revealed he now uses an iPhone.]

DR: Let me ask you about how you came to this position. You grew up in Alabama.

TC: I did. In a very, very small rural town between Pensacola and Mobile on the Gulf Coast.

DR: Were you a star athlete in high school? A star scholar? Were you a tech nerd?

TC: I'm not sure I would say I was a star anything. I worked hard at school. I had some reasonably good grades. The benefit I got in my childhood was being in a family that was a loving family and in a public school system that was good. That's a huge benefit, and honestly a benefit that many, many kids don't have these days.

DR: You went to Auburn. How did you do there?

TC: I did pretty well. I really got into engineering in a big way, and industrial engineering.

DR: Then you went to work for IBM.

TC: I did. I started as a production engineer out designing manufacturing lines. At that time, robotics were beginning to take off, so we were focused on automation. I wouldn't say we successfully focused on it. But I learned a lot from going through that as well.

DR: You were there for about twelve years, and then you joined another company called Compaq, which at the time was one of the biggest manufacturers of personal computers.

TC: They were number one at the time.

DR: You're there for about six months and you get a call from Steve Jobs, or somebody working for him, saying, "Can you come and join Apple?" Apple was modest compared to Compaq. Why did you take the interview and join Apple?

TC: It's a good question. Steve had come back to the company and was essentially replacing the executive team that was there at the time. I thought, "You know, this is an opportunity to talk to the guy that started the whole industry."

Steve met me on Saturday. Just minutes into talking with him, it was like, "I want to do it." I was shocked myself. But there was a sparkle in his eye that I'd never seen in a CEO before. And there he was, sort of turning left when everyone was turning right. In everything that he talked about, he was doing something extraordinarily different than conventional wisdom.

Many people were abandoning the consumer market because it was a bloodbath. Steve was doing the exact opposite. He was doubling down on the consumer at the time. Talking with him, and the types of questions he asked were also different. I did literally, before I left, think, "I hope he offers me the job, because I really want to do that."

DR: Did your friends tell you this was not a good idea?

TC: They thought I was nuts. Conventional wisdom was, "You're working for the top personal computer maker in the world. Why would you ever leave? You've got a great career ahead." It wasn't a decision that you could sit down and do an engineering kind of analysis saying here are the pluses and here are the minuses. That analysis would always say, "Stay put." It was this voice in your head saying, "Go west, young man. Go west."

DR: In hindsight, this was the best professional decision of your life, I assume.

TC: Maybe the best decision of my life. I'm not sure you need to put *professional* in that.

DR: When you got there and you were working for Steve, was it better than you thought? Worse than you thought? More challenging than you thought?

TC: Liberating is the way I would describe it. You could talk to Steve about something very big, and if it resonated with him, he would just say, "Okay," and you could do it. It was a total revelation for me that a company could run like this. I was used to these layers and bureaucracy and studies—the paralysis that companies can get into. Apple was totally different than that. I realized that if I couldn't get something done, I could just go to the nearest mirror and look at it, and that was the reason.

DR: Steve's health was such that he couldn't continue to be the CEO. He told the board that, and you were announced as the CEO around August of 2011. When you became the CEO, did you feel that Steve would say, "Here's what I was interested in doing, and you fulfill my goals"? Or did you feel you had your own view on what you should do? How did you balance the two? You were succeeding a legendary figure.

TC: It's not as sequential as that. We have a really open company. Most of us could finish the other person's sentences even when we might disagree with them. It wasn't a matter of Steve having this secret file or something. He was always sharing his ideas.

My view at that time was, he was going to be chairman and he would do that forever, and that we would figure out the relationship change there. Unfortunately it didn't turn out that way.

DR: You have a product that is the most successful consumer product in the history of mankind, which is the iPhone.

TC: There was a sense that it was a profound product, that it was a game changer. If you go back and watch the keynote where Steve announced it, you can feel his passion in it and the way he describes it. I still remember it like it was yesterday.

DR: How many iPhones have now been sold?

TC: Well over a billion.

DR: Let's talk about some of the values that you've been espousing. One is privacy.

TC: We see privacy as a fundamental human right. To us, it's right up there with some of the other civil liberties that make Americans what they are. It defines us as Americans. We see that this is becoming a larger and larger issue for people. We take a minimum amount of data from customers—only that which we need to provide a great service. Then we work really hard to protect it with encryption and so forth.

DR: You've also talked about the importance of equality. Why is that important to you?

TC: As I look at the world, many of the problems come down to the lack of equality. It's the fact that the kid who is born in one zip code doesn't have a good education because they happen to be born in that zip code.

It's someone in the LGBTQ community who is fired because of that. It's someone who has a different religion than the majority and therefore is ostracized in some way. Very simply, I think if you could wave a wand and everybody in the world would treat each other with dignity and re-spect, there are many problems that would go away.

DR: You exposed your own personal life, giving up some of the privacy that you've said other people should have. Why did you do that?

TC: I did it for a greater purpose. It became clear to me that there were lots of kids out there that were not being treated well, including in their own families, and that kids need someone to say, "Oh, they did okay in life and they're gay, so it must not be a life sentence in some way."

We were getting these notes from kids, and it would tug on my heart even more. It got to the point where I thought, "I'm making the wrong call by trying to do something that is comfortable for me, which is to stay private," and that I needed to do something for the greater good.

DR: No regrets?

TC: No regrets.

DR: So did your parents live to see your success?

TC: My mother passed away three years ago. But my father's still alive.

DR: Your mother lived to see you be the CEO of Apple.

TC: She did.

DR: Did she say, "I always knew you were going to be successful. And can you help me with my iPhone?"

TC: Well, I did get both of them an iPad, and I finally convinced my father to start using iPhones. They treat me like they did twenty years ago and forty years ago and sixty years ago.

DR: He calls you with tips about what to do? Or tells you how not to do things?

TC: If I do something he doesn't think is good, he tells me about it.

DR: You're obviously a pretty public figure. Have you ever thought that maybe you could run for president of the United States? Because you've seen the president up close.

TC: I'm not political. I love focusing on the policy stuff. With the dysfunction in Washington between the legislative branch and so forth, I think I can make a bigger difference in the world doing what I'm doing.

DR: Of all the CEOs I know who have run major companies, you are the lowest-ego, most self-effacing person I've seen in this kind of position. Have you ever noticed that you're different than other CEOs? How do you maintain this modest demeanor when you're running the biggest company in the world?

TC: When you work at Apple, there's a high expectation on everyone to perform and to contribute. Because of that high bar, you never quite get there—including the CEO, including every job in there. So I never feel that way very long, if I ever felt that way.

GINNI ROMETTY

Former Chairman, President, and CEO, IBM

"I have always had the viewpoint that every situation is a
learning opportunity. . . . People say to me, 'When you hire
people now, what do you look for?' and I will say one
of the biggest traits I look for is curiosity."

F ounded in 1911, IBM became during the 1950s, '60s, and '70s the
world's dominant computer manufacturer and technology company. But it did not capitalize fully on the personal computer and software revolutions, and was not seen as sufficiently customer-friendly
and tech-savvy compared to Microsoft, Apple, and many Silicon Valley
leaders.

The result was a near bankruptcy in the 1991–92 period. But Lou
Gerstner, recruited from RJR Nabisco, and with limited technology experience, was brought in as CEO and is widely seen as having "rescued"
IBM during his tenure as CEO from 1992 to 2001. Gerstner was succeeded from 2002 to 2012 by Sam Palmisano, a career IBM executive,

who worked to keep the company competitive with the tech revolution of that period.

When Palmisano retired, he was succeeded by another longtime IBM executive, Ginni Rometty. Her appointment surprised many. Women had rarely been given the CEO position in major tech or computer companies, and certainly not at a company as large (some 350,000 employees) and iconic as IBM.

Because I had recruited Lou Gerstner to chair Carlyle upon his IBM retirement, I had heard about the talented Ginni Rometty, and was not overly surprised when she became CEO. In Lou's view, and also Sam Palmisano's, she was clearly the most qualified person within IBM to lead the company and to address its major challenge: the technology world was changing so rapidly that IBM's products and services were often not competitive with those of younger, more nimble technology companies. Being a woman had no bearing on her selection.

Ginni served as CEO from 2012 until 2020. She is credited with transforming IBM from top to bottom during her tenure, making it more nimble, customer-friendly, and relevant. For that effort, she has acquired a strong reputation in the business and technology communities, especially for making the company more of a factor in the cloud-computing sector with its $34 billion acquisition of Red Hat in 2019 (the largest acquisition in IBM's long history), and for her work to ensure that people from all socioeconomic backgrounds benefit from the digital economy.

I have worked with Ginni on the Business Council, World Economic Forum, and other matters over the years, and always admired her intellect, focus, poise, and leadership skills. This interview took place at the Bloomberg studios in New York in June 2017.

In the interview, Ginni described her less-than-silver-spoon upbringing. Her single mother had to raise four children with limited financial resources. But as Ginni relates, she used a scholarship to get an engineering degree from Northwestern and, after a few years at General Motors, joined IBM in 1981.

So how did Ginni Rometty rise to the top? What does she see as the essential qualities for leadership? Certainly one of those qualities is curiosity. She attributes her rise to her constant interest in learning, in asking questions about subjects she wants and needs to learn more about. The same interest in constantly learning is the skill that she always sought in hiring and promoting others at IBM.

DAVID RUBENSTEIN (DR): When you wake up in the morning and you realize you are the CEO of one of the largest and best-known companies in the world, and you're a female and you have beaten a path to get there that was quite hard, do you say, "Look at all that I've achieved. I'm incredibly proud of what I've done"? Is it fun to be the CEO of IBM?

GINNI ROMETTY (GR): What a way to start. I don't think I had either of those thoughts on that first day. That first day, I just thought about what an honor it was and what a responsibility it is. At that time, IBM was just over one hundred years old. So you wake up that morning realizing you are a steward of something important and enduring.

To your question about fun, I do find it to be great fun. I think it's hard for anyone to do a job unless they find it fun.

DR: Today, as you look at IBM, do you think it has the same strength in the computer world that it had in the '60s?

GR: What makes IBM great is that, regardless of our offerings, the market conditions, or the political environment, we have always helped change the way the world works. And to do that, a technology company has to reinvent itself over and over.

I go back to the beginning, way back in 1911. When IBM started, it wasn't IBM. It made cheese and meat slicers. Then it was clocks, then tabulating, then it was an era of the mainframe, which was the back office. Then the company reinvented itself again and got into software and services. Now we're reinventing ourselves again. To me, that art of reinvention is really what makes us unique.

DR: There was that famous situation where IBM was going to get into the PC business and needed to have some software. They put an RFP out and some little company named Microsoft won it. Have you ever thought that if IBM had owned that software, Microsoft might not ever have been heard from? Or nobody ever mentions that at IBM?

GR: Microsoft Office is the operating system you're talking about, of course. And that was a long time ago. I was obviously not there at the time. But it is an interesting question, because there are so many descendants of IBM in the technology industry today. I would say that to be a great technology company, you will invent many things, you will get some things right, you will get some things wrong. In fact, if you don't, you're not going to be able to reinvent yourself.

Today you wouldn't want to be in the PC business, right? That is actually the whole point of our reinvention. People associate tech with growth, growth, growth. But not all technology is high value. So that's a key part of our reinvention, moving to areas where there's profit, where there's value.

DR: Let's talk about your background for a moment. You grew up in Chicago, and you have two sisters and a brother. At one point, your father left your mother, and your mother was not college-educated at the time. How did she support four children?

GR: I continue to learn a lot from my mom, and I give her a lot of credit for all four of us. My mother had a high school degree, but then quickly had us right after that. I was in my early teens when my dad chose to leave.

It was sudden. My mother found herself with four kids, no money, soon to be no home, soon to be no food. We had to go on food stamps. We needed help.

But she was so intent on not letting other people define who she was. She worked during the day and went back to school at night to learn a profession. In fact, she became head of administration for the sleep clinic at Rush Presbyterian Hospital in Chicago.

I'm the oldest, so I had to help out a lot. And there were plenty of people and family that pitched in. But the lesson I learned from my mother is to never let other people define who you are.

DR: You were the babysitter for your three siblings?

GR: I was. I went to PTA meetings, bugle lessons, all sorts of things.

DR: Did you get paid anything for the babysitting?

GR: I didn't get paid. I probably should go and sum that up.

DR: You must have done reasonably well in high school, because you went to a very good school. You got a scholarship to go to Northwestern?

GR: I did. I'm proud. But we all had to find ways to put ourselves through school.

I sometimes say, "I'm the underachiever." My brother and sisters have been incredibly successful.

My brother went to Dartmouth. My sister went to Northwestern for her undergraduate and graduate degrees. My other sister went to Georgia Tech for her MBA. As an undergrad, she played softball at Ohio State. They've all done great.

That really is the work ethic my mom instilled in us. She never complained. She never said much. But we all saw what she did.

DR: You graduated from Northwestern, and then, although you had a scholarship from General Motors, you weren't required to go work there. But you felt you should?

GR: This was an effort to get women and minorities into businesses. General Motors had a program in which they went to some of the best schools and said, "We'll pay your tuition, your room and board, everything." It was a professor who said to me, "Hey, you ought to go look at this program."

And in return, I would work there in the summers. Otherwise, no strings attached. I had a wonderful set of internships with them. When I graduated, I did feel a sense of real obligation to first go to GM. I had lots of other offers. I had a computer science and engineering degree.

DR: Were there a lot of women taking those courses in those days at Northwestern?

GR: What do you think?

DR: Were you the only woman?

GR: No. But I was probably the only woman in many of those classes, even then.

DR: Did you think you had a chance to rise up in that profession because there were so few women in it?

GR: I never thought about it that way, and I don't know how many people do. I always liked math and science, always, and so I never had a doubt. Nowadays, a lot of my nieces, my nephews, they'll change their majors all through college. I never did change my major. Once I went to Northwestern, I said, "It's engineering," and I just stayed with it.

DR: A year or two ago, you gave the commencement address at Northwestern. What's it like to go back to your alma mater and give the commencement address? Did friends of yours come up and say, "I always knew you were going to be successful"?

GR: There's a saying I like—I think about it in business a lot—"Success has a thousand parents, and failure is an orphan."

It was a nice thing to do. You do have that sense of going home for something.

DR: You were at General Motors for a couple years, and then you heard of an opportunity to go to a company called IBM. Who persuaded you to do that?

GR: That was my husband, Mark. People sometimes think, "Oh, you must have had a long, thought-out career plan." I'm sorry to tell you it was not that way. I had been working at General Motors, and while I liked what I was doing, I really liked technology and this idea of applying it to lots of different industries.

It was as simple as my husband saying, "Hey, I have a friend whose dad worked for IBM. Why don't you just call him?" I think it was my husband who actually set the interview up, to be honest with you.

DR: Did he get a finder's fee?

GR: I'm still paying that finder's fee.

I went to interview, and I was hired. I'd been at GM a few years. IBM did not do many professional hires. The typical thinking was, hire people out of university and train them. We're a very different company today. I was probably one of their very first professional hires.

DR: When you went to IBM, you started out in the engineering area?

GR: I started out as a systems engineer, and I worked in banking and insurance. I've had many experiences through my years there.

DR: For a while, you were in the consulting area.

GR: I did many different things at IBM—technical sales, marketing, strategy—through all the different parts of the company, but yes, there was a time when I started our consulting group.

DR: When you started doing these things, did you begin to think there was a chance you could be the CEO? Or did you think IBM, like many companies, was never going to make a woman CEO?

GR: No, it never entered my mind that IBM would make a choice based on gender. Never. IBM, for all my time there, has always been the most inclusive company I've known. I'd never thought about that. I always felt if you do great in your current job, it earns you a right to the next job.

DR: At some point, you're pretty much in the running to be the CEO. Were you surprised when Sam Palmisano, your predecessor, called you and said, "You're it"?

GR: I was surprised. I already had a great job at that time.

DR: Do you think that a woman, to rise up to be the head of IBM, had to be better than the men? Or it really didn't make a difference?

GR: I don't think at IBM it made a difference.

DR: You get the job, and now you're becoming one of the most power-ful women in the world, certainly in the business world. Do you feel a

certain responsibility as a woman CEO to mentor other women and to
speak out on issues relating to women?

GR: I have grown to be comfortable with being a role model. I think
many of my colleagues would say that, as we came through our businesses, we always wanted to be noticed and rewarded for what we did,
our contributions.

I would always think, "This has got nothing to do with gender,"
right? Almost blind to that. Over time, though, I really came to learn and
see how important it is that there be role models, and you have to accept
the fact that you are a role model on the appropriate things.

Another memory sticks out in my mind. Ten, fifteen years ago I was
down in Australia giving a financial-services presentation. I thought I'd
done an okay job at this. A man came up to me afterward, and I thought,
"He's going to tell me either this is great or he disagrees." And he looked
at me and he said, "I wish my daughters had been here." It's funny, the
sort of moments that you remember.

Any of us in these positions of any kind of influence, we are a role
model for someone. And women do need role models. We're still a small
minority that run these companies. They need role models who say,
"Yep, that's possible. I can be that." It's hard to dream to be something if
you don't see other people like you.

DR: Are you disappointed or surprised that, if you take the Fortune 100
or Fortune 200 companies, there are relatively few female CEOs still?

GR: I would have hoped by now there would be more. And so I think
there should be a very conscious effort, in fact, to keep women in the
workforce—to do everything you can to keep them in their jobs, to keep
going.

One of our newest benefits is shipping breast milk for babies for
mothers who are nursing, so they can keep working if they want to.
Keeping women in the workforce, to me, is one of the most important
ways to then create the pipeline for these roles.

DR: IBM had a policy for a while—maybe you instituted it—where you
could telecommute, but it didn't seem to work. Have you kind of gotten
rid of that policy? Was that something that was helpful to women?

GR: This is such a misconception. We never abandoned our policy; we have a great mobility policy. I have thousands of people who work remote all the time, or at times, at home. We have a great focus on mobility, work/life balance, et cetera.

However, for anybody running a company in this day and age, one of the things you need is speed. Let me tell you a little bit about how we've been modernizing the way people do their work. In many ways, we mirror the transformations our clients are going through.

As for how people do their work, you often hear about little companies able to work fast, right? They're nimble, they're small, they're agile. We've been at it a number of years, and I think we're the largest example of agile in the world.

So what does it mean if you want to get speed in a big company? Not just a little start-up—we're 350,000 people. So, we set about it in a couple of fundamental ways.

One is we've built design thinking. In fact, we have thirty-two labs around the world.

We've hired every design graduate there is on this planet. And the idea is that everything you use, like your phone, is simple. We're an enterprise company, business to business. But that same simplicity should be found in our work too. Whatever you're building, the process has to start with the end user in mind.

Next thing, we built agility at scale. Easy to say; super hard thing to do. But we've done it. It means that you train people in how to be agile, in small, multidisciplinary groups. And they work incrementally, producing minimum viable products. They're also co-located, which goes to your question about mobility.

Why do you do that? You do it for speed. We've spent well over a billion dollars renovating work spaces all over the world, open spaces for collaboration. There are a number of professions within IBM where we do want people co-located. I think that's what you're referring to.

To me, it's a new way of working. It's the right way of working. We can see the benefit of it. As I say to a lot of my colleagues, this idea of design thinking married with agile work methods, co-location, modern tools, that's the work environment. That does mean some people will not be able to work remotely. They need to come in and work with their colleagues together.

DR: Let's talk about the life of a CEO of a large company. How much time are you on the road?

GR: Probably 50 percent.

DR: Seeing customers or employees or government officials?

GR: All of the above, around the world.

DR: And customers, they're mostly interested in what? When you meet with them, you're trying to tell them why IBM is better than somebody else?

GR: Always in some way, of course, but many clients look at us as a bit of a mirror image. Years ago, they'd be saying to me, "Wow, that's a lot of change." And I can remember saying, "This is coming to a theater near you."

I believe our transformation mirrors what every company is going through. You'll rebuild yourself around data and the cloud. You're going to have to change how you do the work. And you're going to have to work on who the people are who do the work.

In our case, we've divested $10 billion of businesses and acquired sixty-five different companies to help build the portfolio. We've moved into entirely new products and services—something we called, to give our investors a signpost, strategic imperatives—around cloud, data, artificial intelligence, security. New businesses that now make up fifty percent of our revenues.

But portfolio's one thing; how you do your work is another. I tell clients that you have to change how you do your work.

DR: How do you measure your success as CEO? Is it share price? Is it earnings? Earnings per share? Revenue growth? What metric are you most focused on when you look at your company and when you talk to your board of directors?

GR: What I am most focused on and the board is most focused on is transforming IBM for this next era, this next cognitive era.

DR: Is there any frustration on the job? There must be something you don't like.

GR: The challenge is always to do things faster and faster. That's my own frustration—how to get things to happen faster and faster. That is the world we live in. It's about how fast you get things done.

DR: When you were at Northwestern, could you ever have imagined that you would be in this position now? And as you look back on it, what would you say is the secret of your having risen? Is it that you worked harder? You were smarter? You were nicer? What leadership tips should women and men know if they want to have your trajectory and career?

GR: I don't think it was any of the things you listed. If someone said, "Only name one thing you did," I think it's this idea of being a constant learner, of always being willing to say to yourself, "You don't know everything and you can learn something," from whoever. From this interview, from whoever you talk to—it doesn't have to be people you work for.

I have always had the viewpoint that every situation is a learning opportunity, and perhaps that was it. It's that curiosity. People say to me, "When you hire people now, what do you look for?" and I will say one of the biggest traits I look for is curiosity.

When we hire, we look for a propensity to learn, not just what you know in the moment, because it's so temporal. That was perhaps the biggest quality. I say to people, "If you don't have a natural curiosity, then you need to develop one." To me, that's what takes you forward.

DR: What would you like to see as your legacy? What would you like people to say about you five or ten or fifteen years from now?

GR: It's not about me. It's that IBM, once again, reinvented itself for the next era, uniquely positioned with great technology and the brightest people in the world. And that we've made the world work better, in health care, on education, on making this world safer. To me, if we help the companies of this world reinvent themselves and run better, that has a positive impact on society, and that's a great legacy.

INDRA NOOYI

Former Chairman and CEO, PepsiCo

"If you're willing to make all the trade-offs that you need to make, you can have it all. . . . There will be heartache, there will be pain, there will be some collateral damage underneath the surface. You have got to live with it."

As I have noted, female CEOs running large global companies are still, regrettably, somewhat rare. Even more rare are companies led by women who are immigrants to the United States. For many years, the most prominent such female CEO was Indra Nooyi, a native of India, who served as CEO of PepsiCo from October 2006 to October 2018.

During those years, Pepsi flourished, as its market value went from $104 billion to $154 billion. The company truly became global in its product reach and appeal, while also reflecting the zeitgeist of the period, producing healthier drinks and food.

On October 3, 2018, Indra stepped down as CEO to pursue other interests, including helping women, from all countries, reach their potential and become, among other things, leaders in their organizations. She continues to serve as a role model for women throughout the world, for she succeeded in a U.S. corporate environment largely led by white, native-born men.

I first met Indra when she was still at the Boston Consulting Group, advising Pepsi and other companies on corporate strategies. From that time on, I marveled at her rare combination of intellect, focus, work ethic, global perspective, and charm.

I stayed in touch with Indra through various Business Council, World Economic Forum, and other CEO gatherings. I have been able to interview her on several occasions, and have always been impressed with her commitment to Pepsi's global and health missions, as well as her recognition that being a female immigrant made her an example for so many.

How did Indra manage to rise to the top of a male-dominated business world; maintain strong family relationships with her parents, husband, and children; and become (and remain) such a visible role model? What is her leadership secret? Indra answered these questions, and many more, when I spoke with her on the PepsiCo campus in Purchase, New York, in November 2016.

In Indra's view, she was very well grounded by her parents—particularly her mother—and taught not to take herself too seriously, and to always be respectful of others. As she relates, there are trade-offs one must make to "do it all," and there are no shortcuts to high-level, profound success. Something must be sacrificed, to some extent.

One area that Indra did not sacrifice while at Pepsi was empathy for her employees. She regularly wrote to the parents of her senior employees, giving them a type of report card (invariably a positive one) about how their children were performing.

How can your mother get a favorable report card from your boss and you not feel undying loyalty to that boss? The report card on Indra from her PepsiCo employees was similarly positive—indeed effusive.

DAVID RUBENSTEIN (DR): Did you think, when you were a young girl in India, that you were going to grow up to be the CEO of a large company like Pepsi?

INDRA NOOYI (IN): This is like a dream come true. I pinch myself every day to say, "Is this really happening to me?" If you trace my roots and go back to where I was born and brought up and where I am today, those two points will never connect. To be here, in the United States, running such a large company, it's almost an unbelievable thing that's happened to me.

DR: You grew up in a very close family. When you were very young, your mother would, at the kitchen table, say, "Why don't you pretend you are prime minister of India?" What was she trying to teach you?

IN: She was a very bright woman, and she didn't go to college because her parents didn't think girls should go to colleges, and they couldn't afford to send her to college. In a way she lived vicariously through her daughters, so she kept pushing us to be whatever we wanted to be. "Dream big," she would always tell us, "but at eighteen I am getting you married off. But you can dream big until then."

So at the dinner table, virtually every day, she would sit down and have this conversation about "Give me a speech as if you were the president." One day it would be prime minister, one day it would be chief minister, and she would always critique us. She would never give us a compliment. She would just tell us: "No chief minister would do this, no prime minister will do this." She kept pushing us to be better and better and better, and if we got one compliment from her, we said, "Wow, we must have done really well."

So she really raised the bar constantly on us. She gave us hopes, but then anchored us firmly on the conservative South Indian values of you have got to get married at eighteen—which didn't happen, I want to tell you, but that's what she kept telling us.

DR: If you don't get married at eighteen, it's a disgrace at that time?

IN: That's the way she framed it for us. The other side was that my father and my grandfather said, "Dream, do whatever you want, just get a good set of grades at school so that your mother can get you married off." That was my upbringing. They had these checks and balances at home.

DR: You got some degrees in India, and then you decided to get a degree from the Yale School of Management. When you said to your parents, "I am going to go to Yale, which is in Connecticut in the United States," what did they say?

IN: This is perhaps the biggest mystery of them all, because my conservative mother and my supportive father actually allowed me to come to the United States. It shocked the hell out of me. I would have thought my mother would have fasted for days and thrown a temper tantrum. She didn't. She actually came to the airport and saw me off. They even bought me an airline ticket. Even today I wonder how they did it. What caused them to do it?

But they both were very supportive. They had enough people around here to look in on me and make sure I had a support system, but they encouraged me to go and live out my dreams.

DR: When you graduated, you began to go into various strategy positions. Where were you initially?

IN: I left Yale and went to the Boston Consulting Group in Chicago and spent six and a half years there. It was perhaps one of my most formative experiences, because being in strategy consulting—especially in BCG at that time, which is sort of the father of strategy—allowed me to see the problems of companies in a holistic way. It wasn't just marketing or just operations or supply chain or whatever, but every aspect of the company. It gave me ten years of experience in six years, and I became a better person because of that.

DR: How did PepsiCo hear of you?

IN: A headhunter called me one day and said, "Look, PepsiCo would like to talk to you." I came in and talked to Pepsi, and the rest is history.

DR: They gave you the job of being in charge of strategy.

IN: Yes. Head of corporate strategy.

DR: I assume everybody comes up to you and says, "Make Pepsi taste different" or "Make the Frito-Lay chip different." Do you get advice from people all the time, and do you ever listen to it?

IN: They give me ideas on products, how our existing products taste, and what new products we ought to be developing. They give me ideas and feedback on our commercials. They give me ideas for commercials, packaging. I get ideas for everything.

The most important thing is to keep both ears open, because you never know if a nugget of an idea can actually translate to a big success in the company. One of the things I have learned is not to dismiss the ideas. I catalogue all the ideas I get, then I send it out to my people, saying, "Hey, I listened to this group of people talk about our products and this is what I heard. Is there something here? Should we be doing something about it?" So I listen to everybody.

DR: Do you do some of the testing yourself?

IN: One of the greatest things about my job is I can actually taste and test products when they are in the early stages. Just to give you an idea, during our annual planning cycles I must taste somewhere between fifty and a hundred products over three days, whether it's snacks or beverages or Quaker products or Tropicana products—everything that they are thinking of launching over the next three years or five years. They will show me prototypes and I can give an opinion—not that my opinion is the only thing that counts, but I can give an opinion.

There is something else I do, David, which might sound a bit corny, but I am going to tell it to you. Anytime I visit anybody's home, within the first half hour I make it a point to find my way into the kitchen, and I am opening cupboards to see what products they have. To me it is very important that if I visit somebody in their home—anybody who invites me, it could be a friend or anybody—they have got to have Pepsi products.

DR: Is it harder to be a CEO now than it was ten years ago?

IN: The financial crisis in fact changed the world enormously. The world has not really recovered from the financial crisis. You have had geopolitical upheavals all over the world.

On top of that, technology disruption is absolutely rewriting the rules of most companies. What kind of jobs are you going to keep in the company? How are you going to digitize your value chain? How is e-commerce going to impact your business? There is some technology that's impacting every part of the company.

In this last seven years in particular it's been a real challenge to run a large company, because you have got to be a foreign policy expert, you have got to be a technology person, you have got to be able to talk to the front line, you have got to be able to talk to world leaders. CEOs have had to do a lot just to be able to manage their companies and keep them going in this incredibly troubled global environment. So it has been a challenge.

DR: Not long ago, an activist showed up and said, "Maybe you should spin off your Frito-Lay business, your snack business." What was your response, and how did you keep the activist happy?

IN: My job is not to keep an activist happy, my job is to make sure this company is managed for the next generation and is performing very, very well, and if the activist is happy in the process, so be it. I am an internal activist. I own thirty-three times my salary in PepsiCo stock; my entire net worth is in this company, so if an activist or anyone outside has a great idea on how to improve shareholder value that sustains, I listen to them.

So I listened to the activist. I have my own personal convictions and I have a superb board of directors. So I shared with them the strategy of the company, which you know I am very transparent with them about, and I told them where we are headed and where the activist wanted us to go. It was very clear to the board, as it was clear to me, that that was more of a short-term strategy, and what we were embarked on is really the long-term strategy. The board backed me, the courage of our convictions prevailed, and we are exactly where we were before the activist came, and are performing very well.

DR: Let's say it is very good, but most people would say that Pepsi-Cola and maybe Coca-Cola are not that healthy for you. So you must have heard that argument before. How does PepsiCo under your leadership try to make products like Pepsi healthier?

IN: Products like Pepsi-Cola were invented many, many years ago when society was completely different. There was more undernutrition than there was overnutrition, and at that time people felt that drinking products with that much sugar was all right. Society has changed, and it behooves us to change with society.

What are we doing overall? We are launching more products with zero or very low sugar. We are taking Pepsi itself and reformulating it for lower and lower sugar levels. The idea is to train the consumer to start accepting carbonated soft drinks with lower sugar levels.

Now, the challenge is that overnight you can't train the consumer to do that. You have got to step them down piece by piece, so that when we get to a level that is, you know, fifty or sixty calories per eight ounces or seventy calories per twelve ounces, they are comfortable with the product. That's the journey we're on.

DR: What about snack products? They have been criticized for having a lot of salt. How are you trying to make those healthier?

IN: Let me just give you a good piece of news. A single bag of Lay's has less salt than a slice of bread.

DR: Really?

IN: Yes, because it's surface salt. For bread you need it as a leavening agent. In soup you need it as a preservative. With potato chips, it's a surface salt, so it's actually three ingredients in a bag of Lay's: a little bit of salt, potatoes, and heart-healthy oil. So you can eat your bag of Lay's with a smile on your face. That's my first advice.

DR: I'm sure I would eat them with a smile on my face, but I wonder whether I would gain some weight.

IN: No.

DR: I won't gain weight?

IN: You exercise.

DR: Not enough.

IN: Whatever! I think you should be fine.

DR: Suppose somebody says, "Look, I don't care about being healthy, I just want to eat a great snack." What snack is going to make me the happiest?

IN: Fritos. Oh my God, you would feel like you died and went to heaven.

DR: You have over two hundred thousand employees. How can you possibly relate to them? Do you do it through e-mails? How do you keep your employees informed about everything when you have so many?

IN: We do videos, we do e-mails, we do town halls and forums every quarter. Every time I travel, we meet with the employees and I do town halls in that town or country. Occasionally I write very personal letters to the employee base as a whole. For example, when my kids were going to college, I wrote a personal letter to everybody saying, "I am going through tremendous separation angst." Or if I felt our employees were not calling their parents often enough, I'd write a letter about why it's important they call their parents. Whatever is on my mind on a personal basis. I want them to know me as a person rather than just an executive. I am very accessible to them, and I talk to everybody, from the front line to my senior executives.

DR: A number of years ago you spoke at the Economic Club of Washington and made a speech that I thought really captured a lot of people's attention. One of the things you said was that you write letters to your senior officers' mothers to kind of give them a report card of how their children are doing. Do you still do that, and what was the theory behind that?

IN: I have to take you back a few years to when I first became CEO. I went back to India to visit my mother, who was in India at that time. My father had passed away and my mother was there, and I stayed at the hotel because the home was a little bit more rugged and I wanted the comforts.

She told me I had to dress up and show up at home at seven in the morning. I wondered why, but you know when Mum gives you instructions, you just follow them. When I got home and I sat in the living room, a stream of visitors and random people started to show up. They would say hello to me and then go to my mum and say, "You did such a good job with your daughter. Compliments to you, she is CEO." But not a word to me. When I watched this interplay going on, I realized that I was a product of my upbringing and that my parents, if my father had been around, should both get the credit, because it's what they did for me and to me that allowed me to be who I was that day. It occurred to me that I had never thanked the parents of my executives for the gift of their child to PepsiCo.

So I came back and I started to write my direct reports to other senior executives' parents narrating the story, my cultural background, what happened when I went to India. Then I wrote a personal paragraph of what their child was doing at PepsiCo and said, "Thank you for the gift of your child to our company," and it opened the floodgate of emotions. Parents just started to communicate directly with me. It's been an amazing experience, because I now write to about four hundred executives' parents.

DR: When you write a letter to their parents, what do the executives say? Do they say, "Don't do that," or do they say, "I'm glad you told my mother or my father how well I am doing"?

IN: Our executives actually get very emotional about it, because their parents have never received such a letter, and their parents are now getting a letter that is always a positive report card. I'm not going to write anything else. Their parents are so delighted about receiving this letter, they tell their neighbors, their uncles and aunts. Then the executive says, "This is the best thing that happened to my parents and the best thing that happened to me," so the executive feels proud.

DR: Some people who have heard your story would say, "This person has it all. She's a woman who's become the CEO of a great company, she has a husband she has been married to for more than thirty years, two happy and healthy daughters who are gainfully employed." Is it possible for anybody, certainly a woman in our society, to have it all? Do you feel you have had it all?

IN: On a relative basis, yes, I have had it all. I'm very fortunate to have a wonderful husband, two great kids, a very tight-knit family, an awesome job with a great team. But to get here and to stay here there have been lots of trade-offs, lots of sacrifices, a lot of collateral damage. But somehow I have had the strength to power through all of that.

Can you have it all? That's the big question. If you have the right support system, if you have an understanding spouse, if you want to be married, and if you're willing to make all the trade-offs that you need to make, you can have it all. But while you do all that, there will be heartache, there will be pain, there will be some collateral damage underneath the surface. You have got to live with that.

DR: When you became the president of PepsiCo, you came home one day. Your mother was there and she asked you to get some milk, and—maybe you could tell the story better than I could.

IN: Way back in 2000, I was just informed about nine-thirty at night by a phone call that I was going to be president of the company. I went home to tell my family that I was going to be president of PepsiCo, and Mum opens the door. She was living with me at that time. I said, "Mum, I have got news for you," and she said, "Before the news, go get some milk." I said, "It's ten o'clock in the night. Why should I get milk?" I noticed that my husband's car was in the garage. I said, "Why didn't you tell him to get the milk?" She said, "Well, he came home at eight and he was very tired so I let him be. Now, you go get the milk."

You know you never question your mum. I went and got the milk, came back, sort of banged it on the countertop, and I said, "I had big news for you. I have just been appointed president of PepsiCo, and all that you care about is the milk." She just looked at me and she said, "What are you talking about? When you walk in that door, just leave that crown in the garage, because you are the wife, the daughter, the daughter-in-law, and the mother of the kids, and that's all I want to talk about. Anything else, just leave it in the garage. Don't even try this with me anymore." So I think with Mum you don't try anything.

DR: But she must be very proud that you are the CEO.

IN: I think she is, but she keeps me very grounded.

DR: What is more difficult—being a woman and being a CEO, or being an immigrant and being a CEO, or being a combination of all three? What do you think has caused you more difficulty, and what did you have to work to overcome more?

IN: I don't know if it is difficulty. Being a woman, an immigrant, has had its positives and its negatives. It's had its positives, because people take notice of you because you are so different. You walk in the room, and people say, "Oh, she's a different sort of a person—female, immigrant, tall." All these work together.

It's been difficult, because they think, "How will she know how to run this great American company?" So it has been both a positive and a negative, but I would say on balance more of a positive.

DR: Do you think a woman today has it easier than when you became CEO, or do you feel that you still have to work harder to be a woman CEO than, say, a man who is the CEO of an equivalent company?

IN: I think it's easier today, only because there are a few more of us in positions of power. But I think from a personal perspective, it's got nothing to do with women or being in this position. I have the immigrant fear: I am always afraid that if I fail, I may have to go back to something that I don't want to go back to. That fear always motivates me, and I drive myself to be better and better and better at my job every day.

DR: You are a role model for many women. Do you see yourself as a role model, particularly for women from India or from outside the United States?

IN: I don't have a choice but to be a role model. I feel a privilege to be the role model, whether it is for women, for minorities, for Indian women for sure. Everybody looks up to me and wants to learn from me and get my advice. There are so few of us, we have to play the role of being the role model, and we have to make sure we do a good job because we have to set the standard for others who might follow in our footsteps.

DR: I read that one time your husband was saying, "Indra, you are spending all your time on Pepsi, Pepsi, Pepsi. What about me?" What was your response?

IN: Even today, he will tell me, "Your list is PepsiCo, PepsiCo, PepsiCo, then the kids, then your mum, then somewhere in the bottom I sit there." I keep telling him, "You're on the list! Just be happy you are on the list!" But he knows that I love him dearly. He knows that he is my rock. He is my life. But he likes to be higher up on the list.

COMMANDERS

President George W. Bush
& President Bill Clinton

General Colin Powell

General David Petraeus

Condoleezza Rice

James A. Baker III

PRESIDENT GEORGE W. BUSH & PRESIDENT BILL CLINTON

Bill Clinton: "I was most proud that when I left office, we had the broadest period of shared prosperity in fifty years. That is where the bottom 20 percent's income in percentage terms increased more than the top 20 percent's, and nobody was mad at anybody else over it."

George W. Bush: "[I was most proud] that my daughters loved me. As Bill will tell you, it's a challenge to have teenage daughters when you're the president. . . .
Thanks to Laura's guidance and love, our little girls, our family unit strengthened. I think that's a great accomplishment."

The world's ultimate leadership position is now widely seen as that of the United States president. An enormous number of books and studies have been written about presidential leadership, and specifically what makes a great president. There is no simple answer.

Each president is different, and each brings different skills and experiences to the position.

It is not very often that different presidents become close to each other. They have often been rivals at some point. For that precise reason, the close relationship that developed between the Clinton and Bush families might not have been predicted right after the 1992 presidential campaign, when Bill Clinton beat the incumbent George H. W. Bush. But President Clinton and President Bush became good friends as they worked together on tsunami and hurricane relief efforts. And in time, President Clinton and the second President Bush also became quite friendly, working together on the Presidential Leadership Scholars Program.

That program selects talented midcareer professionals in the U.S. for enhanced leadership training and interaction with top government and business leaders. The training is a collaboration between the presidential libraries of George W. Bush, Bill Clinton, George H. W. Bush, and Lyndon B. Johnson. As such, the program focuses on lessons learned from the presidential experiences of these leaders. I have been a supporter of the program, and have also known both President Clinton and President Bush for a number of years.

I have also interviewed both of them before, though separately. The occasion for this joint interview was the final 2017 session of the Presidential Leadership Scholars Program held at the George W. Bush Institute in Dallas.

The friendly relationship between the two former presidents was evident in the interview, and there was more than a fair amount of joking between them. But they were both serious about the responsibilities they undertook as president, and the separate personal qualities and experiences they brought to the presidency.

While being a former president is one of the great jobs anyone can have, both Bush and Clinton agree that nothing is as great as the ability being president provides to have a positive impact on lives in the United States and around the world.

Their paths to the presidency, as they discussed, were so different: One was raised in modest circumstances by a single mother—his father died before his birth—and was an outstanding student leader, a Rhodes Scholar, a young, six-term governor of Arkansas. The other was raised in comfortable circumstances, the son of a U.S. president, but was certainly not an outstanding student or someone who even considered a political career for himself until midlife, and then was thought even by his parents to have only a modest chance to get elected as governor of Texas.

Presidents come from all backgrounds, and draw on different leadership skills. President Clinton had to manage through a hostile Republican House, a special counsel investigation, and an impeachment challenge; President Bush had to manage through the 9/11 attacks, the wars in Afghanistan and Iraq, and the Great Recession. Not easy for either of them, or their families and supporters. But they came to know a fair bit about leadership through difficult circumstances.

Indeed, it has often been written that our greatest presidents are those who rose to the challenge in the most difficult of times—Abraham Lincoln during the Civil War, or Franklin D. Roosevelt during World War II.

Both Presidents Clinton and Bush had to rise to the challenge, and their mettle was certainly tested during these times. It might be thought that they are pleased to now have those pressures behind them. But both seem to realize that, despite the pressures, the presidency enabled them to help so many others—and they do miss that platform.

DAVID RUBENSTEIN (DR): You're now both former presidents. What's the difference between being a former president and president? One day, you have the nuclear codes. You can send nuclear bombs off. Everybody is working for you. And the next day, when you leave office, you have no power. What was the transition like?

BILL CLINTON (BC): Nobody plays a song when you walk in a room anymore. I was lost for the first three weeks after I left office. I kept waiting for the music, you know?

Actually, it's wonderful. Very rarely in seventeen years have I even given a thought to "Well, I wish I were there. I could do this. Or I miss this."

You have to be grateful for the time you have, and then realize you should focus on today and the future. It's both liberating and also it concentrates the memory.

You don't know how many years you've got left, but you feel that the country's given you something priceless, and you owe something back. Each in our own way, we've tried to figure that out. I found it a really rewarding part of my life. I've loved it.

GEORGE W. BUSH (GWB): I woke up in Crawford [Texas], the day after I left the presidency, expecting someone to bring me the coffee. Laura didn't bring the coffee.

The thing that startled me was the sense of having no responsibility. In other words, during the presidency, you kind of become accustomed to the responsibility you have. First it's pretty grave, and then, slowly but surely, it becomes a natural part of your life. Then you wake up the next day and you have no responsibility. That was probably the most stunning thing for me.

DR: When you're president, when you try to do something, you have somebody in the opposite political party, typically, who says it's a terrible idea. It's hard to get things done in Washington, maybe harder than it's ever been now. But it was hard when you were there as well. When you're a former president, do you find it's easier to get things done?

GWB: Yes. It depends on what you're trying to do.

BC: First of all, you have to realize what you don't have and what you do have. It's really true that I loved the job. I loved all the responsibility. It's amazing how much of every day is taken up by things you have to do as president and by the incoming fire.

If you don't deal with the incoming fire, it will undermine your ability to do anything else. If all you deal with is the incoming fire, you can't keep the promises you made when you were running. So it's a lot of trouble.

When you get out, you change all that power for whatever influence you have and whatever your experience and contacts will permit you to do. And you have to decide what to do.

Everybody makes different decisions. President Carter, he's building Habitat for Humanity houses in Canada. It's what he decided he wanted to do. By doing it, he helped Habitat to grow into one of the biggest home-building operations in the world. We all had to make these decisions.

GWB: I don't think it's that easy to get things done, necessarily. For example, one of the great accomplishments in my postpresidency was the building of this building [the Bush Presidential Center] and the installation of programs that we think make a difference. But it was hard work to get there. In other words, there's not an appropriations bill.

DR: [*to Clinton*] You ran against President Bush 41. It was a bitter campaign. He was defeated for reelection. How did you manage later to develop a close relationship? Wasn't that very difficult or awkward at times, because you had run against each other? He had called you names. You had called him names. How did you come together?

BC: It helped that we had some contact before. I represented the Democratic governors when he decided to embrace these national education goals. He asked the governors to help write them, and we started working together. I tried never to take a cheap shot in the Governors

Association. If we disagreed, we said it and went on. We found things we could do together. Sometimes you click with people, and sometimes you don't.

GWB: I have a different take on what I think is one of the most unique relationships in U.S. political history. I think it starts with Bill Clinton being a person who refused to lord his victory over Dad. In other words, he was humble in victory, which is very important in dealing with other people. And Dad was willing to rise above the political contest.

It starts with the individual's character. Both men, in my judgment, displayed strong character, and therefore their friendship was able to be formed.

Now, why do I have a friendship with him? Well, because he's called a brother with a different mother. He hangs out in Maine more than I do.

DR: When you were running in 2000, you were campaigning against some of the things that the Clinton administration had done?

GWB: We're both baby boomers, and we're both Southern governors. We had a lot in common. He got along with people in his legislature. I got along with mine. We had friends in common. So there was a natural ability to respect and like each other. If you disagree with someone, it doesn't mean you don't like him.

BC: Also, I recognized that he was forty-four days older than me, so I called him on his birthday and I said, "I'm calling you on bended knee, because this begins my forty-four days of respect for my elders."

GWB: When I was president, I would call Bill. He was very helpful. He knew a lot about a variety of issues, particularly international affairs, that I was interested in. I knew I could count on him for good advice, and he was gracious in receiving my calls.

DR: President Clinton, you've done something that was unique. All of us who have gone to school recognize that sometimes there's somebody who's the student body president, who's the class president. Everybody thinks this person could be president of the United States. But none of them actually have made it except you. What drove you to keep being such a leader? Most people burn out.

BC: I also lost two elections along the way, which kind of keeps you humble. First of all, I think all that stuff's way overrated. I think I got elected because we're the last generation that was born without a television. I was ten years old before we got a television. I grew up in a conversational culture, where people actually talked and listened to each other.

I don't know how these people make it today. The average television clip of a president on the news is eight seconds. Snapchat's ten seconds. Twitter's 140 characters.

My life revolved around meals. My father died in a car wreck before I was born, so I spent a lot of time with my grandparents and their generation. My great-uncle was the smartest guy in our family. He presided over conversations, and he involved the kids in them.

He taught me that everybody's got a story and most people can't tell it, and that's sad. And that people are inherently interesting if they can get out of their own way. So I was taught to listen and to look. I really think that's what it is. I always thought I'd have a better life if I could help somebody else have a better life too. I liked it. I don't care what anybody says. All these people who tell you they were born in a log cabin they built themselves are full of bull.

DR: What was the biggest surprise the first day you were in the Oval Office? You learn the secrets, the nuclear codes. You learn all the crises that we might be getting into. When did it hit you that you're president of the United States, you're the most powerful man in the world? When did it first hit you? The first day, the first week, the first month?

BC: Harry Truman said that the most amazing thing about being president is you spend so much of your time trying to talk people into doing things they should do without your asking them in the first place. What surprised me—it may be because I had one of the best gigs, I was the governor of a small Southern state—you're so far removed from the American people that it's hard for them to see you as a three-dimensional person.

It really surprised me how easily I could be turned into a two-dimensional cartoon instead of a three-dimensional human being. You have to discipline yourself about what to talk about, how to talk about it. You have to keep remembering there are all these layers between you and people that didn't used to be there. That surprised me. I thought I was a pretty good communicator, and I just fell on my face four or five times till I figured out how to do it.

DR: You became president at a very young age. You were forty-six years old. If you had been president at fifty-six or sixty-six, do you think it would have been different? Would you have had less energy at that age or more experience?

BC: I think I would have been better in some ways if I had been older. But I would have been not as good in some ways, because sometimes you get a bunch done because you're too dumb to know you can't do it. You show up and you keep trying to do it and something happens.

DR: President Bush, when your father was president, you obviously were in the White House. You saw what he did right and what he might have done wrong. Did you take any lessons from that? Were you trying to separate yourself from your father in some ways?

GWB: No, I learned a lot from watching him. I wasn't interested in separation from him, and he wasn't interested either. We've got a great father-son relationship.

My most startling moment came right after the inaugural parade. I decided I was going to go in the Oval Office to see what it felt like. Unbeknownst to me, Andy Card [Bush's chief of staff] had called up to the Residence and asked Dad to come in. I was sitting in the Oval Office at the desk there, kind of just taking it all in, and in walks my dad. I said, "Welcome, Mr. President." And he said, "Thank you, Mr. President."

DR: Wow, that must have been something. What was it like when your mother walked into the Oval Office the first time and you're the president of the United States?

BC: She started laughing out loud, it was so ridiculous, you know? The idea of it, that it could have ever happened. On the other hand, when I started running, she was the only person who thought I had a good chance to win. Nobody else did. Hillary and Chelsea were undecided at the beginning.

It made me feel good, because my mother had a pretty tough life. She was widowed three times. She got up at five every morning and got herself ready and was at work by seven and then did everything she could to take care of me. So I was proud to be able to show it to her. She was ill then. She lived a little less than another year.

GWB: You want to know what my mother said? "Get your feet off the Jeffersonian table."

DR: Some people call living in the White House kind of a prison, because you really can't get out very much. Or do you really enjoy it and it's a great thing? You've got all these servants there, and you go to Camp David when you want.

BC: If you've lived an informal life—even though I spent almost a dozen years in the Governor's Mansion in Arkansas—it's very different. I basically was self-supporting from the time I was nineteen, and it took some getting used to.

But I developed a real respect and affection for the people who worked there. I developed an enormous amount of respect for the Secret Service and the risks they take. I've adjusted myself accordingly. And I loved living in the White House.

I remember very vividly the last time I got off of the helicopter, Marine One, and walked into the White House as president before I would soon be gone and he would be there. I was consciously aware that I was going in there more optimistic about America than the first time I walked in. More idealistic. I never got tired of it.

DR: [*to Bush*] And did you like living in the White House?

GWB: Yeah, I did. It's great. They really pamper you. We knew a lot of the staff. They were the same people who worked there when Bill was there, and many of the same when Dad was there. So Laura and I got to know them when we went to visit.

But it's great. It's really, really a historic place. It is comfortable. I loved every minute of living there.

DR: So tell us, what's it like at Camp David? Is it a great place to have a retreat and relax? Or is it really overrated?

BC: It's a great place. I loved it most at Thanksgiving, because I'd bring all our family in. And I liked it when Chelsea could bring her friends up there. At least you're under the illusion that you have, while you're on the ground, more freedom of movement, more wandering-around time. It's great just to get away.

DR: [to Bush] Did you like it?

GWB: Yes. We went there a lot, and probably used it more than any president. Maybe Ronald Reagan used it more. One reason we went a lot is we could invite our friends. One of the great delights of the presidency was to invite friends we grew up with in Midland, for example, and show them the Oval Office or show them Camp David.

The other thing I liked about it a lot is that I love exercise, and the place is set up for hiking, running, mountain biking. There's a wonderful gym there. And I found it to be liberating.

DR: [to Clinton] Your exercise is you played golf. You obviously have lost weight since you left the presidency. You've gone on a vegan diet. Isn't that hard to do?

GWB: Less burgers.

DR: How did you do that?

BC: Not when you have a quadruple heart bypass and you want to live to be a grandfather. I didn't give it a second thought. I realized that I was highly prone to arterial blockage. I literally wanted to see if I could live to be a grandfather. Unlike him [indicating Bush], who comes from great genes, I am now the oldest person in my family for three generations, man or woman.

GWB: Wow.

BC: I said, "I think I'd like to hang around. I'm kind of having a good time being alive. It'll be over soon enough, and I think I'll just stretch it out as long as I can."

DR: You two are among only thirteen people in our country's history who served two consecutive terms as president. What do you think is more enjoyable—being president of the United States for two terms, or former president of the United States for thirty or forty years?

BC: It depends on how you keep score. You've got to live a long time as a former president to have the impact on as many people as you can as president. I've tried to do as best I could on that, but if you gave me the choice, I'd serve two terms.

GWB: Me too. The reason why is the decisions you make have a monumental effect on a lot of people. It's exciting to be in that kind of environment. It insists that you use all your skills and your energy in order to affect policy in a positive way. The interesting thing about the presidency is it's often defined by the unexpected. Which makes the job doubly interesting.

BC: It's very interesting, though. A lot of our most successful former presidents are one-term. John Quincy Adams went back to Congress for sixteen years and became one of our most important antislavery advocates. William Howard Taft became chief justice. Herbert Hoover came out of retirement and wrote the Civil Service Act. They did a lot of good things. George and I have been blessed, because we were reasonably young. Barack Obama's young. You can be double lucky. You can serve eight years as president and then do some other good things.

DR: John Kennedy was once asked at a press conference, "Would you recommend the job?" And he said, "Not to others right now, I guess. Wait till I've finished my tenure." But would you recommend the job to people? Would you say it's worth the aggravation factor and all the hard work to become president?

BC: In a heartbeat.

GWB: Same.

DR: Our country's had roughly 550 million people over the course of our history. Forty-five of them have been elected president. What would you say in your eight years in the White House you are most proud of having done?

BC: I was most proud that when I left office, we had the broadest period of shared prosperity in fifty years. That is where the bottom 20 percent's income in percentage terms increased more than the top 20 percent's, and nobody was mad at anybody else over it. It was shared across racial and religious and regional lines. Did I abolish inequality? No. You can't in a market society. But at least we found a way to have more shared prosperity, including three budget surpluses.

If everybody's got a decent job and something to look forward to in the morning, about 90 percent of the other problems go away. Whatever arguments we might have, let's say about health-care policy or any other social policy, it will all become less significant if people think they can start a business and keep a job and educate their kids. Then families are stable, communities are more stable, and all the other problems get smaller.

DR: [*to Bush*] What would you say in your eight years you were most proud of?

GWB: That my daughters loved me. As Bill will tell you, it's a challenge to have teenage daughters when you're the president. It's a challenge anytime to have teenage daughters. Thanks to Laura's guidance and love, our little girls, our family unit strengthened. I think that's a great accomplishment.

BC: Me too. You know what I think? This is what I think a lot of people don't believe about people like us. If you take it seriously, your most important job until your kids are out of the house is being a father or a mother.

DR: [*to Bush*] One of the things that you are now famous for is taking up painting. How did you decide to pick up painting, and why does it give you so much pleasure?

GWB: Because it heralds our veterans. I painted because I was bored. This foundation and institute take up time, but not enough. My exercise program wasn't taking enough. I read Winston Churchill's essay "Painting as a Pastime" and I basically said, "If that guy can paint, I can paint."

DR: President Clinton, since you left the presidency, you've changed your diet and done other things, but what gives you the greatest pleasure now? Is it the Clinton Global Initiative?

BC: Yeah, building my foundation and trying to fund it. It got so big so fast that it just took up all my time. I'm trying to make it more entrepreneurial. But our health initiative now provides AIDS medicine to more than half the people in the world on treatment. And the Clinton Global Initiative has improved more than four hundred million lives.

You have to just keep at it all the time. And at first I thought, "Oh, I don't want to do this." But I did. I'm a workaholic, and I didn't think I could be a gifted painter. I think he would tell you the best thing that can happen to you when you're in politics is to be consistently underestimated.

GWB: I was pretty good at that.

DR: If somebody wants to be president of the United States, is the quality that is most important hard work, intelligence, optimism, luck? What do you think it takes for somebody who says, "I want to be president; I want to be like you"?

GWB: Humility. It's really important to know what you don't know and listen to people who do know what you don't know.

BC: I also think you have to begin with the end in mind. That is, you have to say, "Yeah, you've got to win the election. But why in the heck are you running?"

That's the other thing I noticed about him. When he ran for governor against Ann Richards, he didn't say, "Ann Richards is a klutz." He said, "I want to be governor, because I want to do one, two, three things." A couple of them I didn't agree with, but he had an agenda.

If you want to be president, realize it's about the people, not about you. That's what a lot of these people who are real arrogant in office forget. Time passes. And it passes more quickly than you know.

You want to be able to say, "People were better off when I quit. Kids had a better future. Things were coming together." You don't want to say, "God, look at all the people I beat. Or the people I worked over." The most important thing is to be humble, to listen, to realize everybody's got a story—all the things I learned as a kid.

GENERAL COLIN POWELL

Former Chairman of the Joint Chiefs of Staff and Former U.S. Secretary of State

"I've always taken on every job I've had with, 'What am I trying to do? What's the purpose? What's the vision? Why are we here? What are we doing?' Then get that down to the lowest person in the organization, and make sure they have whatever they need, whether it's diplomatic weapons or real weapons of war, and make sure that I took care of them and gave them every opportunity to be successful. That's what leadership is all about—inspiring followers."

Colin Powell's rise to the most senior military and civilian positions in the federal government—chairman of the Joint Chiefs of Staff and secretary of state—might not have been easily predicted during his youth. He was the son of Jamaican immigrants living in New York, an indifferent student, a geology major at City College of New York, with no well-formed career plans or ambitions.

But Colin joined the U.S. Army following his ROTC training. He overcame racial discrimination, while rising in a series of military combat training and Pentagon assignments before achieving the military's highest position during the presidency of George H. W. Bush. He is the only African American to hold the position of chairman of the Joint Chiefs of Staff.

It was during that time that Colin first came to universal public attention, for he was the military official responsible for the effort to dislodge Iraqi troops from Kuwait in 1990. With that effort's enormous success—in part due to the "Powell Doctrine" of assembling and utilizing massive force—he became one of America's most prominent and admired individuals.

As events unfolded, the victory in Kuwait seemed relatively easy. The military fighting stopped within just a hundred hours. But for that to occur, Colin Powell had to use his military commander skills, working to develop and implement a successful combat approach, and then working closely with the military leader on the ground, General Norman Schwarzkopf. He also had to use his civilian commander skills, lining up support for his costly and time-consuming approach with the president, the secretary of defense, the White House staff, and, of course, Congress, which ultimately was asked to provide legislative approval for the undertaking.

The combined military and civilian leadership needed in this effort was something that few in the country could have provided as well as Colin Powell.

When he retired from the military in 1993, Colin wrote his bestselling book *My American Journey*. Its success further intensified the considerable pressure for him to run for president in 1996 as a Republican against President Bill Clinton.

Ultimately, Colin decided that he did not have the requisite passion to run for office, and forswore any political campaign, though he did agree to return to public service as secretary of state during the first term of President George W. Bush. In that role, Secretary Powell had to deal with the aftermath of the 9/11 terrorist attack on the World Trade Center, and also the invasion of Iraq in the effort to destroy weapons of mass destruction believed to be possessed by Saddam Hussein.

Colin returned to private life after President Bush's first term, and continued his earlier focus on many civic and philanthropic activities, including America's Promise Alliance, the organization he helped to start in 1997 to improve the lives of young people. He also created the Colin Powell School for Civic and Global Leadership at his alma mater, the City College of New York, to enable students there to become the next generation of our country's leaders.

I have come to know and greatly admire Colin over the past few decades through various philanthropic and civic organizations, and at events in Washington and New York. And I have had the chance to interview him at a number of business and nonprofit events.

This particular interview for *Peer to Peer* was held at the Colin Powell School at CCNY—an undertaking of enormous pride for Colin and his family—in November 2017. I am proud to be a charter supporter of the school. In the interview, Colin recognizes that his remarkable military and civilian life of leadership was not always successful. For instance, he was asked by President Bush to make the public case to the United Nations that Saddam Hussein had weapons of mass destruction, thereby justifying the invasion the U.S led.

Of course, there were no such weapons. Colin had relied on our best intelligence sources, but they were wrong. He relates in the interview his embarrassment at having been so wrong. In truth, he had not been anxious to make the case to the U.N. But President Bush asked him to do so, and Colin felt, as the leader of the State Department, and with his well-established international credibility, that he had to be the individual to assume this responsibility.

To Colin, that is what leadership entails. A leader, in his view, has to be the person who gives followers their inspiration, their desire to get the task at hand done. And he has done that throughout his remarkable career, only a small part of which could be considered in this interview.

DAVID RUBENSTEIN (DR): You grew up in the Bronx?

COLIN POWELL (CP): I was born in Harlem, about a mile from here, and I grew up in the South Bronx section of New York—the Hunts Point section.

DR: And your parents were immigrants from—?

CP: Jamaica.

DR: Did you enjoy New York as a young boy?

CP: I thought it was a wonderful place to be a kid. It was such a diverse place that I really learned this is what the world is. The world is full of people of different backgrounds, cultures, colors, you name it. And, of course, the City College of New York replicates that perfectly.

DR: Did you learn Yiddish there?

CP: I learned a little Yiddish working for six years in another corner of the South Bronx, at a place called Jay Sickser's, which sold baby furniture and carriages and toys.

He was a Russian Jew. There was me. There was an Irish driver, an Italian salesman in the store. After I had been doing this for a couple of years with Jay, he came up to me and he put his arm around my shoulder and he says, "Coli, Coli"—a Jewish/Yiddish diminutive—"Coli, Coli, don't think you can stay here at the store. This will go to my daughters and to their husbands. I want you should get your education and go somewhere and do something."

I had no intention of staying at that store and being what's called a "schlepper," somebody that just drags boxes around.

It touched me so deeply that I remembered it for the rest of my life and wrote about it in my memoir. He thought enough of me to tell me that I should get my education and move up. And that's what I did, and CCNY was the source of that education.

DR: Did you ever think that one day you would be the chairman of the Joint Chiefs and the secretary of state of the United States?

CP: No. People ask me about this all the time. It usually starts out with "What year did you graduate from West Point?" I didn't go to West Point. I couldn't have aspired to go to West Point. "Well, did you go to the Citadel, or did you go to Texas A&M or Virginia Military Institute?" I say, "No, they wouldn't let black guys in then."

It was beyond any possible level of aspiration or expectation, but it happened. Why did it happen? Because I got a quality public school education that I didn't know was of that high quality at the time. Elementary school, junior high school, high school. And then CCNY let me in, with my modest average. And it was ROTC and CCNY that really made the difference.

DR: And you were a geology major? Did you think you were going to go into the geology world?

CP: No, I was a geology major because I busted out of civil engineering, okay? Now you know. That didn't need to come up, David. Thank you very much.

DR: When you graduated, when you're in ROTC, you have an obligation to go into the military.

CP: I graduated in '58 and then went to Fort Benning, which was still in a segregated state, in a segregated city—Columbus, Georgia. I knew well that on post I was like anybody else, but as soon as I left post, there were places I could not go, stores I could not go into, places I could never think of even ordering a hamburger. I was thrown out of hamburger joints in Columbus, Georgia.

DR: They just would say, "We don't serve you"?

CP: It was even worse than that.

I stopped at a little hamburger joint late one night, and I knew I couldn't go in, so I just went to the window and asked for a hamburger. This nice white lady from New Jersey said, "I'm sorry. I don't know why, but I can't serve you. You can go around the back." I said, "No thanks," left, and went back onto the base. That was in early 1964.

Then the Civil Rights Act of 1964, the Accommodations Act, was signed in July, just before July 4. On July 5, I went back to that hamburger joint and they served me. What America discovered is that segregation was not just a burden for blacks; it was a burden for whites, who were living in a crazy system.

DR: You went to Vietnam, and you were injured. And you came back to the States, and you went back again to Vietnam?

CP: Yes, about five years later. I went back and got injured again.

DR: When you came back again, your career really took off. You became a White House Fellow?

CP: I did. I was one of about fifteen people who would serve one year in Washington in one of the offices of the cabinet. In my case, I worked in the Office of Management and Budget, and I learned a lot about government in that year.

DR: After your White House Fellowship, you did what?

CP: I went to Korea to command an infantry battalion. I consider that one of the most rewarding years I've had in the army. We were just starting out under the volunteer army, and it was my opportunity not only to train these young people but to give them a GED education.

DR: And English as a second language. You eventually went to Europe?

CP: I was in Europe as a young lieutenant for two years. Then I was pulled back into the Pentagon once again to work for Caspar Weinberger.

DR: He was then the secretary of defense.

CP: He was the secretary of defense, and I was his senior military assistant. We became exceptionally close. After two years, it was time for me to move on and get back in the army, and they got me an assignment in Germany, where I was going to take command of a division.

DR: That was a great job at the time?

CP: It was a great job. It lasted four months.

DR: Because what happened was, there was the Iran-Contra scandal?

CP: Yes.

DR: Then the new national security advisor, Frank Carlucci, came in and he wanted you as his deputy.

CP: Yes. I said, "Frank, it can't be that important." He says, "It is that important." Then I said to myself, "Okay, see if you can risk your entire career by saying the next sentence." I said, "Well, Frank, if it's that important, why doesn't the president call me?" Half an hour later—

DR: You get a call from—?

CP: "Hello, General Powell. This is Ronald Reagan." "Yes, sir." "I really, really want you to come back here—" I can tell he's reading the talking points Frank gave him. "I really, really want you to come back here and be the deputy national security advisor." "Yes, sir, I'll be right there." And that's it.

DR: So you came back?

CP: Yes. Nine months later, Frank got assigned to become the secretary of defense, and I'm thinking, "Good. I can go back to the army now."

Then one day I was chairing a National Security Council meeting, and suddenly the door opens and the president walks in and goes to the head of the table. Frank comes around to the side, and while the meeting is going on, he rips off a piece of paper and scribbles something on it and sends it down the table to me. I open up the little piece of paper, and it says, "You're now the national security advisor." No interview, no nothing.

So the last year and a half of my time in the White House was with President Reagan. It became an extremely close and strong relationship.

DR: When the administration ended, you went back into a military position?

CP: Yes.

DR: But not that long afterward, President George Herbert Walker Bush, the president of the United States right after Ronald Reagan, said, "I need you to be chairman of the Joint Chiefs of Staff."

CP: I was in Atlanta, Georgia, with a great command, a beautiful house, nice headquarters, and I'm at a conference in the Baltimore area with all the army's senior four-star generals, and I get a call: "Secretary Cheney, now the new secretary of defense, wants to see you." I said, "Uh-oh." So I go to the Pentagon in chinos and a polo shirt, and go into his office, and he says, "President Bush wants to make you the chairman."

DR: You became the chairman of the Joint Chiefs of Staff, the highest military job?

CP: Yes.

DR: Early in the Bush administration, Saddam Hussein invaded Kuwait. Was it clear to you that we should go in and try to kick him out?

CP: Well, it was clear to me that this was a horrible invasion that could not be allowed to stand. The first challenge was to make sure he didn't go south into Saudi Arabia. General Norman Schwarzkopf was the commander in this region. He and I were pretty close, and we talked about all of this.

DR: You invented something that became known as the Powell Doctrine.

CP: Not quite. It was invented by a *Washington Post* reporter who came to see me one day, and he said, "I'm writing an article about the Powell Doctrine." I said, "Great, what is it?"

He said, "What you always say and what you did when we invaded Panama and took out Manuel Noriega. One, make sure you go to war after all diplomatic and political possibilities have been dealt with. There has to be a clear political objective, not just a military objective."

The second part of the Powell Doctrine is—I used the term *overwhelming force* once, but what I've always said is *decisive force*, so that people don't think you have to have a gazillion troops, just have what you need to have a decisive outcome.

DR: You get the order from the president to kick Saddam Hussein and his troops out?

CP: When that decision came down that we could not find a diplomatic solution, I received the order, and I gave the order to Norm, and we were ready.

It was the only conflict I've ever been in or read about in history where I could say to the president of the United States, "There is no question about the outcome." The Iraqis had made several horrible mistakes.

They put their line of soldiers right on the border with Saudi Arabia, and they were stuck. They couldn't move. Airpower would not let them move. They had four divisions along the coast, and they were very light. All we had to do was keep these two forces in place, and go around them—the left hook, as it's also referred to.

And that's what we did. The night we launched the ground attack, after air attacks for several weeks, I told the marines who were right opposite the Iraqis, "Attack, but don't get decisively engaged. I don't want to lose a bunch of marines. I just want you to freeze the Iraqis in place." Same thing on the coast: "Amphibious operations, but you're not going to shore. Just freeze them, because we're going to go around them all."

Being marines, they did what they were told, but some found ways to penetrate the fire barriers that the Iraqis had put in place—the fire trenches, the barbed wire, the minefields—and cut a path right through the Iraqi army facing us. Military doctrine says, "Exploit a success like that." So we told the marines, "Go." They burst right through the Iraqi force and were heading to Kuwait City before we even launched the left hook.

DR: Ultimately the war is over, and you write a book about your life called *My American Journey*. When you were doing your book tour, people said, "This man should be president of the United States."

CP: It had never occurred to me. Suddenly the book came out and it caught media attention, and lots of people were coming to me saying, "You need to run." Well, I didn't ever think of running, and I had no particular passion to run, but I felt an obligation to consider the matter.

And so I did. You know, I'm a serviceman, and I try to do what I think is right. Many in the Republican Party did not want me to run as a Republican. They even put out a statement saying, "We don't want him in the party."

DR: Because you were too moderate?

CP: Yes, probably because I was too moderate.

DR: Any regrets about not having run?

CP: No. Why?

DR: Some people say it's a great job.

CP: Prove it.

DR: When you decided not to run, a lot of people were disappointed. You stayed in the private sector, and then George W. Bush is elected president. He calls you and says, "I'd like you to be secretary of state"?

CP: I sensed he was the kind of Republican that I would want to be. And so I was pleased to be able to go back in the government and serve my country.

DR: So you're secretary of state, and then 9/11 happens. When did you realize that the government would have to be involved in some kind of military confrontation?

CP: You can't let something like that go by without doing something about it. My job was not to immediately get involved in military matters, but to pull the international community together.

It was a very rewarding experience. For the first time in NATO's history, they invoked what is called Article Five, which said, "If any member of the alliance is attacked, we are all attacked." So they were all on our side.

DR: Subsequently, we turned our attention to Iraq, and President Bush decided that we would do an invasion of Iraq, to go after Saddam Hussein.

CP: What I said to the president was, "Mr. President, you need to understand that if you take out this government, you would become responsible as the new government. You become responsible for twenty-seven million Iraqis who will be standing there, looking at us. You take on great responsibility. Are you sure you understand that and you want to do it?"

We were in private when having this conversation, and he said, "What's the alternative?" I said, "The alternative is to have the U.N. be in the first position. They're the ones whose resolutions have been violated. So let's have a diplomatic approach."

DR: President Bush said, "I agree with your idea of going to the U.N. and convincing them"?

CP: He did. Before taking military action, he wanted to present our case to the United Nations, publicly. And so on a Thursday afternoon, I was in with him and he said, "Would you take the case next week?"

DR: To the U.N.?

CP: Yes.

DR: You made the case that Saddam did have—or we thought he had—weapons of mass destruction when it turned out he didn't?

CP: Right.

DR: Do you think you were embarrassed by that, or do you think that the U.S. was embarrassed? Do you think that had we known Saddam didn't have weapons of mass destruction, President Bush would have gone ahead anyway?

CP: No, he would not have gone ahead. I asked him that specific question when we were going through this. I said, "Mr. President, if Saddam Hussein can prove that he has no weapons of mass destruction, then you do not have a basis for war. Are you prepared to accept that, even if it means Saddam Hussein will stay in place?" Hesitantly, he said, "Yes, I will accept that."

I went out and spent three days at the CIA with the intelligence communities, and prepared the document that I would present. Every word in there was approved by the CIA, was written by the CIA. And so we went. I gave the presentation. It seemed to go well. I was confident that it went well. But then within a few days or a couple of weeks, it started to fall apart.

So, yes, I was more than embarrassed. I was mortified, because even though the president had used the same information, Congress had used the same information, Secretary Donald Rumsfeld, Condoleezza Rice, all of us had used the same information, I'm the one who made the biggest presentation of it. It all sort of fell on me.

DR: Today, in hindsight, would you say the invasion was a mistake?

CP: I'd say the execution of the invasion was not done properly. We abandoned the Iraqi army without any discussion back in Washington, and then we abandoned something worse, the Ba'ath Party, and said that anybody who worked for the Ba'ath Party could not work in the new government. Those were two monstrously bad strategic decisions, and we did not have enough force in there to do what we wanted the Iraqi army to do, and the place fell apart.

Right now, Iraq has a democracy. It's tricky, but it's a democracy. They have elections, and they are trying to restore order in their country. I think it's bad that we went about it in such a terrible way. In my humble judgment—others will not agree with me—if they come through this difficult process they're in now as a democracy, no weapons of mass destruction, no Saddam Hussein, then I think you'd have to judge this differently than what's being judged now.

DR: You've had an extraordinary life in public service. Did your parents live to see your success?

CP: They both saw me make colonel. And they were very proud of that.

But my father was failing, I could see that. He died about a year and a half later. So he didn't see me make general, but Mother was there when I was promoted to general. She stood there in this line of people, very proud. She was only about this tall, five foot three or so, and there was the secretary of defense and the deputy secretary of defense and all these generals watching, and she was very proud. She and my wife pinned my stars on. From then on, in an almost Yiddish experience, she would say to everybody, "My son the general."

DR: You've seen many great leaders in your career—political leaders, military leaders. Obviously, you've been a great leader yourself. What is it in your view that makes a person a great leader?

CP: A person who understands that they're leading followers. A person who understands that they are there to put a group of human beings into work that has value, that has a purpose, and that the leader will give them the inspiration needed to achieve that purpose, and the leader will make sure they have everything they need to get the job done.

So I've always taken on every job I've had with "What am I trying to do? What's the purpose? What's the vision? Why are we here? What are we doing?" Then get that down to the lowest person in the organization, and make sure they have whatever they need, whether it's diplomatic weapons or real weapons of war, and make sure that I took care of them and gave them every opportunity to be successful. That's what leadership is all about—inspiring followers.

There's a story about Lincoln I've always appreciated. In the early days of the Civil War, he would go to the old soldiers' home outside of the swampy area of Washington, up in the north part of the city. There was a telegraph office there, and one night a message comes in, and the telegraph operator writes it down. "Mr. President, it's not good."

And he hands it to him. The message says: "The Confederates have just raided a Union outpost out by Fairfax Station, and they've captured one hundred horses and the brigadier general." Lincoln sighs and says, "Oh God. I hate to lose one hundred horses." The telegraph operator asks him, "What about the brigadier general?" And Lincoln's reply was, "I can make a brigadier general in five minutes, but it's hard to replace one hundred horses."

Somebody framed that quote and gave it to me the day I made brigadier general, and it has been on my desk ever since. To this day, it's there. If you came to my house now, you'd see it. It always reminded me that "Your job, Powell, is to take care of the horses. Don't worry about being a brigadier general. Take care of the horses, the soldiers, the employees, the clerks, the students, the faculty, whatever it takes to be successful in whatever it is you're trying to achieve."

GENERAL DAVID PETRAEUS

Former director of the Central
Intelligence Agency; Partner in the Global
Investment Firm KKR; Chairman of
the KKR Global Institute

"I'm a particularly great fan of Teddy Roosevelt.
The 'Man in the Arena' speech has always captivated
me. 'The credit belongs to the man who is actually in the
arena whose face is marred by dust and sweat and blood; . . .
who, if he fails, at least he fails while daring greatly.'"

General David Petraeus may be the best-known U.S. military combat leader since the Vietnam War era, in part because of his successful leadership of the "Surge" in Iraq, which came nearly four years after the U.S. invasion and turned around a failing war. A similarly successful effort to shore up a faltering U.S.-led coalition in Afghanistan, though different in scope and anticipated outcome, cemented Petraeus's reputation as an exceptional combat leader, and especially as a leader of troops in extremely difficult counterinsurgency missions.

All leaders take risks, but the risks that combat leaders take are somewhat different. Their decisions can lead quickly to deaths and casualties, so they need to be very precise and decisive in their orders and directions, and need to instill discipline, teamwork, and confidence into their troops. No one wants an indecisive or uncertain military commander leading the troops.

David Petraeus's military career, begun at West Point, might never have continued had he not recovered from two close brushes with death: an accidental gunshot wound to his chest during an aggressive live-fire exercise when he was a lieutenant colonel, and a free-fall parachute landing that fractured his pelvis when he was a brigadier general. In both cases, his will to survive, to regain exceptional physical fitness, and to be an extraordinary leader overcame medical challenges that might have ended the military careers of others less driven and focused.

Where did this drive and leadership skill come from? What made David Petraeus a military and civilian legend? The general addresses these questions in a *Peer to Peer* interview held at the Bloomberg studios in New York City in front of a live audience in March 2017.

I had not really known Petraeus during his military career. But after he left government service, which culminated in fourteen months as CIA director, and joined the private equity firm KKR, I began to see and talk with him at various business and public policy conferences.

As he explained to me, Petraeus believes that strategic leadership—leadership at the very top—involves performance of four critical tasks: 1) getting the big ideas (i.e., the strategy) right; 2) communicating the big ideas effectively throughout the organization; 3) overseeing the implementation of the big ideas; and 4) engaging in a process to determine how the big ideas need to be revised and refined in response to what has been learned and to changing circumstances. In his view, these tasks have to be performed superbly by strategic leaders to succeed in the military world and also in the civilian world.

Of course, accomplishing these tasks in a truly large organization may be easier for someone with the drive, intellect, courage, and presence of General Petraeus. But this intellectual construct of leadership will no doubt be of help to any leader, even if he or she is not a four-star general.

DAVID RUBENSTEIN (DR): Let's talk about how you came into the military. Your father was a Dutch sea captain. He met your mother, who was from Brooklyn, through church at the Brooklyn Navy Yard during World War II, during which he was the captain of a U.S. Liberty ship, and married her during the war.

DAVID PETRAEUS (DP): That's correct. During the war, my father sailed with the U.S. Merchant Marine. He was from the Netherlands and was a graduate of the Dutch Merchant Marine Academy. He was at sea with a Dutch ship in 1940, when the Nazis overran Holland, and the ship couldn't go back to Rotterdam. So it sailed to the United States and docked in the Brooklyn Navy Yard, where most of the crew signed on with the U.S. Merchant Marine.

DR: You grew up in New York City?

DP: No, about fifty miles north of the city—about seven miles north of West Point, in fact. I could actually run home from West Point, and I did on a few occasions—when authorized to do so, of course.

DR: When you were growing up, what was your nickname?

DP: Peaches. An announcer at a Little League baseball game couldn't pronounce my name the first time I came to bat as a nine-year-old. He said, "P-p-p-peaches." And that sort of stuck. It followed me all the way through my time at West Point, in fact.

There was a young woman working a summer job in the West Point laundry who had been a high school friend of mine. She would send me notes in the laundry that came back after we sent it out every week. Some upperclassmen intercepted and opened one of the notes and it started, "Dear Peaches." And so it jumped to West Point.

DR: So it stuck.

DP: It jumped the air gap to West Point.

DR: You graduated near the top of your class. When you graduated, did you decide you wanted to make the military your career?

DP: I wasn't sure I wanted to be a career officer when I graduated. In fact, I was in the premed program at West Point. I loved that particular body of academic inquiry, and it was also the highest academic peak to scale. It was known as the toughest.

All of a sudden, I found myself in my senior year and had earned a slot in the program, which was only open to 1 percent of the class—nine cadets—and I realized at that time I wasn't absolutely certain that I wanted to be a doctor. I had just wanted to climb that particular academic mountain. So I picked infantry instead, and I had a wonderful, wonderful experience over the subsequent thirty seven and a quarter years.

DR: You got married just a few weeks after you graduated to the daughter of the commandant of West Point.

DP: Yeah, actually, he was the superintendent, the overall commander at West Point, and a three-star general. His daughter and I met on a blind date—which was a bit awkward, I must say, when I found out who my blind date was. And it was awkward for her when she learned that neither her mother nor the woman who set it up knew me at all well either!

DR: But it wasn't nerve-racking, your dating the superintendent's daughter? Wasn't that kind of complicated?

DP: It was very complicated. We tried to do it clandestinely for a while. That was not very successful. I took a lot of flak over that, but it was worth it as we'd really hit it off.

DR: So you graduated, you got married, and you went into the infantry. You were working your way up, and then two incidents occurred where you almost lost your life. Not in combat.

DP: Well, the first was some fourteen years after my commissioning, when I was a young lieutenant colonel commanding an infantry battalion. It took place during a very aggressive maneuver live-fire exercise, with live hand grenades, supporting machine-gun fire, riflemen all over, and so on. Jack Keane—who was a one-star general then, and ultimately the vice chief of staff of the army and a four-star, as well as a great mentor—was with me.

We were walking behind the soldiers executing the exercise. One of them knocked out a bunker with a grenade and then his M16 rifle, spun out of it, tripped, and fell down. We think that as he did, he probably squeezed, because when you're about to take a blow you tense up—including his finger that was on the trigger—and an M16 round went through my chest. Luckily, it went over the A in PETRAEUS, on the right side of my chest, rather than over the A in ARMY on the left side, over my heart.

DR: So what happened? You had a bullet in there?

DP: Actually, the bullet went right through my chest and blew out of my upper back—leaving a much bigger hole in the back than in the front. Of course, the medics started working on me very quickly. Of course, shock set in. And I initially said, "Hey, guys, don't worry about me. Just go ahead. Do a quick after-action review, figure out what went wrong, and drive on." They were all rolling their eyes, recognizing that I wasn't totally with it.

They got an IV running. They got a medevac aircraft in. It picked me up. General Keane went with me, held my hand the whole way. We landed at the post hospital and went into the emergency room.

In fact, the bullet had nicked an artery, but not severed it, though none of that was clear at that time—though if an artery had been completely severed I probably would have only lasted a few minutes. The doctor did a quick assessment and looked me in the eye and said, "This is really going to hurt." He took a scalpel and cut an X in my side right down to the ribs, pulled the skin back, and shoved a plastic tube right into the lung to try to get suction going so that the fluid buildup would drain out. And it did. That's what I think saved my life.

Then I was put back on the medevac helicopter and flown down to Vanderbilt Medical Center [in Nashville, Tennessee], with General Keane still at my side. Of all people, the surgeon on call that day was Dr. Bill Frist—later the majority leader of the Senate. Some folks have jokingly said, "Petraeus was dying to meet Bill Frist."

Dr. Frist and his team performed thoracic surgery, found and cauterized the artery that had been nicked, pulled out the bone and other damaged material, and sewed me up. I was transferred to our military hospital after a few days, and I was out of the hospital a few days later.

DR: They didn't want you to leave that soon. You did fifty push-ups to make sure that they knew you were okay. Is that right?

DP: It's the only time I ever stopped at fifty, David.

DR: Okay. I've never even gotten to fifty.

DP: I wanted to get out of there. Recovery was going fine for me. There was no reason to keep hanging around. In fact, I was walking laps in the hospital corridors. I'd put all my tubes and monitoring devices in a wheelchair and push it around. I think it was driving them crazy.

DR: The other incident was when you were skydiving, and your parachute didn't quite work. You broke your pelvis. What is that like?

DP: It was horrific. I was a brigadier general then. That was actually worse in terms of pain, because my pelvis fractured front and rear. Your body is literally in two parts. I rode an ambulance all the way in, and every single crack in the road was agony.

DR: Did you ever skydive after that?

DP: I was told by General Keane, who was by then a four-star: "Dave, no more skydiving." I said, "Roger, sir, you give me a division command, and I'll quit skydiving." I quit. And later took command of the 101st Airborne Division. So no more free fall, but I did make more military static-line jumps after I was fully recovered. In fact, the first one was over a lake so that the landing wouldn't be so hard if the deployment of my parachute pulled apart what the surgeons had put back together!

DR: So they gave you a command.

DP: I was very privileged. And not just any command, but the 101st Airborne Division (Air Assault), the same division General Keane had commanded, and the one in which we'd both been serving when I got shot.

DR: You had a number of important jobs in the military. Ultimately the decision was made by President Bush to invade Iraq. You were a commander there and went over with the first part of the military that went in. It was supposed to be relatively quick. When did you realize, "This isn't going to be as easy as we had thought"?

DP: First of all, we actually did, in a matter of weeks, topple the regime, although there was stiff fighting along the way at various points. To be sure, what was predicted by some folks prior to the invasion—which was that Iraqi units were going to surrender and come over to our side and help us establish order—did not prove out. Nor did the predicted Iraqi last stand in Baghdad.

But there was, as I noted, tough fighting along the way. In fact, I had a nagging sense fairly early on, probably in the first week after the massive dust storm blew through, that the assumptions we'd been given before the invasion were not going to prove out.

I had Rick Atkinson, the *Washington Post* reporter, already a two-time Pulitzer Prize winner, accompanying me, riding in the back of my Humvee and helicopter. I remember turning to him at one point and asking, "Tell me how this ends, Rick—because I'm not sure this is going to go according to script." The idea that we were just going to topple Saddam and his sons and some of his closest henchmen, and then everybody else would stay in place, there would be a political negotiation and we would hand Iraq over to them, obviously proved unfounded.

DR: Do you think it would have been different had we not decided to get rid of the entire Saddam army and instituted the de-Ba'athification process?

DP: Those were huge mistakes. We used to have a question on the wall of the operations center in our headquarters that asked: "Will this operation take more bad guys off the street than it creates by its conduct?" The same is true of policies. Firing the Iraqi army without telling them what their future was—this meant throwing out of military service hundreds of thousands of young soldiers, without telling them how we would take care of them during their transition—was disastrous. So was firing tens of thousands of Ba'ath Party members without an agreed-upon reconciliation process. As a result of those decisions, we created hundreds of thousands of people whose only incentive was to oppose the new Iraq rather than to support it. The seeds of the insurgency were sowed as a result of those decisions.

DR: You led the effort to get control of Mosul, is that right?

DP: Yes. We were in southwest Baghdad, which is where we'd been told we were going to be based after the fight to Baghdad. All of a sudden we got an emergency order to get up to Mosul. The city was out of control. There was a small U.S. unit up there, and its members had killed seventeen civilians the day before when the unit was confronted by a violent demonstration. Within thirty-six hours or so, we conducted one of the largest, longest air assault operations in history, well over 260 miles. We had 250 helicopters in the 101st Airborne at that time, and we used just about all of them to put as many of our soldiers on the ground in one lift as we possibly could and then to cover them with an armada of attack helicopters overhead.

We immediately blanketed the city with our soldiers, literally pushed right into the city, calmed it down, stopped the looting and all the rest of that, established security, and then gradually took control of it. Then I went to work with a team, very intensively, to set up an interim government, and we had that established within a little more than two weeks of arriving. That was hugely helpful, as we desperately needed Iraqi partners and assistance. Keep in mind that we hadn't even had maps of Mosul until just before the air assault operation to occupy the city, which had two million people. Having an interim government in place, with a provincial council whose members obviously knew the province much better than we did, was hugely helpful because Nineveh Province, of which Mosul is the capital, has a very diverse population, with numerous different ethnic and sectarian groups, as well as tribes, elements of society, and institutions—all of which needed representation in the interim council.

DR: Early on in the war, it was thought that "shock and awe" would be all that was necessary. All we have to do is show a lot of missiles going off, and that would be the end of the war. That concept doesn't really work.

DP: That's right. It was not enough. I think it did generate shock and awe here and there, but again, there were certainly plenty of folks still fighting, shooting at us with various weapons systems, including rockets, artillery, tanks, other armored vehicles, and regular and special forces. We had casualties and lost heavy equipment and so on. But ultimately, of course, there was no stopping the U.S. and coalition forces, and Saddam and his henchmen all fled or were captured.

DR: President Bush decided to invade Iraq in part because of the theory that they had weapons of mass destruction. That information came from the CIA, among other places. When you became the head of the CIA, did you ever dig into it and say, "Where'd you get that information from?"

DP: I didn't dig into that very much, as the subject had been exhaustively revisited by various commissions—and as I had lived the whole experience as well! But I dug deeply into some other issues, such as the use of enhanced interrogation techniques, something I'd personally opposed over the years for two reasons: One is that I think they're wrong: they violate international law and the Geneva Convention and so forth, all of which we support and promote. Two is that I just never thought they were as effective as the proponents of them believe they are. As Jim Mattis colorfully said, "Give me a beer and a cigarette, and I'll get more information than by waterboarding."

To put it more simply, the most skillful interrogator seeks to become the detainee's best friend during their interaction. I offer this having been the commander who oversaw the holding of more detainees in Iraq than at any other time—twenty-seven thousand of them—and later the commander in Afghanistan who also oversaw more detainees than before or after, as we were conducting surges in each case. So I had considerable experience with what works with detainees. Treating them humanely while still eliciting information from them is the way to go about it, unless you are in a so-called ticking time bomb situation, in which case you may need to, and should, engage in more robust activity, depending on the nature of the particular threat.

DR: You had never before had people working for you directly who were killed in combat. What was it like to have the command of people who were dying?

DP: It's a chilling experience. I remember the radio call when our first soldier was killed. Hearing such a report takes the wind out of you. Your blood goes cold. I also remember hearing when a sister unit—the Third Infantry Division, which really spearheaded the fight, along with a marine division, up to Baghdad on the ground with M1 tanks and Bradley Fighting Vehicles—I remember monitoring their net, because we were all fighting north together, and hearing that they'd had a number of heavy vehicles blown up. That was also chilling, especially as there was not much expectation that our tanks could be knocked out by the weapons the Iraqis had. Frankly, reports of casualties continued to be very tough to hear or read throughout my time in the war zones, which was the vast majority of my final eight years in uniform.

DR: You were there for how long before you were sent back to the States?

DP: The first tour was a yearlong deployment—and it came some seven months after I'd returned from a year in Bosnia. I was back home from the first year in Iraq for a couple of months and was asked to go back over to do an assessment, for the commander of U.S. Central Command and the secretary of defense, of the Iraqi security force effort. I came back, reported out to Secretary Donald Rumsfeld, and he said, "Great report, great recommendations. Now go back home, change command, get back over to Iraq, and implement what you've recommended."

DR: Have you thought if you hadn't written such a good report, maybe you wouldn't have been sent back?

DP: Secretary Rumsfeld had an interesting concept of rewards for a job well done. That next tour was fifteen and a half months. I remember that in the final week or so of it, he came over to Iraq, spent time with us, and literally patted me on the back and said, "Well done, Dave." I thought, "This is really sort of nice."

Then he said, "On the way home, I want you to come through Afghanistan." I replied, "You know, Mr. Secretary, that's not exactly the most direct line between here and home." But obviously we came home through Afghanistan and we did an assessment of the situation there for him on the way home.

DR: You finished your second tour of duty in Iraq and went back to the United States.

DP: Yeah. Then I had about fifteen months at Fort Leavenworth, Kansas, as commander of the Combined Arms Center. It was really quite an extraordinary command, overseeing a vast number of training centers, bases, and organizations. In fact, it had such considerable responsibilities that my predecessor termed it "The engine of change for our army." When I asked the chief of staff of the army if he had any guidance before I headed out to Kansas, he told me, "Shake up the army, Dave." And that's what the team there and I sought to do. We revamped the whole process of preparing units, leaders, and soldiers to go to Iraq and to Afghanistan. And we published a much-needed counterinsurgency field manual, which became the intellectual foundation for all that we did in that effort in the States and then in turning around the war in Iraq and later in Afghanistan.

DR: Once again, you write a very good report. You oversaw the counterinsurgency manual. It was so good that people said, "Maybe this person should be in charge of the current counterinsurgency effort." So you were asked by President Bush to go back to Iraq and lead the so-called Surge.

When he said, "I'd like you to go lead the Surge," did you say, "I've already served two tours of duty in Iraq, and I don't need to go back a third time"?

DP: Not quite, David. No, I said, "It would be a privilege to do that." It's the same thing I said when President Obama sat me down several years later, and said—with no pleasantries, and no one else in the room except for a photographer, who took some quick photos and left—"I'm

asking you as your president and commander in chief to go to Afghani-
stan and take command of the International Security Assistance Force."
And I answered, "The only possible answer to a question like that, Mr.
President, is yes."

DR: How many troops did we have in Iraq at the time that you went
back with the surge?

DP: We had a bit under 140,000 U.S. soldiers, sailors, airmen, marines.
The coalition countries had some tens of thousands of additional troops.
Then the U.S. added about 25,000 to 30,000 additional forces during the
course of the Surge, so we ultimately reached 165,000 American men
and women in uniform.

I'd just want to point out here, David, that the surge that mattered
most was not the surge of forces, it was the surge of ideas. It was the
change in strategy. It was really a 180-degree shift from consolidating
on big bases and getting "out of the faces of the Iraqi people," to going
back and living in the neighborhoods with them. Because doing that was
the only way we could secure the people, and that also meant retaking
control of numerous areas that we had prematurely transitioned to Iraqi
control. We also had to recognize the need to reconcile with as many
of the rank and file of the insurgents as was possible, as we understood
that you cannot kill or capture your way out of an industrial-strength
insurgency.

DR: So we had about 140,000 American troops. We sent over an additional 25,000 to 30,000. And that was enough, given the techniques you
used, to bring Iraq to a stable position, relatively speaking?

DP: Yes. We were able, with the new strategy and additional forces,
to reduce the level of violence dramatically, by some 85 percent or so,
during the course of the eighteen-month period that was the duration of
the Surge. In so doing, our forces truly turned around a country that was
on the verge of an all-out civil war.

DR: The president then asks you to head the U.S. Central Command,
which is in charge of U.S. military operations in the Middle East?

DP: Yes, Central Command is responsible for an area that includes twenty-one countries, from Egypt in the west to Pakistan in the east, Kazakhstan in the north to Yemen and the pirate-infested waters off Somalia in the south. We were very proud that it had 90 percent of the world's problems at the time.

DR: After someone heads one of these commands, usually they become chief of staff of the army, and then maybe chairman of the Joint Chiefs of Staff. So you're rising up, then one day President Obama calls you into the Oval Office and says, "I'd like you to give up the Central Command and go back and be a military commander in Afghanistan." What did you think about that?

DP: It was an extraordinary circumstance, obviously. And if the president calls on you and asks you to do something, I think you do it.

DR: You didn't say, "Let me think about it. Give me a few minutes"?

DP: I think you say, as I noted earlier, that the only answer to a question like that can be yes. In the previous case, for the Surge in Iraq, it was actually Secretary Robert Gates who called me. In fact, he reached us while my wife and son and I were on a freeway heading north out of Los Angeles Airport to Valencia for what turned out to be the last time I saw my father just before I went to the Surge.

My wife was driving, and I took the call from Secretary Gates on a cell phone. I actually wanted to have a little bit more of a conversation than just answering yes.

So after saying yes, I added, "Mr. Secretary, I'd like to be sure you understand who you're getting as your commander. Because my advice, when it comes to drawing forces down and so forth, will be based on the facts on the ground and our mutual understanding of the mission that you have assigned us. It will be informed by an awareness of all these other issues with which you and the president have to deal—congressional politics, domestic politics, coalition politics, budget deficits, strain on the force, you name it. But in the end, my advice and my recommendations will be driven by the facts on the ground.

"And that's important, because what I'm basically saying is, I'm going to give it to you straight. I'm not modifying my advice based on issues you have to deal with, although I will obviously support whatever decision you and the president ultimately make."

DR: You went to Afghanistan. What did you conclude? Did we really have an effort to successfully get rid of the Taliban or reduce their impact?

DP: That's a good question, because as I said in Congress, in my confirmation hearing for that command, I did not believe that we would be able to flip Afghanistan the way we flipped Iraq. I really did believe we could do in Iraq what we ultimately did. But the conditions in Afghanistan were vastly different.

To be sure, what was eating at me early on in Iraq was whether we could do it fast enough, whether we would have sufficient results to report to Congress in September 2007, when I knew I had to return to Washington for hearings six months into the Surge in Iraq. That was crucial, because congressional support was very tenuous.

But we did achieve significant results in Iraq during the first six months. We reduced violence very dramatically, and we continued to reduce it over the subsequent year. Indeed, there was a gradual further reduction in violence for a good three and a half years after that until, unfortunately, tragically, the prime minister undid all that we had fought so hard to achieve together by taking a series of highly sectarian actions that once again inflamed tensions between the Sunni and Shia and set off a new cycle of violence that took attention away from al-Qaeda and allowed it to reconstitute itself in Iraq as the Islamic State.

In the case of Afghanistan, I was under no illusions that we would be able to replicate what we had done in Iraq. The circumstances were very different and very difficult, even if the levels of violence were nowhere near as high. I'd actually laid the situation in Afghanistan out in the assessment Secretary Rumsfeld asked me to do. The very first slide in that briefing—of course PowerPoint is the means of communication of the modern general—said: "Afghanistan does not equal Iraq." And then I listed the significant differences between the two countries.

So there was not going to be the prospect of a dramatic improvement in Afghanistan similar to what we had achieved in Iraq. But we did accomplish our mission in that year, which was to halt the momentum of the Taliban—because they were on the march at the time. In fact, we actually reversed the Taliban's momentum in some key areas. And we also performed our other tasks, accelerating the development of the Afghan security forces and select Afghan institutions so that we could begin the transition to them of security tasks in some areas, which we initiated as well.

So, we did accomplish those missions during that year in Afghanistan, while also continuing to achieve the overarching goal there, which is still a valid and important mission for the United States in Afghanistan. That is to ensure that Afghanistan is never again a sanctuary for transnational extremists the way it was when al-Qaeda planned the 9/11 attacks there and conducted the initial training there—doing that when the Taliban ruled the bulk of the country, I might add.

DR: While you were in Afghanistan, the effort to capture Osama bin Laden was going forward.

DP: Capture or kill.

DR: Capture or kill. You were alerted to that. You were not directly involved. How were you alerted, because you weren't directly in the chain of command for that decision?

DP: I was alerted while back in Washington for a series of meetings with the president on the drawdown in Afghanistan and then for my confirmation hearing for the position of director of the CIA.

I returned to Afghanistan shortly after that. And a week or so later, on the night of the operation, I was back in Kabul, the only one in our headquarters who knew about the operation. So I got up myself, no aides, no anything else, around eleven p.m. We had a Joint Special Operations Command post at the NATO headquarters in Kabul where I was located.

I strolled in there and surprised them. They asked, "What are you doing in here, sir?" I asked everybody to leave except for one officer whom I knew very well. In fact, it had been one of his platoon members who shot me in the training accident twenty years earlier.

We then connected to a number of highly classified "feeds" so that we could monitor the operation and be prepared to execute various contingency plans had things gone wrong. Most of the special operations forces that conducted the operation, the headquarters element, in particular, normally worked for me. But that night they were working for the CIA, because it was a covert action, conducted under different authorities than the military, which meant the chain of command ran from the president to the director of the CIA, Leon Panetta, then to Vice Admiral McRaven, and then to the SEAL Team Six Unit that conducted the operation.

That was quite a night, especially given the rocky start, when the lead helicopter had a very hard landing and was not going to be able to fly out of the compound. But, interestingly, at the end, there were no high fives or anything like that. Rather, we brought the other folks back into the command post and refocused on the twelve or so operations going on in Afghanistan that night, many of which were more demanding in terms of the enemy and the terrain—but none of which were remotely as important strategically. Regardless, the war went on.

DR: After you'd spent the better part of your twelve and a half months in Afghanistan, the president told you, "I'd like you to come back and be the head of the CIA." Doing that meant you had to give up your military career, essentially.

DP: I didn't have to, but I chose to. The president and I talked about that before he made the decision to nominate me. I agreed that taking off the uniform would be the best approach. I thought it was very important not to have folks think that I was going to turn the CIA into a military headquarters.

DR: Was it emotional to give up your military career at that point?

DP: It's very emotional to take the uniform off for the last time. There was a wonderful retirement parade and ceremony and speeches and a final medal. And you go home and take off the uniform, realizing that you have just left the institution in which you've spent your entire professional life. But I had the prospect of this extraordinary new opportunity, being director of the CIA, and that was very exciting. The CIA is just an incredible group of men and women—silent warriors, as they are described. Like the military, they also raise their right hand and take an oath. But they know they're not going to get a parade or any public recognition along the way. They can't even have the joy that most of us have in talking about what it is that we do on a daily basis with our friends and neighbors—or, in many respects, with their own families.

DR: When you got to the CIA, did you say, "These are all the secrets the country has, and geez, there's not as many secrets as I thought"? Or did you say, "These are incredible secrets"?

DP: On a near-daily basis, almost throughout my time there, it was "Are you kidding me? Seriously? Really?" There are some extraordinary secrets there.

DR: You've briefed President Bush 43, and you've briefed, many times, President Obama. What's the difference between the two in briefing them?

DP: You have to keep in mind that Bush 43 was the one I briefed most significantly, on a weekly basis, in fact, together with my great diplomatic partner, Ambassador Ryan Crocker, during the Surge in Iraq. We had a weekly video teleconference for an hour every Monday morning at seven-thirty eastern standard time, the president with his national security team around the Situation Room videoconferencing directly with us.

He had gone all-in on the Surge. He had put it all on the line. He'd frankly overridden the advice of most of his advisors. Very few people were really strongly behind the Surge. General Keane, by the way, and retired by then, was one of those who was very supportive of the Surge during a meeting with President Bush.

So President Bush was absolutely intimately involved in that.

But we weren't doing the surge in Iraq anymore by the time President Obama arrived. Iraq was really in a pretty good place. And the question was, how quickly could we draw down without jeopardizing what we fought and sacrificed so hard to achieve? President Obama famously did his homework, studied the issues, deliberated on them. The Afghan policy review that was conducted in the latter part of his first year was extraordinary. I don't think any president has ever engaged the national security team nine or ten times directly in the course of making a decision like that.

DR: You are considered one of the great military leaders of our generation and maybe any other generation. What is leadership to you?

DP: I think leadership, especially at strategic levels, the very top, encompasses four critical tasks. Whether you're the commander in Iraq or Afghanistan, or the CEO of The Carlyle Group or KKR or Amazon, you have to get the big ideas right. You have to communicate those big ideas effectively through the breadth and depth of your organization. You have to oversee their implementation. And you have to determine how to refine the big ideas—and then do it all over again.

Each of those four tasks has subtasks, of course. Overseeing the implementation includes metrics. It has your battle rhythm; how do you spend your own time? We had a whole matrix for a generic three-month period showing how I sought to spend my time. You have to provide energy, example, encouragement, determination, and so on. And you have to drive the campaign's execution.

Most important, and the final task, one that's often forgotten, you have to have a formal process for determining how the big ideas need to be revised, refined, maybe shot and left on the side of the road intellectually, so that you can do it all again and again and again.

These tasks are critical in the civilian world as well. Think of Netflix. Four times they've gotten this right, reinvented themselves. They decided early on that "We're going to put Blockbuster out of business by mailing CDs to people." Worked all the way through that. Then they sat down and said, "Okay, Blockbuster's going out of business, and now others are doing this. But now Internet connectivity is fast enough. We can get movies to our customers by having them downloaded."

They do all that, it works, then they realize, "Okay, others are doing that now too." And then they make a huge bet, I think it was $100 million, on *House of Cards* and other shows. "We're going to create our own content." Reed Hastings oversaw all of that, and he is a truly admirable, innovative, and impressive strategic leader who continues to get it right. And then they did it again when they bought major studios and decided to make big productions.

DR: Who are the military leaders you've most admired over time?

DP: I think that Ulysses S. Grant is hugely underrated, although now he's finally once again getting his due. He was the hero of the world, really, after he left the White House and traveled around the globe on this famous tour. He wrote fantastic memoirs, and then the Southern historians ran him down for the first fifty years of the past century. But gradually, regard has returned.

Grant was the only general, I believe, in U.S. history who was brilliant in combat tactically, at the division level and below; brilliant operationally, with multiple divisions, especially at Vicksburg, one of the greatest maneuver campaigns of all time; and brilliant strategically, when he developed the strategy for the entire Union force and essentially won the war for the North, because the eventual battlefield victories ensured the reelection of President Lincoln. Remember that Lincoln was running against General McClellan, who had pledged, if elected, to reach a peace agreement with the South that would have ended the Union as we knew it.

You know, David, people forget, the Northern victory was not inevitable. The idea that the Union forces were just ultimately going to grind down the South was not certain until Grant made it so. Had it not been for the overall strategy he developed, and the subsequent victories of General Sherman at Atlanta and then General Sheridan in the Shenandoah Valley, President Lincoln could have lost the election of 1864. And had General McClellan won, he would have sued for peace, and we might not have the United States as we know it now.

DR: What political leaders do you most admire?

DP: There have been a number who have gotten the big ideas right over the years and deserve the respect of all of us. Certainly those who are on Mount Rushmore deserve that. I'm a particularly great fan of Teddy Roosevelt. His "Man in the Arena" speech has always inspired me. "The credit belongs to the man who is actually in the arena, whose face is marred by dust and sweat and blood; . . . and who, at the worst, if he fails, at least fails while daring greatly."

CONDOLEEZZA RICE

Former Secretary of State and
National Security Advisor; Professor,
Stanford University's Graduate School of
Business; Senior Fellow, Hoover Institution

"I thought I was going to rise up and be a great
concert pianist. My parents were people who had me
convinced that even if I couldn't have a hamburger
at Woolworth's lunch counter, I could be president
of the United States if I wanted to be. In my
family, you were going to achieve."

"My father once said to me, 'If somebody doesn't
want to sit next to you because you're black, that's fine,
as long as they move.' In other words, don't take
somebody else's prejudice on you. It's their fault, their
problem, not your problem. Don't be disabled
by people who may have prejudice."

When she was growing up in the 1960s as an African American girl in heavily segregated Birmingham, Alabama, Condoleezza Rice and her parents certainly did not foresee her future as a national security advisor or a secretary of state. They dreamed she might develop into a classical pianist; she certainly had considerable talent in that area.

But fate has a way of changing the best-laid plans. Rice's education at the University of Denver did involve a good deal of music instruction, but it also had a fair bit of public policy, especially under the direction of Dr. Josef Korbel, the Czech scholar who was Madeleine Albright's father.

That ultimately led Rice to a PhD in political science, and a teaching position at Stanford, then the provost's position there, following a time on the National Security Council as a Soviet specialist under President George H. W. Bush. At former secretary of state George Shultz's suggestion, she assumed a role advising then governor George W. Bush on foreign policy during his 2000 presidential campaign.

The rest is history, as Condoleezza Rice (better known to her friends as Condi) became the first African American woman to be appointed to the two positions she held under the second President Bush. How did she rise to these heights, overcoming the prejudice she often faced in areas typically dominated by men and whites?

Rice discusses these matters, as well as her views on leadership, in the *Peer to Peer* interview I had with her at the Bloomberg studios in Washington, D.C., in May 2018, in front of a live audience.

Through my relationship with both President Bushes and my involvement with the Council on Foreign Relations, the Aspen Strategy Group, and the Kennedy Center, I had known Condi somewhat over the years, but had not previously interviewed her. In our discussion, held around the time of the publication of her fifth book, *Political Risk: How Businesses and Organizations Can Anticipate Global Insecurity*, Condi makes clear that she thinks great leaders, like Nelson Mandela, have a vision of where they want the world to go, and they typically have the requisite intelligence and humility to get their followers to move that vision forward. In Condi's view, arrogance and hubris are generally not going to enable a leader to fulfill a vision and attract followers.

On discrimination, her father instilled in her the view to not consider herself a victim, to not allow someone else to control her life. As he
reminded her, she could not always control her circumstances, but she
could control her response to those circumstances. That advice is often
harder to follow than to articulate, but Dr. Condoleezza Rice obviously
has had no such problem in her career at the height of global policy-
making and leadership.

DAVID RUBENSTEIN (DR): If President Trump called you and said, "I really need you to come in and help your country," what would you say?

CONDOLEEZZA RICE (CR): I would say, "Mr. President, there are so many wonderful people who can help our country. Here's my number in Palo Alto, and do give me a call if there's anything you want to talk about." I'm really happy.

DR: From time to time, your name has been mentioned as a vice presidential or presidential candidate. Can you say for sure you're not likely to run for either of those positions?

CR: I can say that with even more certainty, because you have to know your DNA. I don't have the DNA of a politician. I love policy. I don't love politics. It is just enervating for me.

DR: You grew up initially in Birmingham, Alabama, in a segregated South. Some of your friends were in the terrible Birmingham church bombing. Did you ever think that, from a beginning in the segregated South, you would ever rise up to the kinds of positions you held?

CR: It never occurred to me, more because I thought I was going to rise up and be a great concert pianist.

My parents were people who had me convinced that even if I couldn't have a hamburger at Woolworth's lunch counter, I could be president of the United States if I wanted to be. In my family, you were going to achieve. You were going to go to college. David, I'm not even the first PhD in my family.

DR: Your father had a PhD.

CR: My father and my aunt Theresa, my father's sister. I always say, if you think what I do is kind of weird for a black person, she wrote books on Dickens, of all things.

DR: You were an only child?

CR: I was an only child.

DR: Your parents obviously focused a lot on you. You had all the lessons that you could have had. You were a ballerina.

CR: I had every lesson known to humankind, some of which I was good at, and some of which I wasn't. But they kept me going. I had French lessons. My mother decided that every well-bred young girl should speak French. So, at nine years old, I was dragged off to French lessons on Saturdays.

I had ballet lessons. We had etiquette lessons. I was, of course, a pianist. So yeah, my parents kept me very, very busy.

DR: And your mother was a schoolteacher?

CR: My mother was a teacher, and also a musician.

DR: One of her students, I understand, was Willie Mays?

CR: My mom taught Willie Mays in high school. I asked him once, "Do you remember my mother? She taught you ninth-grade English." He said, "She told me, 'Now, son, you're going to be a ballplayer, so if you need to leave a little early, you go ahead and do that.'" I thought, "That doesn't sound exactly like my mother, but it's a great story, so I'm going to hold on to it."

DR: Your father was a Republican.

CR: Yes, he was. The way that it happened was that my father and my mother, before they were married, went down to register to vote. The poll tester looked at my father—big, tall man, football player—and said,

"How many beans are in this jar?" And of course my father couldn't answer the question. So the man said, "You don't pass the test."

My father went back to his church, and he asked a man who was one of his elders. Mr. Hunter said, "Oh, Reverend, don't worry about it. I'll tell you how to get registered. You go down there, and there's a clerk who's a Republican. She's trying to build the Republican Party. And if you'll just say you're a Republican, she'll register you."

So my father went down, and he said he was a Republican. He got registered. He never forgot it. He remained a Republican the rest of his life.

DR: You went to the University of Denver. Madeleine Albright's father, who'd been a very famous international political scientist, was your professor.

CR: He was the one who got me into international politics. I actually went to DU as a piano major but graduated with just enough units to be a political science major. If you look at my transcript, I've got a hundred units of music and forty-five in political science.

DR: You then went to Notre Dame to get a master's, and then you went to Stanford later?

CR: I went to Stanford on a one-year fellowship—the Arms Control and Disarmament program, learning the physics of nuclear weapons and how many warheads could dance on the head of an SS-18.

I learned something very important from that experience. Stanford was looking to diversify its faculty, and it engaged in a very smart way to do affirmative action. To this day, I believe affirmative action is still necessary, which means you look outside of your normal channels to find people. They had in their midst a young black woman who was a Soviet specialist, and they offered me a job. They said firmly, "When it comes time for your reappointment, which is after three years, the fact that you came through this appointment will mean nothing at all."

I remember saying, "That will give me time to see if I like you and time to see if you like me." Which I don't think a dean at Stanford had ever heard from a prospective assistant professor.

DR: You got tenure, and you were recruited to come to the George Herbert Walker Bush White House staff.

CR: I went to be the White House Soviet specialist, and got lucky enough to be the White House Soviet specialist at the end of the Cold War.

DR: You were there when the Berlin Wall went down. Did the president say, "Let's jump up and down and take credit for this"?

CR: The minute the Berlin Wall fell, a bunch of us went over to the Oval Office. "Mr. President, you have to go to Berlin. You have to go for Kennedy. You have to go for Truman. You have to go for Reagan." He looked at us, and he said, "What would I do? Dance on the wall? This is a German moment, not an American moment."

I'll never forget that, because it was just so much George H. W. Bush—self-effacing, modest, a great sense of humility. And it was the right thing. He was absolutely right.

DR: You saw him recently at Barbara Bush's funeral. Did you have a chance to talk to him?

CR: I had a chance to talk to him and tell him how much I love him and loved Mrs. Bush. That's a generation that's going to be missed. They were people who understood kindness and humility and gentility. They made their mistakes, most certainly, but when you think about that family and what George H. W. Bush did as a public servant, it makes you think of a wonderful time for our country.

DR: Bill Clinton came along and defeated your boss in the 1992 election. Were you shocked by the outcome?

CR: I was. I'd already gone back to Stanford. I became provost. I was surprised. But President Bush had done what he needed to do. I don't think there will ever be a full accounting of the way he did the diplomacy at the end of the Cold War, with respect for [Mikhail] Gorbachev and never humiliating the Soviet Union. Not dancing on the wall.

One of the last things Gorbachev did before he went out to sign the paper that would collapse the Soviet Union and allow Boris Yeltsin to become president of the Russian Federation—he called George H. W. Bush. And he said, "We did good things, didn't we? History will judge us well." I said to President Bush, "Do you realize how extraordinary this is?"

He was George H. W. Bush. He said, "I never thought about it." I said, "That the president of the Soviet Union, in his last act before the collapse of the Soviet Union, called the American president, essentially to seek his affirmation?" That was a very big deal. But that's the way he was.

DR: Another member of the Bush family decides to run for president— George W. Bush. You become national security advisor, the first woman to be national security advisor. Then 9/11 happens. Where were you on 9/11?

CR: On 9/11, I was at my desk. You'll remember that President Bush was actually at that education event in Florida. Just to show you our pre-9/11 thinking, I did not go with him that day.

My assistant came in and said a plane had hit the World Trade Center. First we thought it was an accident. I called President Bush. Then, a few minutes later, we learned the second plane had hit the World Trade Center. We knew now it was a terrorist attack.

Then it was just a procession, over the day, and really the next several months, of Hobson's choice after Hobson's choice after Hobson's choice for the president of the United States. The United States had not been attacked on its own territory since the War of 1812. We had no structures, no institutions for internal security for the country. It was flying without a compass.

DR: Subsequently, President Bush decided to invade Iraq, to topple Saddam Hussein. In hindsight, was that a mistake? Had you known that there were no weapons of mass destruction, would you still have gone forward?

CR: What you know today can affect what you do tomorrow, but not what you did yesterday. We simply believed, as all the intelligence agencies around the world did, that he had weapons of mass destruction, that he was reconstituting them, that he was doing it quickly.

It was on that basis that we decided we finally had to do what the international community had been threatening to do, which was to have serious consequences. In retrospect, I don't know, if we had known, what we would have done.

I will say this: I still think the world's better off without Saddam Hussein. He was a cancer in the region. And while Iraq went through an extraordinarily difficult time, the thing I would do differently is how we rebuilt Iraq.

We made a lot of mistakes postwar. But I will say this: I would rather be Iraqi than Syrian today. Iraq has a chance now to be a stabilizing element of the new Middle East, because they have an accountable government. The Iraqi Kurds and Baghdad are finally finding some way of dealing with one another. It's a very different place.

The Arab Spring was going to happen, and I think Iraq would have made Syria look like child's play. So you never know what you prevented. You'll never be able to bring back the lives lost, and you'll never be able to deal with that. But I think, in the long arc of history, Iraq will turn out okay.

I wish we hadn't left in 2011. The one thing that might have made me think differently about it was to think that we would have stayed with a few troops in Iraq to help them make the transition.

DR: President Bush is reelected. You're the first African American woman to be secretary of state. What is it like to represent your country?

CR: I loved it. I loved going out and representing the country. Every time I stepped off a plane that said THE UNITED STATES OF AMERICA, I just got chills about it. When I was actually sworn in, I took an oath of office to a constitution that once accounted my ancestors as three-fifths of a man. I took that oath of office in front of a portrait of Ben Franklin, sworn in by a Jewish woman, Supreme Court Justice Ruth Bader Ginsburg, who was my neighbor at the Watergate.

And I thought, "What would old Ben think of this?" Because in some ways, it showed how far our country had come. I always felt, when I was out there, that I could speak about the hard road to democracy, about the importance of institutions becoming more inclusive over time to people who were having those challenges, because I personally experienced them.

DR: Since you left government, you've written four books. You have a new book about the political risk that businesspeople should take into account when they're making business decisions. Why is this an important consideration?

CR: When people used to think about political risk, they thought largely of the socialist dictator who might expropriate your property or nationalize your industry. Now the sources of political risk are multiple, and they're sometimes surprising.

A person who gets on your airplane and sees your flight attendants treat somebody poorly and has a cell phone and documents it—United Airlines. That's political risk. A supply chain that's deep into China, and now there's consideration of a trade war with China. That's a political risk.

What we wanted to do was to say, "There are lots of sources of political risk. Look around corners. Look at your industry and say, 'What are my sources of political risk? And what's my risk appetite?'" We didn't want to say, "Don't do things because they're risky."

I mentioned the Russians. Cyber is a whole category of risk in and of itself.

DR: Is your point that businesses, when they make significant decisions, should take into account political risk as well?

CR: Yes. And they should constantly be surveying the landscape for how those risks are multiplying and changing.

DR: As you look back on your extraordinary career, what would you like people to think of as your major accomplishment?

CR: With my government career, I hope that people think I represented the United States well. I hope that people think I represented our values, especially that we stand for people who have no voice for themselves.

That people who are suffering in jail cells and putting their lives on the line for the very rights that we almost start to take for granted—you can say what you think, and worship as you please, and be free from the knock of the secret police at night—that we advocated for that. And we believed that no corner of the earth should live in tyranny.

With my academic career, I hope that people think I helped a whole new generation of kids, many generations of kids, find themselves and recognize that it wasn't ever my job to tell them what to think. It was my job to make sure they thought in a rigorous and systematic way, and maybe a few leaders I trained will take that to their leadership positions.

DR: You've obviously seen great leaders around the world. What are the qualities that you think great leaders actually have—and the qualities that people who aren't great leaders fail to have?

CR: Integrity is at the center of being a great leader. Once you lose people's trust, you have nothing. Great leaders are visionaries. By that I mean that they see the world as it should be, not as it is. I think of Nelson Mandela and how, sitting in a jail cell for all of those years, he did not think, "When we finally are in power, blacks are going to dominate whites," rather than thinking of a multiracial, multiethnic South Africa that would be for all South Africans.

Most importantly, I think great leaders have a sense of humility about what they can achieve.

DR: Humility.

CR: Versus arrogance. Arrogance and hubris are recipes for disaster. My parents were great people. They always taught me that you need, personally, to do three things. If you're going to lead, and if you're going to be successful, the first thing is try to be twice as good. In other words, work hard enough to be confident that you've worked hard enough to be twice as good.

Secondly—and remember, I'm growing up in segregated Birmingham, Alabama, so they were trying to armor me in some ways—never consider yourself a victim, because when you think you're a victim, you've given control of your life to somebody else. You may not be able to control your circumstances, but you can control your response to your circumstances.

Thirdly, something that I particularly tell minority kids and women and others who are from populations that have been in one way or another marginalized: my father once said to me, "If somebody doesn't want to sit next to you because you're black, that's fine, as long as they move." In other words, don't take somebody else's prejudice on you. It's their fault, their problem, not your problem. Don't be disabled by people who may have prejudice.

JAMES A. BAKER III

Former Secretary of State, Secretary of the Treasury, and White House Chief of Staff

---

"I have always followed the 'Prior preparation
prevents poor performance' mantra. I think those things
made a difference. I was brought up to believe that if
you start something, you finish it, or you do
everything you can to finish it."

Over the past half century, the U.S. government has had a fair number of individuals serve at the highest levels with extraordinary distinction and success. But it is difficult to think of any nonelected official who served in as many different roles with such great distinction or success—and such bipartisan admiration—as James A. Baker III.

Over a twelve-year period, in between running several successful presidential campaigns, Jim Baker served as President Ronald Reagan's first chief of staff (his performance there is universally seen as the gold standard); as Reagan's second-term secretary of the treasury (where he helped produce the country's first major tax reform in more than a quarter century); and as President George H. W. Bush's secretary of state (where he helped produce the coalition that ended Saddam Hussein's invasion of Kuwait).

How were these results possible for a man whose family urged him to stay out of politics and government, who had been a lifelong Democrat, and who had also been the director of two campaigns against his future boss Ronald Reagan?

In this interview, Jim Baker describes his unlikely and unanticipated rise from Houston corporate lawyer to the heights of international diplomacy. The interview was held in May 2018, at Rice University's Baker Institute, established after his government service to foster education and dialogue about public policy.

I had already been privileged to interview Secretary Baker many times, for he had become a senior counselor to Carlyle for twelve years following his government service. During that period, I traveled extensively with him, and could see firsthand the enormous respect with which he was held in absolutely every part of the world.

When you get to spend time with great or famous individuals, it is said that you see their flaws up close, and perhaps your admiration declines a bit. That was not the case here. From afar, I had admired Secretary Baker's legendary government service. He always seemed to be so well organized, to surround himself with talented advisors, to achieve his key objective, to negotiate with unusual patience and skill, and to remember that the ultimate credit must be publicly given to the president for whom he was working.

As I came to know Jim Baker quite well, my admiration and respect for him increased—and it was extremely high to begin with. In part that was because of his human qualities as a friend and colleague, and in part because of the skills that he brought to any task: intellect, focus, knowledge, perspective, charm, and a well-developed sense of humor.

In the interview, he attributes his success, and his record of leadership in so many areas, to the mantra drilled into him as a youth by his father: Prior preparation prevents poor performance.

Jim Baker was always prepared. That preparation, combined with the other skills mentioned above, enabled him to achieve results other government leaders could only dream about.

DAVID RUBENSTEIN (DR): Do you miss the days when everything you did was on the front pages, making world policy? Or are you quite happy with what you're doing now?

JAMES A. BAKER III (JB): I only miss our not having been reelected in '92. We were getting a lot of things done, and we could have continued doing some things. But I have to tell you, life after politics is pretty dang good. You're your own boss. You set your own schedule. You do what you want to do. There's a lot to be said for that.

DR: Let's talk about your career and how you came to be in the positions that you held. You are a native of Houston. Your family has been here for quite some time.

JB: Since 1872.

DR: To be precise. When you were growing up, did you want to be secretary of state, secretary of the treasury, or White House chief of staff?

JB: No, I was raised by a family that didn't really participate in politics. Politics was thought of as a dirty business. Really good lawyers didn't involve themselves in politics. I had a grandfather whose mantra for the young lawyers coming to work for Baker Botts, the family law firm, was "Work hard, study, and stay out of politics." That's the reason I used that title for my most recent book. I was pretty much apolitical.

DR: Were you a star athlete? Were you a student leader? What was your great interest?

JB: I was a reasonably decent athlete. I would not say I was a student leader. As a matter of fact, I almost flunked out of Princeton University my freshman year because I'd gone to a prep school in Pennsylvania, the Hill School, which was very strict. We couldn't have dates. I couldn't have girls visit there. When I got to Princeton and got all that freedom, and I could go to New York, I didn't spend much time studying.

DR: You went into the marines, though, before you went to law school.

JB: That was a very maturing experience for me. I loved the Marine Corps, and I love it to this day. As you know, there's no such thing as a former marine. When you're a marine, you're a marine.

DR: My father was in the marines. I understand it. After you finished your service, you came to the University of Texas School of Law. You did quite well. You were ready to join Baker Botts, the family firm. What happened?

JB: They had a nepotism rule, but I was hopeful. One day my dad came home from work, and he said, "Son, tomorrow the firm's going to give some consideration to waiving the nepotism rule for you because you've got the grades, you're on the law review, and so forth and so on, and you're the fourth James A. Baker in a row that would practice there."

He came home the next night, and he said, "Well, the firm decided not to waive the nepotism rule." I was very down about that.

In retrospect, it was the best thing that could ever have happened to me. If I had succeeded, it would have been because my dad was there. And if I had failed, people would say, "Well, what do you expect? He's only here because his dad is here." So it was a good thing for me that they didn't want me to come there.

DR: Growing up, your father was a tough taskmaster. He had a certain set of principles about preparation.

JB: He kept telling me, "Son, prior preparation prevents poor performance." He called it the five p's. It is a mantra that sort of got in my life. I could probably say, since we're here at the Baker Institute, that I thought it might ought to be the six p's: "Prior preparation prevents piss-poor performance."

DR: Your father didn't say that, but this is your addition to the family mantra?

JB: That's right. It's an amendment.

DR: So you're practicing law. You're minding your own business. You're playing tennis with someone named George Herbert Walker Bush. And then all of a sudden, he asked you to help him in his campaign. That's after your wife dies of breast cancer?

JB: That's correct. She died of breast cancer at the age of thirty-eight. Barbara and George were the last non–family members to see her before she died. We were close even then. George came to me. He said, "Bake," he said, "you need to take your mind off your grief and help me run for the Senate."

I looked at him. I said, "Well, George, that's a great idea except for two things. Number one, I don't know anything about politics. And number two, I'm a Democrat." "Well," he said, "we can fix that latter problem." And we did.

When I'm talking to a room full of Republicans, I say I got religion. When I'm talking to a mixed crowd, I say I switched parties.

DR: You switched parties and helped him in the 1970 election for the Senate.

JB: I'd been a little bit bitten by the political bug then. Not totally or completely. But they asked me to be state finance chairman of the Republican Party of Texas, and I did that.

DR: Then you were offered a chance to come to Washington when Gerald Ford was president. You were offered the position of deputy secretary of commerce. How did you quickly become somebody who was in charge of finding delegates for President Ford in his race in 1976 against Ronald Reagan?

JB: First of all, for the job of deputy secretary of commerce, they usually try to find a business-lawyer type. That's what I had been. George Bush put in a big good word for me.

But the second tragedy struck after I'd been at Commerce for about six months—the second tragedy that changed my life. Jerry Ford's delegate hunter in his campaign for the nomination against Ronald Reagan was killed in an automobile accident, and they needed a new delegate hunter. I didn't know anything about delegate hunting, but I found out about it.

DR: To remind people, in 1976 Gerald Ford was president, but he had never been elected. He was going to run for election. His main opponent was Ronald Reagan. It came down to a very, very tight convention, and your job was to get the delegates for President Ford. And how did it go?

JB: That was the last truly contested national convention of either major political party in this country. It went right down to the last ballot. It was very tight. We were chasing a very small pool of uncommitted delegates. Reagan was very strong. He almost knocked off an incumbent president. But we were able to prevail. We used, I will say, the full resources of the White House to get there.

I used to tell people, "I've been to more state dinners than anybody in the world." As a delegate hunter for President Ford, I used to bring uncommitted delegates to state dinners. Then I became secretary of state and had to go to every state dinner, which I did.

DR: The election is against Jimmy Carter, who is way ahead. Ford comes back. They have debates. But ultimately, Ford loses narrowly to Carter.

JB: That's because you were in the White House advising him.

DR: Well, that was later, when he lost.

All right. You have now managed a campaign for president that lost. You decided to go back to Texas?

JB: Yes. I tell people, every time we lose an election I come back here. A lot of people stay up there in Washington. I don't do that.

DR: You decided to run for attorney general of Texas.

JB: I'd been bitten by the political bug, because that convention was really close. It was very exciting. By the way, we only lost that election by

10,000 votes out of 81 million votes that had been cast. You turn 10,000 votes around in Iowa and Hawaii, Ford would have been president. Carter would never have been president.

I was bitten by the bug. But I had practiced law for eighteen years, and I was coming back here. I said to myself, "Maybe you ought to try your hand at this political game."

DR: While you were campaigning, somebody came up to you and said, "You look like Jim Baker."

JB: I had gotten a lot of press time as Ford's national chairman. A lot of TV time. People used to recognize me, but they couldn't really come up with a name. This guy one time did that. He said, "Anybody ever tell you that you look like Jim Baker?" I said, "Yes, often." I thought, "Boy, this is a big deal." Then the guy said, "Doesn't it piss you off?" That's when I realized, David, I wasn't going to win that race.

DR: In 1978, you get a call from your friend George Bush, who says, "Guess what? I'm going to run for president. I want you to help manage my campaign."

JB: That's correct. I helped George Bush because he was my close friend.

DR: Ultimately, he did not get the nomination.

JB: No. Reagan got it.

DR: I don't think you thought that George Bush was going to be picked as vice president.

JB: I was in the suite with Barbara and George and a few of our campaign staff. We thought it was all over when Walter Cronkite came out and said, "Ford is seriously considering joining the ticket with Reagan."

DR: When Walter Cronkite said, "It would be like a co-presidency if Ford was the vice president for Reagan," Reagan got upset with that. He said, "This isn't going to work." And he ultimately called George Bush.

JB: That's correct. I took the call. It was Drew Lewis, who was working for Reagan. He said, "Governor Reagan would like to speak to Ambassador Bush." I handed him the phone. He said, "Yes, sir? Yes, how are you? Yes, sir." The only question I think Reagan asked him was, "Will you support my position on abortion?" And Ambassador Bush said, "Yes, sir. I will."

DR: You were given the task by Ronald Reagan to help on the debates.

JB: To help negotiate the debates and help prepare for them.

DR: Was it difficult to prepare Reagan for the debates? People were not confident that he was a good debater.

JB: A lot of his close-in people didn't want him to debate. I wanted him to. His pollster wanted him to. I believe Nancy wanted him to. I always thought he was terrific in front of the camera. The red light goes on, and he's perfect.

DR: Reagan wins the election. What do you think you're going to be offered, if anything?

JB: I don't think. I don't know. But I had heard that my name had surfaced as a potential White House chief of staff. I said, "That's not possible. You don't go to somebody who's run two campaigns against you and make them your White House chief of staff." And guess what? I don't think it'll ever happen again in American politics. Not the way we're going today anyway.

DR: But Ronald Reagan did offer you the job, and you became chief of staff of the White House. Was it as much fun doing that job as it later is talking about it?

JB: It's the worst job in government. I tell everybody that. I tell the people who have been nominated for that job, or appointed to that job, "You got the worst job in government, because you're right at the intersection of politics and policy."

For me, it was even worse because I was an interloper. I wasn't a Californian.

They didn't give me credit for being a conservative. I wasn't a Reaganite. And there were a lot of people that tried to take me out. But the Gipper was always there for me. So was his wife. And so was Mike Deaver, and Stu Spencer, and a whole host of other people.

DR: Reagan was an amiable person. You found him to be quite easy to work for. It was said that you had to give him a joke every day. He liked to hear a joke every day.

JB: He loved it.

DR: He would give you a joke every day at the beginning of the day.

JB: He was the best joke-teller you ever heard. I can't repeat them, though.

DR: You became secretary of the treasury. During that time, among other things, there was the most significant rewriting of the tax code we'd had for fifty years or so.

JB: In a revenue-neutral way. We didn't grow the deficit to do it.

DR: The 1986 Tax Reform Act. How did you get that through? Congress was controlled by the Democrats in those days.

JB: President Reagan was very good about reaching across the aisle. We worked with the Democratic leadership in the House to make that happen. It wasn't easy.

DR: You got that done. And then your friend George Herbert Walker Bush says he wants to run for president. Reagan's two terms are going to be up. George Bush is vice president. And he asks you to help run his campaign. Were you reluctant to leave as secretary of the treasury to do that?

JB: I was going to do it if he asked me to. I didn't like the idea of having to get back into the grubby nitty-gritty of politics.

DR: Bush is behind for quite a bit of the campaign. He catches up, wins. Then do you say, "I'm ready to go back to Houston?"

JB: No. He knew I wanted to be secretary of state.

DR: And he offered you that right away?

JB: The next day.

DR: As secretary of state, you had to deal with a number of problems. One of them was the invasion of Kuwait by Saddam Hussein. Your job was to go around and get the coalition put together and also to raise the money to pay for it. Was that hard to do?

JB: It's the first and only time it's ever been done. I tell people that it was a textbook example of the way to fight a war. You tell the world what you're going to do. You get the world together with you to do it. You go do exactly what you said and nothing more, nothing less. You bring the troops home. And then you get other people to pay for it.

That's never been done before. I don't know when it's going to be done again, but that's the way to fight a war.

DR: The Cold War actually ends during George Bush's presidency. The Berlin Wall falls. Why did you not recommend that Bush go over there to Berlin and kind of remind everybody we'd won the Cold War?

JB: And dance on the wall.

DR: That's exactly right. Why not?

JB: This was President Bush's decision, and it was absolutely the right decision. He got a lot of grief for it. If he had gloated and been triumphal, we would never have been able to conclude what we were able to subsequently conclude with Gorbachev and Shevardnadze, the two leaders of the Soviet Union who, by the way, made the decision not to use force to keep the empire together and whom history will treat very, very well, in my opinion.

DR: What do you think was the reason you were so successful? Was it that you were trained as a lawyer, that you were harder-working than everybody else, smarter, more clever, surrounded by better people?

JB: Lucky.

DR: A little bit more than that probably.

JB: I had wonderful parents who instilled a solid work ethic in me. And, by the way, I never wing it. I have always followed the "Prior preparation prevents poor performance" mantra. I think those things made a difference. I was brought up to believe that if you start something, you finish it, or you do everything you can to finish it. That sort of thing.

But I was there at a wonderful time. Here's what I really think was the best thing for me: I had tremendous associates and assistants. They really performed beautifully. I was the beneficiary of a lot of that.

DR: In your time as secretary of state, who were the one or two most impressive foreign leaders you met?

JB: I dealt with some outstanding leaders. I think of Gorbachev. I think of Thatcher. I think of Shevardnadze—a former Soviet apparatchik who changed entirely.

DR: You met Gorbachev many times. You were impressed with his intellect and his abilities.

JB: Yes.

DR: He seems to have done an incredible job of actually changing the course of the world—maybe unintentionally to some extent.

JB: Much of it was unintentional.

DR: Does President Trump call you for advice very often?

JB: No. No.

DR: Some people watching might ask, "What are some words of advice for Congress or the administration from the great former secretary of state, secretary of the treasury, chief of staff Jim Baker?"

JB: We absolutely have to understand that one of the biggest threats facing our country and facing our democracy is the political dysfunction we have today. When I was there twenty-five years ago with Reagan, with Bush, with Ford, we reached across the aisle and we got things done. It happened with Carter. It happened with Clinton.

That doesn't happen anymore. That's truly tragic. There are a lot of reasons for it. But we need to cure that.

DR: Your great pleasures are still hunting and fishing.

JB: Yes. And I like playing golf. I still go to the office. I'm still a senior partner at Baker Botts. We have a mandatory retirement policy at age sixty-five, but there's an exemption.

DR: For Bakers.

JB: If you have been chief of staff at the White House, secretary of the treasury, and secretary of state.

DR: Well, they should have that exemption. Let me just say that after you left government, I had the privilege of working with you for about fifteen years in business and other things. It was one of the great pleasures of my life, getting to see you up close, somebody I'd read about. I hope everybody else can follow your leadership and do the kind of job you did for our country. Thank you very much for your service.

DECISION-MAKERS

Representative
Nancy Pelosi

Adam Silver

Christine Lagarde

Dr. Anthony S. Fauci

Justice Ruth
Bader Ginsburg

REPRESENTATIVE
NANCY PELOSI

Speaker of the U.S. House
of Representatives

"We have to be a model to women. Do not fear any of
this, have no fear. Know your own power. Be yourself.
Go out there and fight the fight, because you know your
why. You know why you decided to get into the arena.
You know what you care about. You know how to get
a job done, and you can draw support from other people."

Nancy Pelosi came from a well-known political family in Baltimore,
but as the only girl in the family, she was not expected to be an
elected political leader. Women in the 1950s and '60s were not generally
expected to run for office, let alone become national political leaders.

But Pelosi had some different ideas. After her five children were
essentially grown, she ran for Congress and, after serving for almost

twenty years, she became the first woman to serve as Speaker of the House of Representatives.

When the Democrats in the House lost their majority in the 2010 midterm elections, she remained their leader and was elected again as Speaker when they regained the majority in 2018. No woman in American political life has held as much power for as long as Nancy Pelosi.

How did she accrue so much power? She recognized that increasing power in Congress was derived from the ability to raise an enormous level of campaign contributions for other members. And from the time Nancy Pelosi became the House Democrats' leader, she also mastered the necessary skill of lining up votes and enforcing discipline among the troops. She used these skills to ensure the difficult-to-achieve congressional passage of the Affordable Care Act.

I have known the Speaker for a good many years. She attends many of the Kennedy Center's signature events, as well as events in which I am involved at the Smithsonian and the Library of Congress. We have also bonded a bit because we share a hometown—Baltimore—and an affection for some of its traditions.

How did she rise from housewife and mother of five to be a member of the House of Representatives (from her adopted city, San Francisco) to Speaker of the House, and the most politically powerful, influential, and impactful woman in the country's nearly 250-year history? I asked Speaker Pelosi these questions and many others before a very large audience at the Economic Club of Washington, D.C., in March 2019.

The Speaker recounts that she went into elective politics to solve social problems—such as the fact that one in five children in the country lives in poverty—and that she has stayed in politics for the same reason. But there is no doubt she also stays in the political arena to serve as a role model for women. She makes clear that she knows other women are watching her, and that she is regularly fighting as hard as she can for the causes in which she believes.

Nancy Pelosi is trying, as she relates in the interview, to show that women can be effective leaders if they get in the arena and use their skills to show how to get the job done. That type of strong leadership is what Speaker Pelosi no doubt felt she was showing as she led the House of Representatives' historic effort in 2019 to impeach President Donald J. Trump, and as she led the House's unprecedented efforts in 2020 to deal with the COVID-19 pandemic.

DAVID RUBENSTEIN (DR): You have said that being the mother of five and the grandmother of nine has been helpful to you in government service—in giving you a kind of experience. Is it more helpful in dealing with your caucus or dealing with the White House?

NANCY PELOSI (NP): I want to say to all moms out there, place a gold star on that experience that you have. Whatever, shall we say, opportunities you are faced with, it's about managing time and personalities and diplomacy and quartermaster and logistics and all the rest. It's a multitasking wonder, and I just congratulate all moms and dads for what they do. It's not about managing people, it's more about managing time.

DR: You were elected Speaker—the first woman to be Speaker—and then you recaptured the speakership after eight years as minority leader. How do you compare the relative pleasure of being the first female Speaker to being the first Speaker in sixty years to recapture the speakership?

NP: When I was running for leadership in the Congress, or for Speaker, the last thing I could ever say to someone is "You should vote for me because we should have a woman." You just had to prove that you would do the best job.

But when I became the Speaker, it was quite an overwhelming feeling that we had broken a marble ceiling in our country. I always thought the American people, David, were much more ready for a woman president than the Congress of the United States was ready for a woman Speaker.

The first meeting that I ever went to as a leader—not yet Speaker—with President Bush as president, I was going to the White House for my first meeting as the leader of my caucus. I didn't feel apprehensive about it, because I'd been to the White House many times, as an appropriator, as a member of the Intelligence Committee. They're the two places I was forged in Congress. I just went. But as the door closed behind me, I realized that it was unlike any meeting I had ever been to before.

It was unlike any meeting any woman had been to before in the White House, because there was a small meeting—the president, the leadership of the House and Senate, Democratic and Republican. I was going in there not as an appointment of the president, with my power and presence derived from a person, but derived from the power of my caucus.

As I sat there—and President Bush was ever gracious, welcoming— all of a sudden it was so crowded on my chair I could barely acknowledge what he was saying, I was so distracted with what was happening. I realized that sitting there on that seat with me were Susan B. Anthony, Elizabeth Cady Stanton, Lucretia Mott, Sojourner Truth, Alice Paul, you name it. They were all there, right on that chair. I could hear them say, "At last we have a seat at the table." And then they were gone, and my first thought was, "We want more. We want more."

DR: Since you've been a leader in the House, you've dealt with three presidents: President Bush, President Obama, and President Trump. Can you compare their relative styles?

NP: Well, they aren't relative, but I thank you for the question. It's an important one from a historical standpoint. Here's the thing: first of all, I completely and entirely respect the Office of the President of the United States, and I respect the people who voted to elect a president of the United States.

It's with complete respect that I encounter whoever the president is. I always make it my practice not to suggest to any president, Democratic or Republican, anything that is not in his interest. Do I go in with my agenda and say, "You should do this"? No. [I say,] "This is in the public's interest, the national interest."

President Bush was the governor of Texas. President Obama was a state senator and a United States senator. They brought to the office some level of experience in government and some level of knowledge of issues of the day. It was a little bit easier, if you use the word *relative*, to relate and speak shorthand about the issues that we had ahead.

We worked very closely with President Bush, even though I disagreed with him mightily on the war in Iraq, but that did not prevent us from working together to pass the biggest energy bill in the history of our country, passing legislation related to taxes that helped poor children, poor families in our country—all kinds of issues that we worked together on. We had a good working relationship.

President Obama, of course, as a Democratic president, we had a very special relationship then. But you still, even though it's your own party, have your differences of approach or degree or timing and whatever.

DR: President Trump?

NP: I pray for our country every day, I always have. But I do think there's something to be said for experience, knowledge, judgment, and surrounding yourself with people who know things. I always say to people, when they say they want to run for office, "What is your vision for our country? What is your why? Why should we be attracted to what you have to say? What do you know about your subject, your focus?"

If it's climate, if it's economic vitality, if it's education—whatever the subject, what do you know about your specialties so that your judgment can be trusted in one arena and perhaps transferred to another? What is your strategic thinking about issues, how to get something done? And how do you draw people into your orbit so that you are a leader and can advance in that?

When you make a judgment about a candidate, that applies to a president as well. There's something to be said for, whatever your vision is or whatever your connection is to the public, that your judgment is guided by evidence, data, facts, truth, knowledge, and that is a place where we have some work to be done.

DR: In the old days, twenty years ago, thirty years ago, freshman members of Congress were generally quiet for a few terms. They weren't supposed to say very much. That seems to have changed.

Is it harder for you to convince your senior members that the junior members need to have more time to express themselves? Is it difficult to manage the caucus when you have freshman members who get so much attention?

NP: No, it's a joy. It's an invigoration. It's what our founders intended—elections every two years. Every two years. I have to say this, because I'm really proud that in the Congress of the United States, this Congress, we have over a hundred women members serving at the same time. Over a hundred women.

With all due respect to everyone who has served, our caucus is over 60 percent women, people of color, LGBTQ. Over 60 percent of our caucus. That's remarkable, right? And that diversity is our strength. I say to the members, "Channel our exuberances. Our diversity is our strength, but our unity is our power." It's really important, especially for women and newcomers to the Congress, to know, this is not a zero-sum game. Somebody else's progress or success in the public arena is a plus for all of us. It isn't a zero-sum game—if you have this, that subtracts from something else. Again, I thrive on the diversity.

DR: In recent years, you have been vilified by the Republicans and people on the right. In the most recent campaign, 132,000 ads were run against you, just using your name.

NP: One hundred thirty-three thousand.

DR: Has this been personally difficult for you, to be so vilified? Or you take pride in the fact they recognize you're very powerful?

NP: My goddaughter, Katie, sent me something on my phone after the election. It said, "Your power is the reason your opponents come after you," or something like that.

This is what I say, because I have set an example to other women: Don't be too shy about things. Assert yourself and take credit and the rest of that.

But here's the thing. If I were not effective, they wouldn't be doing these ads. They fear me because I'm a master legislator. I just know how to do it because that's what I was doing. I wasn't running for leadership, I was legislating.

I have a following in the country that supports me at the grassroots level and across the board. So they have to take me down. I have to show other women, we're in the arena, you're in the arena. Once you get in that arena, you've got to be prepared to take a punch. You've got to be prepared to throw a punch too.

We have to be a model to women. Do not fear any of this, have no fear. Know your own power. Be yourself. Go out there and fight the fight, because you know your why. You know why you decided to get into the arena. You know what you care about. You know how to get a job done, and you can draw support from other people.

And that's why they come after me. If I were not effective, they wouldn't take out 133,000 ads against me during the campaign. But we won a very decisive victory.

DR: You never considered running for president?

NP: No. I didn't consider running for Congress. That doesn't mean that people haven't suggested it.

DR: Sala Burton, who represented California's Fifth District in Congress until her death in 1987, was a good friend of yours. When she was on her deathbed, she asked you to run for Congress. Had you ever thought of running yourself?

NP: No.

DR: What did your children and your husband say when you said you were going to run for Congress?

NP: Well, here's the thing. I had no interest in running. As you mentioned, when I was born my father was in Congress, a member from Baltimore. When I was in first grade, he became the mayor of Baltimore. When I was at Trinity College, he was still the mayor of Baltimore. It was the only life that we knew.

We were born into a family that was devoutly Catholic, fiercely patriotic, in love with America, proud of our Italian American heritage, staunchly Democratic. That connection between our faith and how we exercised our belief in the Gospel of Matthew, "When I was hungry," how we just treated people with a spark of divinity, each of them worthy of respect, we're all God's children—that's how we were raised, to have responsibility to other people. That's what our parents instilled in us.

But I never ever thought, nor did anybody else around me think, that I would ever want to run for office. However, I did volunteer in the Democratic Party to support other candidates.

When we moved to California, my kids and I used to go to the library and sort books and do all the things that you do as a volunteer. The mayor called me one day and he said, "I know you love the library. I want to appoint you to the library commission." I said, "You don't have to do that. Save that for somebody else. We'll always volunteer, we love the library."

Now, he wasn't known as a feminist, Mayor Alioto, but he said this: "Nancy, if you're doing the work, get official recognition for it. You become a member of this commission, you have a vote, you make decisions. People care about what you think."

So I did that. And I'm still close to the library. The point for other women is, get the recognition for what you are doing. I never knew that Sala would want me to run for office. But when she did, I was ready. So I say to people, know your power. Women, know your power. Count everything you've done, including being a mom, maybe starting with. Know your power. Be yourself. Authenticity is everything. Sincerity and authenticity is everything. Don't try to be somebody else, be yourself and be ready, be ready.

DR: And you got elected. It must have been a thrill for your father and mother, who were still alive when you were elected. They came to see you sworn in, is that right?

NP: Yes. My father had been a member of Congress, and as a member of Congress, you have rights to the floor. So he was on the floor of the House when I was sworn in. That was pretty exciting. He died a few months later. I was so lucky that he was there to see that, and my mother was too.

DR: You obviously enjoy the job. How many more years might you do this? Ten, fifteen, twenty? Any limit?

NP: Jerry Brown, the former California governor, said this to me recently: "There's nothing as liberating as term limits." You just do what you do. I'm on a mission, I'm not on a timetable. But I do have some other things I want to do in life.

DR: Would you say something about your husband? What's it like to be married to the Speaker of the House?

NP: Let me just say, you have to ask him that. However, he does from time to time say, "This isn't what I bargained for." Or "How did this happen?" Here we were just getting married, happily having our children and the rest, and then boom, all of a sudden, one thing and another.

DR: What would you like the American people to know about Nancy Pelosi?

NP: In terms of why I went from the kitchen to the Congress, from housewife to House Speaker, my why is that one in five children in America lives in poverty. To me, it's a disservice to every child in America to not be sure that every child in America has opportunity. This is the greatest country that ever existed in the history of the world, and one in five children goes to sleep hungry at night.

That is my why. I couple that with—instilled in me by my parents—a love of our country that says anything is possible in America. Anything is possible. It gives you hope that if you work hard enough, pray hard enough too, you'll be able to accomplish whatever the goal is.

I just leave you with the thought that this country is the greatest country that ever was. It can withstand anything. But we all have a responsibility.

Thomas Paine said, "The times have found us." The times have found us now too, to channel the energies, respect the diversity, the differences of opinion in our country, and always keep taking it back to the oneness, *E pluribus unum*.

What I want them to know about me is the reason I left home, the reason I get up every morning to go into the fight, is the one in five children who live in poverty.

ADAM SILVER

Commissioner, National Basketball Association

"Having gone to law school, learning those skills,
has been very beneficial. A large part of my job is
being a professional negotiator, whether it's collective
bargaining or relationships that we enter into."

A dam Silver has a job that seems ideal for anyone who really likes professional basketball: commissioner of the NBA. The NBA is extraordinarily successful these days—four decades ago, the league was struggling—and it has made its players and owners quite wealthy and its fans quite pleased. What was once a U.S.-centered league is now really a global multimedia business.

Indeed, professional basketball has become a great sport that is now part of the fabric of American society. Its recent and current stars—Michael Jordan, Magic Johnson, Larry Bird, LeBron James, Stephen Curry, the late Kobe Bryant—have become the role models for many of the country's youth and adults. They have become what the country's best-known baseball players were in the 1950s and '60s, but they are more than that: they are global stars and "influencers."

How did this turnaround and current success come about?

Adam Silver would no doubt give much of the credit to the late David Stern, who was the commissioner for thirty years, and who first hired Adam as a special assistant. But Adam has actually taken the NBA to financial and popularity heights that even David Stern might not have thought possible.

The commissioner's job is multifold: ensure the integrity of the sport, negotiate the collective bargaining agreement with the players, negotiate the national media contracts, represent the league in public and with government agencies, and help the sport to grow and be increasingly profitable and popular.

Adam got the position that led to his working for the NBA for twenty-two-plus years (before becoming commissioner in February 2014) an old-fashioned way. He was a young lawyer who wrote a letter to Stern seeking career advice. He impressed the commissioner so much in their one meeting that Adam was hired shortly thereafter.

I have known Adam for a few years. He joined the Duke board while I was its chair, and we may have bonded over our shared interest in Duke basketball, and our having also both attended the University of Chicago Law School. But I had not interviewed him until our session at the Economic Club of Washington, D.C., in May 2019.

In our exchange, he is too modest to talk about the skill set that enabled him to rise and to succeed so well. But he is clearly intelligent, with a passion for his job and the ability to get along with and please high-powered owners and maintain a strong relationship with the players and the players' union—not an easy task for anyone.

And he clearly showed, at the outset of his becoming commissioner, the leadership that convinced the public that the owners had indeed selected the right person to succeed his legendary predecessor: he responded to the racist comments of an owner by effectively stripping that owner of the ability to operate his team and forcing a prompt sale of the franchise (at a record price)—unprecedented steps for any sports commissioner.

After this interview occurred, Adam and the NBA found themselves in other uncharted waters. He has since navigated tense relationships with China that have tested sports diplomacy as an essential tool for global engagement, and the NBA played an integral role in protecting public health when it suspended its season in March 2020 to help contain and mitigate the coronavirus pandemic. A number of sports, entertainment, and cultural institutions followed suit.

What can be better than being an avid basketball fan and the commissioner of the NBA, and also having everyone say you are doing a great job? Nothing, except not letting it go to your head. And that is never a problem for Adam Silver.

DAVID RUBENSTEIN (DR): Since you've been the commissioner of the NBA, revenues are up. Ticket sales are up. TV viewership is up. The owners' value of their teams is up by about three times. The NBA seems to be at its peak. It's very popular all over the world.

Why do you think NBA basketball is so popular, whereas major-league baseball and professional football aren't quite as global?

ADAM SILVER (AS): Part of the reason is that it's been an Olympic sport since the 1930s. That's made a big difference—and that it's a sport that has been played around the world.

It was actually invented by Christian missionaries. James Naismith was a Christian missionary, and the game was, shortly after it was invented in Springfield, Massachusetts, brought to China.

So it's been global since its earliest days. Part of it is the simplicity of the game. For people who grew up in the States, there's a reason they use basketball in gym class. It's a way to get all the kids quickly involved. It's incredibly difficult to master, but at least the concept of it is easy: you dribble the ball and then you shoot it into the basket. It doesn't require a large amount of space. You can practice it on your own.

Lastly, it's a team sport. It's something that societies think is very important in getting people to learn to work together.

DR: Some people who have bought franchises have done extremely well. The 76ers were bought a few years ago for $300 or $400 million, the Bucks for maybe $400 or $500 million. When Steve Ballmer came in and paid $2 billion for the Clippers, were all the other owners happy because it made their teams look more valuable?

AS: Yes, they were happy. Since Steve bought the Clippers, two teams have sold for more than he paid—the Houston Rockets and the Brooklyn Nets.

DR: One of the most difficult things you had to do after you became the commissioner was to ban the then owner of the L.A. Clippers for making racist comments. Was that a tough decision for you?

AS: Yes. People may not realize it, but he's the only owner who's ever permanently been banned from a sport. I work for the owners collectively. Those are my thirty bosses. I don't work for any one owner. My job is to do what's in the best interest of the league.

I had been with the league for almost twenty-two years before I became commissioner. He had been an owner from before I even joined the NBA. He's someone I had known for a long time. It was difficult. But I had no doubt that it was the right thing to do.

DR: When North Carolina passed its so-called Bathroom Bill, you moved the NBA All-Star Game from there. [The bill included a requirement, since overturned, that transgender people in state-run buildings use the facilities for whatever sex was listed on their birth certificate.] Was that a tough decision?

AS: The league made a decision that we would not play our All-Star Game in North Carolina while that law, HB2, was still on the books. We made a decision that it was not our right to direct a state how it should run itself, but that that law was inconsistent with the core values of the league. We weren't boycotting North Carolina. We have a team owned by Michael Jordan, the Charlotte Hornets, and a minor-league team that was still playing in North Carolina.

But we decided for an event like an All-Star Game, which is a celebratory event, there was a large part of the community that wasn't feeling welcome. We made a decision to move that game, and then, as you know, a new governor came in, Roy Cooper, and the law was changed and we returned to North Carolina.

DR: Would you make a decision like that yourself or do you call the owners up and say, "What do you think?"

AS: I call lots of owners and say, "What do you think?" It's not something that we took a vote on.

It's not just owners that I call. I spoke a lot to Michael Jordan because he owns the team in that state. He's from North Carolina. I spoke to some of our Duke friends before I made that decision. I also spoke to not just our players association and our partners but many of our players who are from North Carolina. I wanted to make sure they understood why we were making that decision. I spoke to many of our corporate partners. But once I take information in, it's my job to make that decision and not to suggest, on a controversial decision, that it wasn't my responsibility.

DR: One of the controversial things in college basketball has been the so-called one-and-done situation, where high school players go to college for one year and then get drafted into the NBA. Are you in favor of continuing that policy? What would you change about it?

AS: When I first became commissioner, I announced that I thought the minimum age for entering the NBA should be twenty instead of nineteen. Roughly eleven years ago, we changed it from eighteen to nineteen. That has to be collectively bargained with our players association.

As commissioner, I became more aware of how the one-and-done situation actually worked in operation, how the recruiting worked. There have obviously been some high-profile criminal proceedings around college sports. In the middle of all that, Mark Emmert, the head of the NCAA, appointed a commission chaired by Condoleezza Rice to look at issues involving college sports, particularly the one-and-done situation. Ultimately Rice and her commission recommended that we return to the eighteen-year-old entry age.

That had an impact on me, together with a better understanding of what is happening to these top players. It's hard even to see it as a full year in college in many cases. Most of them leave once the tournament is over. So I've changed my position. It's a tough one, because not all the teams agree with me on this.

DR: If you're a lottery draft pick in the NBA, the maximum you can get paid for three years is what?

AS: We negotiated with our players association a rookie scale. The number-one pick—I may be off slightly—will enter into a three-year contract at roughly $10 million a year in salary.

DR: After the three years is over, they've made $30 million, forget the shoe contracts, they can get into whatever contract the market will allow. You have a maximum contract. What is that?

AS: We have a salary-cap system. There's a soft-cap system for the team. Then there's a maximum an individual player can make. If there's a fixed pool of money, in essence there's negotiation among the players that a star player should only take so much out of the system. Right now that's about $35 million a year. You can enter into a five-year contract with your own team. But it goes up every year.

DR: Take college athletes like Zion Williamson. Do you think people like Zion should get paid by colleges to play, or should they just say, "We're here for education or to get ready to be pros. We don't want to be paid"? This was a controversy that arose when he was injured this past year.

AS: It's such a complicated issue. They are paid, in essence. They're on scholarship. They get all kinds of benefits by virtue of being at the school. Clearly there's an enormous amount of revenue being generated around them. You and I both know it's money that's reinvested into other athletic programs, and still doesn't pay for itself, which might surprise people.

DR: Virtually no college athletic program, with the exception of two or three schools, actually is profitable. They all have to be subsidized by the university.

AS: We would both agree that's not necessarily the measure of the market value of those players. Part of the reason an economist would say there's so much corruption around college sports is presumably that the player is worth more to the school than the scholarship, which is why markets are broken.

DR: Let's talk about the NBA players themselves. You have fifteen players allowed on a team, and you have thirty teams. So there are 450 people, more or less, in the NBA. How many of those players play more than five years?

AS: The average career is seven years, but it's much longer for All-Stars. Probably the average career for an All-Star is closer to thirteen or fourteen years.

DR: When the players are done, whenever it might be, do they actually have financial problems? Or they've made so much money they can coast the rest of their lives? How do you deal with the amount of money they're getting and what they do with it?

AS: The average player in the league this year is making $8 million. By anyone's math, if you average seven years in the league, you should be set for life—maybe not private equity style, but set for life.

DR: In private equity, you're never set for life.

AS: To the question "Do they have financial issues?"—in certain cases they do. Some of the players who have financial issues didn't make nearly the kind of money players are making now, but some who made a lot of money either were taken advantage of or didn't invest it wisely. It's something that we work very hard on with our players association and directly with our players. We of course don't have control over their money. They're our employees. We have counseling and we have a pension plan.

DR: Four hundred fifty players. How many of them do you think have college degrees?

AS: A small percent. Even if they're not one-and-done, many are coming out after two years or three years. And 25 percent of our league is made of international players, and almost all our top international players became pro at fourteen, fifteen, sixteen. So none of them went to college.

DR: What percentage of NBA games are sold out?

AS: Our arenas this past season were roughly 94 percent full. A lot of our games are sold out.

DR: How does it happen that Jack Nicholson, other movie stars, happen to get those L.A. Lakers seats right on the floor? The team wants them there or they just get lucky?

AS: All the credit goes to the late owner of the Los Angeles Lakers, a guy named Jerry Buss. He ran an incredible franchise and had an enormous number of championships. In addition to fielding incredible teams, he in essence invented what we even call in the league now the Jack Nicholson seats. Jerry came up with that idea of putting a celebrity courtside.

DR: Let's talk about one serious issue I didn't really address before. You've said that players sometimes have depression and they feel isolated. How does somebody who's making $50 million a year and seems to be well respected get so depressed and isolated?

AS: I've said they're no more immune from mental illness than any other sector of our society. Regardless of how much money you're making or your position in life or your family, in some cases it's chemical, in some cases it's environmental, but depression cuts across all socioeconomic groups.

What's changing, though, in our league—and I think it's wonderful—is that players are now willing to talk about these things. The fact that these players are talking about it has had a huge impact on other players.

DR: How do the ticket sales work? The Golden State Warriors make, like, $3.5 million a home game. Do they keep all the revenue from the ticket sales from their home games?

AS: There's something we call a "gate assessment" of 6 percent that goes to support league office costs. Other than that, they keep the revenue from their regular season games. It's a different formula in the playoffs. There's some nuance to it. But in essence, 25 percent goes into a fund, as opposed to 6 percent, during the playoffs.

DR: Who's the most popular player in terms of jersey sales?

AS: I think LeBron James may still be the number-one jersey seller. Steph Curry's up there.

DR: When teams have three or four superstars, is that good for the league?

AS: It depends how that team is developed. Most people would agree that if you draft those players and develop them into superstars, that's a good thing. In a situation where a superstar is joining a team that is already a so-called loaded team, a great team, in terms of wanting parity in the league that's not ideal.

That's where the collective bargaining agreement comes in. The agreement isn't just designed to determine how much players make, but to create competition. If you're a player being drafted into the NBA, you don't want to be drafted by a team that has no chance of winning either.

DR: How do you get to be NBA commissioner? Did you grow up saying, "I want to be NBA commissioner"?

AS: I didn't grow up wanting to be the commissioner. I don't even think I had any sense of what it was. Even when I went to law school, if somebody asked me what the NBA commissioner did, I would have said, "He hands out championship rings and sets the schedule." I wouldn't really have even understood the job.

DR: You graduated from the University of Chicago Law School. You clerked for a federal judge. Then you went to Cravath, Swaine & Moore, a well-known Wall Street firm. How did you go from there to the NBA? A lot of lawyers who are not happy practicing law would love to go work there.

AS: I got incredibly lucky. I had worked at Cravath for about two years. One of Cravath's big clients was Time Warner, and I was working on a lot of media cases, for HBO in particular.

I became fascinated with the media business. While I was working on a particular litigation, I was following what was happening in sports media, the move of sports to cable television, and it was Ted Turner, in essence through TBS and then TNT, who was leading that charge.

David Stern, then the commissioner, was at the forefront of that movement. [Stern died in January 2020.] I didn't know David, but I wrote him a letter and asked him if he could give me some advice about transitioning from law into a media job.

This was pre–e-mail. I wrote him an old-fashioned letter. His assistant called me a few weeks later and said, "He can see you on whatever date." I went over. I met with him for a half hour. He gave me some advice, which I didn't follow. Then, about a month later, he called me and he said, "What are you up to? I have an idea." And after a series of meetings he hired me as his assistant. That was my first job with the NBA.

DR: If you got a letter from a young lawyer today seeking that kind of advice—

AS: I'd pass it to our HR department.

Being commissioner of the NBA is my sixth job at the NBA. For five of those jobs, I worked directly for David. He gave me enormous opportunities. I ended up running an entity called NBA Entertainment, which did television and media and then became the Internet arm of the NBA. Many years later, I became the deputy commissioner of the NBA. Ultimately, you know, David recommended me, but it required the team owners voting me in. That's how the commissioner is determined.

DR: What leadership trait did you have that made David think you deserved to be the commissioner?

AS: It was nothing necessarily unique to me. I was willing to work very hard, and I did work very hard over the years. I certainly love the sport of basketball.

Much of my job now is spent on media. It's the primary revenue source for the NBA. So the fact that I developed an expertise in media over the years was very important.

I think you and I would say the same thing: having gone to law school, learning those skills, has been very beneficial. A large part of my job is being a professional negotiator, whether it's collective bargaining or relationships that we enter into. It was all of those skills.

DR: A lot of your media today, and this contrasts you with the other leagues, is social media. You encourage your players to be involved in social media. You encourage LeBron James and your best-known players to be, if not controversial, to have public views. Why do you do that? And has it been helpful to the NBA?

AS: I certainly don't encourage them to be controversial. I encourage them to be genuine and earnest about their views. I make sure they know that within certain boundaries—more around issues of decency than political speech—that they should feel safe as NBA players.

Ultimately, it's in our business interest to demonstrate to our fans that these are multidimensional people. Social media, as a complement to traditional media, which is really helpful too, allows them to show who they really are. It helps to engage fans in our game.

DR: You're going to stay in this position for the foreseeable future. You're not going to go buy a team, go into private equity, nothing like that?

AS: No plans to go anywhere.

CHRISTINE LAGARDE

President, European Central Bank;
Former Managing Director,
International Monetary Fund

"There are still instances when I walk into a room full
of men and there is this little smile about their face,
which is either 'Here she goes again, she's going to talk
about women,' or 'I wonder what she has to say.'
It's less now, for sure, but when you are in a
minority, that's what you experience."

C hristine Lagarde was for eight years the managing director of the
International Monetary Fund (IMF), a Washington-based organization created after World War II with the goal of ensuring international financial stability and economic growth. As director, Lagarde
frequently had to deal with the world's financial crisis of the moment:

debt defaults in Argentina and Greece, the impact of a post-Brexit Europe, declining growth rates in many emerging and frontier markets.

In addressing these kinds of issues, and in running the sprawling IMF bureaucracy, she invariably was able to get many disparate parties on the same page because of the power of her intellect, the force of her personality, and her considerable charm. She left this position in late 2019 to become the president of the European Central Bank, a somewhat less global organization but with an enormous role in guiding the European economy. Prior to the IMF position, she was the French minister of finance and the managing partner of the multinational law firm—then the world's largest—Baker McKenzie.

Lagarde was the first woman to hold all of those positions. As such, she was both a trailblazer and a role model for women throughout the world. More than just holding these positions, she provided the type of strong, decisive leadership that some thought only a man could provide.

What was the secret to the repeated leadership successes of a French lawyer, who as a youth also showed leadership in a totally different setting as a member of the French national synchronized swimming team? How did Lagarde overcome the frequent discrimination she encountered? She not only held positions that had always been filled by men, but she also found few female coworkers along the way.

I asked these and related questions at a *Peer to Peer* session at the IMF headquarters in Washington, D.C., in September 2018. In the interview, she does not attribute her professional successes and leadership skills to any one factor. But I think it is fair to say that her considerable intellect, self-confidence, and hard-work mind-set are important factors. Too, while she might not say so directly, she probably feels that being underestimated at the outset—and then being able to show her evident skills quickly—has enabled her to achieve success few expected.

For instance, she came to lead the IMF at a time when her predecessor had to resign amid a personal scandal. The IMF's basic credibility and effectiveness were being questioned. By the time she left, Lagarde had restored and enhanced the credibility of the IMF to a level not even imagined by its creators in the post–World War II period.

I spoke at her IMF farewell dinner and said, rather tongue in cheek, that her success might also be attributed to the skills she had learned as a synchronized swimmer, and that perhaps everyone in Washington interested in leading a large organization might begin by learning synchronized swimming. There must be something learned in that sport that is exceedingly valuable later in life.

DAVID RUBENSTEIN (DR): Many people don't know what the IMF actually is.

CHRISTINE LAGARDE (CL): The International Monetary Fund was set up seventy-five years ago by forty-four men—

DR: No women?

CL: Not in those days. So, it was set up by forty-four men in 1944 on the eve of the end of the Second World War, with a view to avoiding major economic crisis, major instability in the world, which in their view led to the war. That's the intention.

DR: Let's go back to how you actually came to this position. You grew up in France. What did your parents do? Were they educators, or were they in government?

CL: They were both professors. My father was a professor of English literature at university and my mother was teaching French grammar, Latin, and ancient Greek. That's the universe that populated my childhood—a lot of literature.

DR: Growing up with parents like that, you must be really good at languages.

CL: I was hopeless. I was really bad, actually.

DR: I doubt that. So you were, I assume, a very good student. You were also interested in synchronized swimming at that time. Can you explain what synchronized swimming really is, and how you came to be on the French national team?

CL: The athletic activities had to do with the riots we had in France in 1968—students who had taken to the streets. My parents were terrified that I would do that too. They allowed me to go to the swimming pool of the club. I could skip school and spend all my time by the pool. I enjoyed swimming at the time. Gradually I became really interested in the synchronized swimming that brought together girls. It's teamwork that required music and liking music, and I had always liked musical discipline and methods. So I joined the team. I did the European championship and many international events.

DR: You still do swimming? Not synchronized?

CL: Oh, yes, including this morning.

DR: Wow, how do you have time for that?

CL: I get up at five o'clock.

DR: That probably helps.

CL: The pool doesn't open until six, so I have to do a bit of gym before that.

DR: What did you study in college?

CL: I had a very classic education. I studied the basic subjects—French, math, English, geography, history, chemistry, and physics, plus some sports, which were not so important in those days in France.

DR: Very often leaders in France go to certain prestigious schools. Did you go to one of those?

CL: No, I failed miserably. The first time I was in love with somebody who was going to become my husband, and I did not study very hard. The second year I did study really hard with a group of others who studied equally hard, but I totally missed the date of registration to take the various exams.

DR: You became a lawyer, though. What propelled you to want to be a lawyer?

CL: I wanted to participate in abolishing the death penalty. When I started law school, the death penalty was one of the tools of criminal law. For personal religious and other reasons, I wanted to participate in eradicating this penalty in the legal arsenal of France. Unfortunately, when I graduated and could have joined that group, the death penalty had been abolished.

DR: You nonetheless stayed a lawyer. Did you practice in France?

CL: I practiced in France for a few years. I was doing as so many young lawyers in those days did: you had to do tax law, you had to do corporate law, you had to do antitrust law, you had to do labor law. Luckily the French president to be elected was François Mitterrand, a socialist, and that government came out with lots of very, very hard labor rules to benefit the unions and the workers. At Baker McKenzie, most of our clients were international corporations or American companies that had invested in France, and I was really busy.

DR: Were there many women lawyers in France in those days?

CL: No, no, no, no. One of the reasons I joined Baker McKenzie was because the managing partner of the Paris office was a woman, and she was then a role model for me.

DR: Baker McKenzie was for many years one of the largest law firms in the world.

CL: It was the largest, yes.

DR: And it was based in Chicago. How did you get to be the head of the entire firm? You're a woman; it's a male firm, more or less. You're from France; it's a Chicago-based American firm. How did you get elected to be the managing director of the entire firm and move to Chicago?

CL: I would love to think that it is pure merit and the quality of the work I was doing.

It's interesting, actually. I became managing partner of the Paris office, and I was doing a decent job. I was picked up by the nominating committee, who selected me to join the executive committee. I was the first woman to be on that committee, and then I went back to practice, happily. But they came back to get me. By that time, it was a mess. The IT budget was completely out of order. The knowledge-management system was a complete disaster, and management was not really trusted. The nominating committee had a tough time selecting somebody, and it's often in those situations that a woman arises. So I was selected as chairman of the firm.

DR: So you are the head of Baker McKenzie, you're living in Chicago. Was living in the Midwest of the United States like a foreign situation since you are from France?

CL: Chicago is a fantastic city—I had lots of friends there and I still have many of them today. I truly enjoyed my six years in Chicago.

DR: You were doing that, and all of a sudden Nicolas Sarkozy gets elected president of France. Did you know him?

CL: It was two years before that. Jacques Chirac was still the president and Dominique de Villepin, the prime minister, was in charge. He's the one who called me to be minister of trade.

DR: You went back and you served as minister of trade for a couple of years. How did you like that job?

CL: I loved it. I really loved it. It was a massive change in my life geographically, socially, financially as well.

DR: I assume the income was not the same as you had before?

CL: It was, like, divided by ten. But it was a job that I most enjoyed in government because I was selling France around the world. President

Chirac knew I was this strange animal that had come out of the private sector and corporate life. But I think he had a lot of respect for me, and I had huge respect for him.

DR: Then Sarkozy does get elected president of France.

CL: Yes. He asked me to be minister of agriculture. Which I had no clue about, but I was prepared to learn.

DR: But you did that for just a few months?

CL: I did that for two months, because then he asked me to become minister of finance. I think he asked me to be minister of agriculture because he knew that it was going to be a World Trade Organization hot potato and he wanted somebody who was acquainted with difficult international issues.

DR: Were you the first woman to be finance minister of a major country in Western Europe?

CL: Yes, yes, yes. I was the first female finance minister for a G7 country and of many countries, actually, over time.

DR: You were a lawyer by training, and all of a sudden you are in charge of the finances for France. Were you worried about not having that kind of background, or did your job as minister of trade help you?

CL: That background helped me, but I recognized right from the get-go that I was going to have to learn enormously and learn from the team from the treasury department. I had to work very hard.

DR: So you did a very good job there, by all accounts. Then the IMF managing director position opened up. Did you really want the job, or did you have to be persuaded to move back to the United States?

CL: So things in my life happened out of the right timing, the right people, and my sense of "All right, let's try it. Let's do it." You know, when

I returned to France as a minister, I had not thought for a second about my pension, my compensation, the reporting lines, how it would work out. I just wanted to do it. I wanted to help the country.

As finance minister, I don't think I anticipated at all that two months into the job, the beginning of the financial crisis would loom as a result of the closure of the two BNP accounts [French investment bank BNP Paribas]. But you just roll your sleeves up and work and team up with people who know what they are doing and who have a good moral compass. It's a combination of all that.

DR: At the IMF, one of the things that you have to worry about is not just countries that are not doing that well and need some money but the economy of the entire world. Your job is to help to promote stability and development and also employment. Are we better prepared around the world for another financial collapse of the type we had ten years ago?

CL: We are better prepared, because at least in certain areas we've learned the lessons. When you look at the banking system, when you look at the ring of supervisors, when you look at the set of regulations that apply, in that particular sector we are much better prepared. The banks around the world have almost solid capital ratios, liquidity ratios, leverage. On all those fronts, I think we've made significant progress.

Risks tend to travel to the fringe. If you look at other areas—asset management, pension funds, fin-tech development—those are areas where I'm not sure we have added the security that we've developed in relation to the banking sector.

Now there are other numbers that are much more worrying. The weight of debt on corporations and households has gone up by virtue of the stimulus and the indebtedness that had to develop as a response to the crisis.

DR: Have you noticed that, when there is a very difficult problem, sometimes the men don't want to do it and give it to a woman to do?

CL: You said it, not me.

DR: None of the men seem to want to take that job because they know it's a no-win situation.

CL: No, they are probably prepared to come and take the job afterward.

DR: You have spoken about the fact that more women should be on corporate boards—in corporate boardrooms and as CEOs. Do you think you have made a lot of progress, and why do you think women should be more represented in these positions?

CL: There is a very clear economic case now that the more women on the board, the more women on the executive committees and management teams, the better the returns, the better the results, the better the profits. So, even if you have a very, very cold heart, no moral imperatives, and no sympathy for women and for the principle of inclusion, you have to consider including women and bringing them to the table and to all the tables.

Have we made progress? Some, yes. When I look at the numbers, they tell me that we have made progress. Do we still have a long way to go? Yes as well.

DR: Did you experience a lot of discrimination because you are a woman as you were rising up in your career? Are you still experiencing it today?

CL: I did experience discrimination, yes, from the first day I interviewed with law firms. I was told back in those days that I would never make partnership because I was a woman. There are still instances when I walk into a room full of men and there is this little smile about their face, which is either "Here she goes again, she's going to talk about women," or "I wonder what she has to say." It's less now, for sure, but when you are in a minority, that's what you experience.

DR: What is the greatest pleasure of being the head of the IMF?

CL: Working with the teams.

DR: What's the worst part?

CL: Having to sit through meetings that endlessly repeat the same things and end up nowhere.

DR: When you are the head of the IMF and you go to have, let's say, lunch or breakfast in a restaurant in Washington or other famous cities, do people come up and ask for selfies? Can you go where you want to go without being bothered? Do people recognize you?

CL: They recognize me, they ask for selfies. Most of the time they are very nice and flattering. It's a lot of ego food that I take and store for the holidays.

DR: Any regrets about your career?

CL: No. No regrets, like Édith Piaf would say.

DR. ANTHONY S. FAUCI

Director, National Institute of Allergy and Infectious Diseases at the National Institutes of Health

---

"You don't dictate to people. But if you let them know what your vision is, hire the best people, and then don't get in their way, those are the qualities of a good leader."

During the COVID-19 crisis, Dr. Anthony Fauci, the director of the National Institutes of Health's National Institute of Allergy and Infectious Diseases, became one of the best-known and most respected individuals in the United States, and indeed the world.

I have known Tony for many years, and have interviewed him on a number of occasions. Part 1 of this interview took place in Washington, D.C., on April 15, 2019. Part 2 took place at the Economic Club of Washington, D.C., on April 28, 2020.

Shortly before that latter interview, I wrote an article about him for *USA Today*. I think that article succinctly summarizes my views about this extraordinary public servant. It is reprinted here by permission:

Some viewers of the daily White House coronavirus briefings may wonder why everyone increasingly defers to a diminutive, Brooklyn-accented 79-year-old doctor, Anthony Fauci. They do because, as I have learned over many years of talking with and more recently interviewing this man, he is without doubt the world's leading authority on infectious diseases.

In any area of human activity or knowledge, there always seems to be one person who is the global gold standard. In the world of infectious diseases, that person is Tony Fauci. The American people—indeed, people around the globe—should be grateful that Tony has dug into this crisis with the same work-around-the-clock, just-the-facts style that he has used while serving under and working with six U.S. presidents.

He is as apolitical as anyone can be. I have no idea whether he is registered with any political party; I suspect that he is rabidly independent. His only focus is on getting the facts out, providing the best health care treatment and information possible, and saving lives.

Tony joined the National Institutes of Health in 1968, after completing his medical training at Weill Cornell Medical Center, and he has led the National Institute of Allergy and Infectious Disease at NIH since 1984—36 years. Hard to believe anyone can run anything that long and still be at the top of his game. But Tony is. During this period, he has dealt with every serious infectious disease challenge—malaria, tuberculosis, HIV/AIDS, the Middle East respiratory syndrome, the severe acute respiratory syndrome, dengue fever, Ebola, to name a few—and now the most serious pandemic since the 1918 flu, COVID-19.

Among Tony's best-known accomplishments, beyond running the institute and training dozens of the world's top infectious-disease professionals, has been helping to discover how HIV leads to AIDS and leading the effort to create (at President George W. Bush's direction) the President's Emergency Plan for AIDS Relief, which has transformed the treatment of HIV/AIDS in Africa and other parts of the developing world. Millions of lives have been saved by this program alone.

More recently, Tony has been an architect and powerful advocate of President Donald Trump's plan for ending the AIDS epidemic in the United States through HIV antiretroviral therapy targeted to disease hot spots.

In his spare time, Tony has been involved with writing or editing more than 1,100 scholarly articles and several textbooks, and, in the process, has become one of the most cited authorities of the entire medical profession.

For these breakthrough activities and his dedicated service, at a government salary, for more than a half-century—he worked at NIH for 16 years before assuming his current role—Tony has received the Presidential Medal of Freedom and a Lasker Award (called the American Nobel by many). He has earned them.

With this long service and universal acclaim, one might think Tony would let it get to his head, at least a little bit. Not the case, though.

He is readily accessible to those who need treatment—he still runs a lab at NIH—or information. Tony still lives in the same house he bought when he first moved to Washington, and it is there that he and his wife, Dr. Christine Grady, have raised their three talented daughters (though none of them chose to attend medical school).

Until the latest crisis, Tony has often commuted to NIH by Metro, typically after running or power-walking several miles for his daily exercise. And when he has been invited to make speeches in the Washington area or on Capitol Hill, he invariably turns down a car and driver for the Metro. (This practice has had to change of late for the obvious reasons.)

There are, of course, many other dedicated federal servants who also value their commitment to the country and its people over financial rewards. But surely no federal civil servant, in any area, can exceed Tony Fauci's long-term and selfless commitment to this country and the health of its people.

I tried years ago, when Tony was approaching a normal retirement age, to see whether he might want, after a normal lifetime of federal service, to take some of his considerable skills and knowledge to the private sector. He quickly said no—money did not motivate him, serving the country did. And he stayed at NIH— to the country's good fortune.

If there is any one medical professional who can help the country deal with the COVID-19 crisis, it is Tony Fauci, an example of the best this country has to offer. He is not a miracle worker. No one is. Nonetheless, Tony has the decades of experience needed to understand infectious disease problems and prescribe treatments that should, in time, provide the requisite comfort, even if in the short term the medicine is painful and inconvenient.

PART 1

DAVID RUBENSTEIN (DR): You've been the director of the National Institute of Allergy and Infectious Diseases of the National Institutes of Health since 1984. Thirty-six years is a pretty long time to be leading an institute at NIH. Is that a record?

ANTHONY FAUCI (AF): It is indeed.

DR: You haven't gotten tired of doing this for thirty-six years?

AF: No, because things keep changing. We get new infectious diseases, new outbreaks, new challenges, so it's almost like a different job every year or two.

DR: A hundred years ago, around 1918–19, about 100 million people in the world were killed by influenza. Why could they not treat it better in those days?

AF: One, it was a pandemic, which means it was caused by a virus no one had any previous experience with. It was a brand-new influenza. Two, it happened to be one that spread very rapidly and that was very virulent. It was a catastrophe.

DR: You're the leading infectious disease person in the United States, maybe the world. How many times a day do you wash your hands?

AF: Several times a day, for a number of reasons. One, I still see patients, so when I go in and out of a patient's room I have to. But even in my office, I have a lot of visitors who, when they come in, I always shake hands with them. So I have a sink not too far from my desk where I can go and wash my hands, I would say at least seven, eight, nine times a day.

DR: Does it look bad if you shake somebody's hand and then you go wash your hands right away?

AF: If you make it obvious to the person.

DR: Let's talk about humans and infectious diseases. *Homo sapiens,* three hundred thousand–plus years ago, had an average life expectancy roughly of twenty years old. Today, average life expectancy in the United States is maybe eighty or something like that. We've extended expectancy by about four times compared to three hundred thousand years ago. Why was life expectancy so short then? Were infectious diseases a large part of the problem?

AF: The answer is yes. Then, as we moved further and further toward modern times, there were different challenges. It wasn't only just infectious disease then but the issue of survival under very severe environmental circumstances. However, if you look at the seventeenth, eighteenth, nineteenth centuries, where there were infectious diseases before the vaccines and antibiotics, many children died, and when children die, the average life expectancy goes down. Right now, we're seeing improvements in life expectancy not only because we've conquered many infectious diseases, but because noncommunicable diseases are being handled better. Hypertension is being better controlled. Heart disease and high cholesterol are being better controlled. People are smoking less. Those are all things that are increasing life expectancy.

DR: The bubonic plague that went through Europe hundreds of years ago—what was that?

AF: That was caused by bacteria called either *Yersinia pestis* or *Pasteurella pestis*—bacteria spread, interestingly, through fleas in situations where the hygiene wasn't very good. A flea would bite somebody, they would get infected.

So there were two types of plague. There was the bubonic plague, where people would get very swollen lymph nodes and they could die from that. It didn't generally spread directly from person to person. Then there was the pneumonic plague, which disseminated through the body, and you could cough and transmit it to somebody.

In the fourteenth century, one-third of the population of Europe died from the plague. It devastated Europe.

DR: But the chance of that happening again is remote?

AF: With that microbe, yes, because it's easily treatable with an antibiotic.

DR: When did vaccinations first start? I remember reading that in the late eighteenth century, some people would get inoculated against smallpox. How did they do that then? When did people first realize you could be inoculated against a disease?

AF: Right. That was in 1796. Smallpox was rampant in society then. A man named Edward Jenner noticed a very interesting phenomenon: that cow maids, the women milking the cows, would get a relatively mild disease called cowpox, which was very much related to smallpox.

Jenner noticed that they would get cowpox and recover from it, and then they would be immune to smallpox. So he put two and two together and said, "If we could deliberately infect people with a version of smallpox—namely cowpox—they would be protected against smallpox."

He actually did an experiment on a young boy, which quite frankly, in retrospect, was unethical. He vaccinated the boy with this cowpox, then exposed him to smallpox and discovered he was protected. So vaccinations all started at the end of the eighteenth century.

DR: What did smallpox actually do to people?

AF: The virus was quite virulent. It killed anywhere between 20 percent to 35 percent of the people it infected. The disease is characterized by high fevers and a terrible blistering rash that can then involve multiple organ systems. So that's the reason for the high rate of death.

DR: When you were inoculated in those days, they would cut a little hole in your skin and then put the disease in?

AF: No, they would take one of the pustules with the virus in it, scrape it, then go to somebody else and just scrape it on the skin to produce an immune response. It was a bit dangerous because, before they had the attenuated part—the more weakened form of the virus used to make vaccines now—you could actually kill somebody using that means of vaccination.

DR: Let's talk about HIV. When did the world first realize there was a problem with HIV, later leading to AIDS?

AF: It was first recognized in 1981. There was a report from the Centers for Disease Control and Prevention of five men, curiously all gay, who were from Los Angeles. They had this strange new disease that no one had ever seen before in which otherwise healthy men were getting infections that only infect people who have tremendously compromised immune systems.

Everybody thought it was a fluke. A month later, in July 1981, twenty-six individuals reported—again, all gay men, from New York, San Francisco, and Los Angeles. Then we realized we were dealing with a brand-new disease. It wasn't until 1983 when the virus HIV was discovered, and in 1984 it was proven to be the cause of AIDS.

Even though we recognized it here in the United States first, it was happening throughout the world. It originated in sub-Saharan Africa, and we didn't even realize how badly Africa was hit until we went there and started testing individuals.

DR: And it originated in humans?

AF: It started centuries ago in nonhuman primates, in chimpanzees. Then it jumped species from the chimpanzees to humans.

DR: Is viruses jumping a species a common thing?

AF: Seventy to 75 percent of all the new infections that humans get infected with come from an animal. It's called zoonotic—meaning it's predominantly an animal virus but jumps to humans for one reason or other, like our encroaching on the environment of the animal or the virus mutating a bit. Influenza is fundamentally an infection of birds. HIV, as we said, came from chimpanzees. Zika and a variety of other infections come from animals.

DR: When did we discover there's a way to moderate the impact of HIV becoming AIDS?

AF: That was when we got drugs that treated the virus. We started off in 1987 with the first approved drug, called AZT. By 1996, we realized that if you gave a combination of three drugs together, you could drop the amount of virus below detectable level, and people who would otherwise face almost a certain death sentence could live essentially normal lives. So right now, if someone is infected with HIV and gets put on this triple combination of therapy drugs, if they religiously take their medication, they could live almost a normal lifespan.

DR: Let's talk about your background. You grew up in Brooklyn. And you went to Catholic school?

AF: Yes. I went to Catholic elementary school and to Regis High School in Manhattan, then Holy Cross College in Worcester.

DR: Did you always know you wanted to be a doctor? Or did you think you wanted to be something more important, like a lawyer or a private equity investor or something like that?

AF: I can't say I always felt I wanted to be a doctor. I was very interested in the humanities. I took classical background courses—likely because I went to a Jesuit school—in Greek, Latin, philosophical psychologies, all the philosophies. So I had an interest in the humanities, but I also had an aptitude and an interest in science, so I figured the best way to combine that interest in the humanities with an interest in science was to be a physician.

DR: Where did you go to medical school?

AF: I went to Cornell University Medical Center in New York City.

DR: After you graduated, you didn't want to go into heart surgery or brain surgery? Or did you say, "I want to be an infectious disease person"?

AF: I wanted to do a combination of infectious diseases and immunology. Immunology is the study of the body's mechanisms of fighting infections. So I did a dual fellowship, after I finished my internal medicine training, in infectious diseases and immunology. I liked it because it's a very exciting field.

DR: Where did you do the fellowship?

AF: Here at the NIH.

DR: So you first came to NIH in 1968. When you were here, there were a lot of other people entering the class with you. Many of them have gone on to win the Nobel Prize—Dr. Harold Varmus, among others.

AF: Mike Brown, Joe Goldstein, Bob Lefkowitz, they all won Nobel Prizes.

DR: So how come you haven't won a Nobel Prize yet?

AF: I'm the stupid one in the group. No, actually, I probably wouldn't have won one anyway, but my work was much more on broader global health issues. They discovered really exciting specific things.

DR: But you have won the Presidential Medal of Freedom, and the Lasker Award, and the National Medal of Science. Is there any award in medicine that you have not won?

AF: The Nobel Prize.

DR: I would nominate you if I knew how to do that. But let me ask you— you have written, coauthored, or edited something like 1,200 articles. How do you have time to do 1,200 articles, run the institute, and also treat patients?

AF: One, my career has been quite long, so that's one of the reasons why there are so many articles. But doing all of that—taking care of patients, running a lab, running a big institute, and getting involved in global health policy—I work a lot of hours. I'm an unapologetic workaholic, and I really love what I do.

DR: How do you stay in good shape?

AF: I used to run. I used to run marathons and 10Ks. About two or three years ago, I stopped running every day. I used to run about six miles a day. Now I power walk about three to four miles a day, every day.

DR: And you generally are not sick?

AF: No, I'm generally pretty healthy, thank goodness, yes.

DR: Are any of your children interested in medicine?

AF: No. I have one daughter who just got her PhD in clinical psychology, so she's going to be a clinical psychologist. Another daughter is a schoolteacher, and my youngest daughter works in the tech world. She works for Twitter in San Francisco.

DR: Now, you're a very prominent person in the infectious disease world. Many people have come to you over the years and said, "Why don't you leave and go into something more lucrative than doing this?" In fact, I came to you once and said, "Why don't you come into private equity? You could figure out how to be an investor in the health-care world. You'd be perfect." You resisted all those entreaties. Why did you do that?

AF: Well, I would have loved to have worked for you, David, but I love what I'm doing and it's so exciting, that really is what drives me. It isn't as if I think those other professions aren't worthy; I just really like what I'm doing.

DR: You've been heading this institute for thirty-six years. As you look back on your career, what are you most proud of having achieved?

AF: There are two things I feel very good about having at least had the opportunity to do. One is to lead the institute that developed lifesaving drugs for HIV infection. I took care of many, many HIV-infected individuals before we had any drugs, and they almost all died. Now, with the work that we did in the institute, we have drugs that save lives and let people live normal lives.

The other thing is something you mentioned before, and that was to develop and be the architect for George W. Bush's PEPFAR program. The development of a global program that has now saved anywhere between fourteen million and sixteen million lives. I'm proud but also humbled about having the opportunity to do that.

DR: So any regrets in your career?

AF: No, actually not at all. I don't have any.

DR: Did your parents live to see your success?

AF: My father actually lived a long time—he lived till he was ninety-seven. He died about twelve years ago. He saw the successes I had in a certain part of my career. My mother died at a very young age, so she did not see me even graduate from medical school.

DR: Your father said he was proud of what you had done?

AF: Yes, very much so.

DR: As you look back on your career, what do you think has made you a leader—and a very successful one—of this institute? What would you say are the characteristics that make somebody a leader?

AF: The characteristics that I've examined and felt were important for my own leadership are things that others have also had. I don't think it's anything unique about me.

One of the things I tell people, because I feel it strongly, is that if you're leading an organization of some sort that has a purpose or a mandate, you've got to articulate to the people you are leading exactly what your vision is and where you want the organization to go. I've seen instances where there wasn't good leadership, where an organization is almost rudderless. They don't know where they're supposed to be going. You don't dictate to people. But if you let them know what your vision is, hire the best people, and then don't get in their way, those are the qualities of a good leader.

———————

PART 2

DR: I'd like to acknowledge all the frontline health-care workers and first responders and servicemen and -women who are helping our country in this very difficult time. Dr. Fauci, thank you very much for agreeing to do this. I know that your time is very precious, and I appreciate your giving us this time.

My first question is, what do you think of Brad Pitt's imitation of you on *Saturday Night Live*? Were you disappointed that somebody else didn't play you?

AF: No, Brad Pitt is one of my favorite actors. And I think he did a great job. He got the raspiness of my voice right. He got the hand movements right. He's got to work a little on the Brooklyn accent, but I think he did a great job. He was really very funny.

What he did at the end was a class act, I thought, when he took the wig off and thanked me and the health-care workers, just the way you did. I've never met him, but he seems like he really is a classy guy.

DR: Did you know that was happening, by the way?

AF: I didn't know until literally a few hours before.

DR: You have been heading up the National Institute of Allergy and Infectious Diseases since 1984. In those thirty-six years, has anything come close to the type of crisis or health-care calamity that we're now having?

AF: Well, we've had multiple emerging outbreaks, both naturally occurring, like HIV, and deliberately imposed upon us, like the anthrax attacks, and then the things that we've recently spoken about—Ebola, Zika, the pandemic flu of 2009. Each of those have different characteristics.

HIV-AIDS started off under the radar screen, slowly. It was not recognized, but has extended over now thirty-eight, thirty-nine years. The total of deaths right now is something like thirty-seven, thirty-eight million, but it's taken place over a very long period of time, and selectively has involved individuals who are in certain demographic groups associated with certain behaviors.

The thing about the current pandemic that's so unique—you asked me years ago what keeps me up at night. What keeps me up at night is the emergence of a brand-new infection, likely jumping species from an animal, that's respiratory-borne, highly transmissible, with a high degree of morbidity and mortality. And, lo and behold, that's where we are right now.

The reason it's so unprecedented, it exploded upon us. Remember, the first recognition that it even existed was the end of December, the beginning of January. Here we are, just a few months into it, and we've had almost a million cases. In the United States, we've had 55,000 deaths. [By late June 2020, that number had risen to in excess of 120,000.]

Globally it's exploded in a way that's unprecedented in a compact period of time. And everyone is at risk, unlike some infections like Zika. If you don't live in a mosquito zone, you really don't have much to worry about with Zika. With HIV-AIDS, if you don't belong to a certain risk category, it is very unlikely you'll get infected, whereas with this, everyone seems vulnerable to a disease that's highly transmissible.

So the short answer to your question, David, this is really unprecedented.

DR: Do you have any doubt that this came about from a wet market in China? Do you subscribe to the view that it might have come from a lab in China, or do you dismiss that?

AF: Well, you never dismiss things out of hand, but you just look at the scientific data. Evolutionary biologists have looked at the evolution of virus mutations in bats over a period of time, with the extraordinary likelihood that they infected an intermediate host that has yet to be identified. Everything is compatible with the virus jumping species from an animal host to a human. That's the first unfortunate step.

The second thing that is really unfortunate for the human species is that this particular virus immediately was able to adapt itself to a high degree of efficiency in human transmissibility. Unlike SARS, which came and then disappeared, unlike some of the bird flus that we've dealt with, where it jumps species from a chick to a human—bad news, but the encouraging news is that it was very, very inefficient at, if not incapable of, going from human to human. This virus has all those bad characteristics, but it's very transmissible and it has a high degree of morbidity and mortality, relatively speaking.

DR: In hindsight, is there anything the Chinese could have done to warn people about how lethal this was, or really was there nothing they could have done?

AF: I think there is something a little bit remiss that people are going to look at when this is all over. Right away, the Chinese said this was a virus that jumped species in an animal market, and that it only goes from animal to human, and there was no evidence whatsoever that it was transmissible from human to human, or, if so, very inefficiently. As they were saying that, it had already become clear that there was human-to-human transmissibility in China.

Not only was it bad for the rest of the world, they hurt themselves. Soon after the realization that there was this new infection—and, to their credit, they put the genetic sequence of the virus up on a public website very quickly—what they also did is by not letting their own health authorities know that there was transmission from person to person, they held something like a forty-thousand-person block party in Wuhan. The worst possible thing you could do is to have a congregation of people when you have a virus circulating that has a high degree of transmissibility.

DR: To date, 55,000 to 56,000 Americans have died from this. What will the likely death toll be, based on all the modeling you are now looking at?

AF: As I've often said, although models are helpful, they're only as good as the assumptions that you put into them, and you can be misled as often as you can be helped. Right now, we're at 55,000. The model now has been upgraded to say that instead of 60,000, it's probably going to be 70,000-plus.

That assumption is based on how we respond. Here is what's going to determine how many deaths we have.

Hopefully everyone will follow the guidelines for opening America again, which were very carefully designed, and which I played a role in making very conservative and very careful. As we open up the country economically and otherwise, when new cases occur—which they will—there's no doubt that they will as you try and relax mitigation—if we have the capability of identifying, isolating, and contact-tracing in a highly effective and efficient way, then the numbers will stay lower.

It may be 80,000 or 70,000, like the model says. If we are unsuccessful, or prematurely try to open up, and we have additional outbreaks that are out of control, it could be much more than that. There could be a rebound that gets us right back in the same boat we were in a few weeks ago.

That's why we've really got to be careful and very circumspect as we go from a lockdown to a gradual, rolling reentry into some sort of normality.

DR: You have said you think it's likely that in the winter this virus could come back, as the Spanish flu of 1918 came back fairly lethally. Why do you think this will come back?

AF: I'm almost certain it will come back because the virus is so transmissible and it's globally spread. Remember, when people are indoors and congregated in the cold dry weather, these kinds of viruses tend to do better than in a warmer climate.

I don't know whether that's going to make a major difference here. What we do know is that right now, as we start to stabilize, places in southern Africa, like KwaZulu-Natal and Cape Town in South Africa, are starting to see the emergence of cases. So it's not going to disappear from the planet, which means as we get into next season, in my mind it's inevitable that we will have a return of the virus—or maybe it never even went away. When it does return, how we handle it will determine our fate.

If by that time we have put into place all of the countermeasures that you need to address this, we should do reasonably well. If we don't do that successfully, we could be in for a bad fall and a bad winter.

DR: So how do you look at testing? In other countries that have taken on testing, the nation has taken on the testing. Here, we're letting the states take it on. Why is that the best way to do it, and if somebody wants to get a test today, can they realistically get one?

AF: Early on, our testing capability was not really properly designed for what we had to deal with in such an acute way. And it actually did fail us early on. I've said that before, so I'm not creating any new dialogue here.

However, we have responded now in a very aggressive way, and appropriately for the way our country is built. Namely, we have engaged the private sector, the big companies who know what they're doing, who do this for a living. Over the past several weeks and into the future, the testing situation has improved very rapidly.

Whether or not we're exactly where we want to be remains to be seen. I think we are either there or getting very close to being there. Yesterday, the plan that was rolled out was a blueprint for testing as we open America again. The thing in that plan that's now different, and everyone should understand that, it is really a true partnership between the states and the federal government, where the implementation on the ground should be at the state level, because they know what they're doing. But the federal government has a role in providing strategic direction and technical assistance.

That's something that wasn't fully in place early on. Right now there's a commitment of that partnership between the federal government being kind of the supplier of last resort but also the group that allows interaction with the states so that we can give them strategic direction and then let them do at the local level what they do very well. So I believe we are much, much better off now than we were several weeks ago.

DR: Do the tests work? Are there a lot of false positives or false negatives on these?

AF: The validated tests that are out there are sensitive and specific. No test is 100 percent perfect.

I think people sometimes get confused about what test you're talking about. There are two major categories of tests. One is a test for the virus itself. With those tests, there are multiple different platforms that get you there—some more rapid than others, using different approaches. But the bottom line, the test tells you whether you are infected or not at this particular time.

There's another test now being worked on—many of them out there have not been validated, but a few have been validated by the FDA—and that's an antibody test. It doesn't test for whether you are infected now. It tests whether you have been infected and likely recovered and now have antibodies, which are proteins that the body produced in response to an infection. And most of the time that protects you against being infected by the same virus again. The degree to which that protection exists still needs to be worked out for this particular virus, because this is the first time that we've had any experience with it.

So one group of tests for the virus is quite solid. The other is working its way now toward being more solid.

DR: What is the status of vaccines? There's a report in the *New York Times* today that your lab and Oxford University are working on something that seems to have worked in monkeys. What's the likelihood that that vaccine could actually turn out to be good for humans?

AF: Certainly it's possible. I'm cautiously optimistic about not only that vaccine candidate but a number of other candidates that we at the NIH are partnering with our pharmaceutical colleagues on, and some companies and countries are developing vaccines totally independent of us. There are going to be a lot of candidates out there. As you know, a few of them are already well into phase one studies in humans to determine if they're safe.

Hopefully we can move along to get an answer to whether they are safe and effective in a timely manner, which I've said right from the beginning would likely be a year to a year and a half. I said that a few months ago. Hopefully, by the time we get to this coming winter, we will know whether or not we have a safe and effective vaccine.

Then the challenge will be to scale it up enough to be able to distribute it meaningfully, both in this country and throughout the world. That's the reason why as important as getting a vaccine that works and is safe is the ability to scale up enough doses so that it isn't confined only to rich countries—that the rest of the world can have access to it.

DR: We never really came up with a vaccine to prevent one from getting HIV. Why are you optimistic we can get a vaccine for this? Because a lot of work's been put into HIV as well.

AF: There's a big difference with HIV, David. Whenever you make a vaccine, what you rely on is the ability of the body to make an adequate response to natural infection.

So we know that measles is a serious disease, but the body clears measles in the overwhelming majority of individuals and leaves those people with an immune response that protects them against reinfection. So measles has already proved the concept that the body can make a good response.

That's not the case with HIV, for reasons that are very perplexing. The body does not make a very good response against HIV that can protect it, which is the reason why, of all the millions and millions of cases of HIV, there have been really no instances of spontaneous removal of the virus from the body purely on the basis of the natural immune response.

However, with other viruses, including respiratory viruses, we know the body does make a good immune response. Many, many, many people recover from coronavirus infection, from this novel coronavirus that is giving us so much trouble. So the very fact that people can mount a natural immune response that gets rid of the virus makes me cautiously optimistic that we can develop a vaccine that can mimic natural infection enough to induce that same sort of response that would ultimately protect people.

There's no guarantee. There's never a guarantee of success. But the fact that the body can do it gives me cautious optimism.

DR: But could the virus that causes COVID-19 mutate such that the vaccine wouldn't be adequate?

AF: That is always possible. It likely would mutate less to make it evasive of the vaccine than to make it a little more or less virulent, or a little bit more or less resistant to a drug. For it to mutate so that the vaccine doesn't work is possible and could occur. That's the reason why you need to do carefully designed and well-controlled studies to look at the efficacy and match it against immune response to the particular virus that happens to be currently circulating.

DR: Why do you think this virus has been so damaging to people who are elderly—people over, let's say, sixty or sixty-five—or people who are African American or other people of color?

AF: If you look at influenza, which we have a lot of experience with, influenza and other types of viruses always hurt the elderly and people with underlying conditions more than they hurt healthy young people.

The interesting thing about this infection is that, for the most part, with some exceptions, people who get into trouble are those who have underlying conditions—mostly hypertension, diabetes, obesity, some chronic lung disease.

We don't fully appreciate and understand what I call the pathogenic mechanisms of this virus. But as we learn more about it, we see that it has a complicated way of hurting the body. If you have an underlying condition, as with many viruses, it puts you at much higher risk, not of getting infected but of actually getting a deleterious consequence.

With regard to African Americans, unfortunately there's a disparity in health that has nothing to do with coronavirus. We've known forever that the African American community suffers disproportionately with diseases like hypertension, like diabetes, that give you a greater possibility of having a poor or adverse outcome.

So it's a double whammy. They disproportionately have these diseases that are bad enough to begin with, and that puts them at additional risk of getting a very poor outcome when they do get infected.

DR: There are 330 million people in the United States who are worried about your health every day. How are you avoiding this virus? Because nobody wants you to be incapacitated. What are you doing to stay healthy?

AF: I'm not doing things that I would recommend to others because my day is just, you know, ridiculous. In the beginning I was foolish, because we had so many things to do that I was getting three hours of sleep a night. That doesn't work very well for more than a few days in a row. So, listening to the advice of my very clinically skilled wife, who was formerly a practicing nurse, the thing I do now that I didn't do before is get at least five or six hours of sleep. That and staying away from people, to the extent that I can, doing everything virtually, the way we're doing now, is I think keeping me okay. I'm running a little bit on fumes. But they're pretty good fumes.

DR: What about your voice? People keep commenting that it's a little raspy. What are you doing? Are you talking too much or what?

AF: It's exactly that, David. In December, unfortunately for me, I got influenza A, H1N1. I developed a tracheitis that gradually was getting better. And then came coronavirus, which had me briefing, at least in my mind, almost every congressman, every senator, every governor, and doing five, six, seven interviews a day. When you get your trachea damaged a little—I probably have a polyp there—the only way you're going to make it get better is to keep your mouth shut. But that's not in the cards right now.

DR: Tell us what the coronavirus task force is like. Everybody sits around saying how everything is great and people argue with each other? What are those meetings like?

AF: No, no, it's a good meeting. We have a good bunch of colleagues in it. It's led by Vice President Mike Pence. Various Cabinet members are there, predominantly Alex Azar. We have Ben Carson. We have Chad Wolf and others who are actually active members. We have medical people—myself, Bob Redfield [Director of the Centers for Disease Control and Prevention and Administrator of the Agency for Toxic Substances and Disease Registry], Debbie Birx [U.S. Global Aids Coordinator & U.S. Special Representative for Global Health Diplomacy], Steve Hahn [Commissioner of Food and Drug Administration]. So we have a good group of individuals who actually go over the data from the night before, what the pattern and the dynamics of the outbreak are, and we address the different issues, some of which you've already mentioned. Things like testing, the ability to have enough ventilators, PPE, plans for the states, interacting with them.

We do that for about an hour and a half or more, then we gather and the vice president and his staff decide what the topic for the press briefing is going to be. Then we brief a little summary after we brief the president. Then we go out and do the press conference.

DR: People get nervous when you don't show up at those press conferences. When you don't show up, is that because you're doing something else that's more important?

AF: The press conferences are often topic related. When there is a topic where it's more appropriate for someone else to be the backup, they do that. For example, yesterday it was testing. The people predominant there were the people involved in testing. I'm a health physician, a scientist, a public health person. I've been involved in most but not all of the briefings. A lot of times when people don't see me, they think there's some problem between the president and me. And that's really not the case at all.

DR: So you're seventy-nine years old, but in great shape. You power walk three miles a day. Power walking means you're walking fast, right?

AF: Power walk means I'm trying to catch up with my wife, who's walking faster than I am.

DR: Your goal is to do this for another ten years or so? How much longer would you like to do this job?

AF: You know, David, that's a good question. You've been asking me that for decades. I'm going to do it until I feel I'm not doing it as effectively as I can. Right now, I think I'm as good as I've ever been, because not only do I still have the energy I had, I have a lot more experience.

DR: Do you think, in hindsight, that had you been a couple inches taller, you could have been a one-and-done college basketball player? Because you were a high school basketball star. Did you aspire to go to the NBA or not?

AF: The answer is that every young kid in New York City who plays in the schoolyards and gets good at it and does well in high school always has aspirations, and often the aspirations are not connected to the reality.

I inherited a couple of things from my father. My father, interestingly, when he was in high school was the New York City champion of the 220- and the 440-yard dash. He was very fast. So on the basketball court, you couldn't catch me on a fast break. However, I also inherited his height. And I found out something that's the rule in basketball—that a very fast five-seven point guard who's a good shooter will always get crushed by a very fast six-three point guard who's a good shooter.

DR: I had the problem I wasn't a good shooter either. I wasn't anything, so I didn't get very far either.

Tony, thank you very much for this. Thank you for what you're doing for the country. Stay well. Get some tea and honey. Keep your voice in shape. And keep working as hard as you can. Thank you.

AF: Thank you very much, David. It's always a pleasure. Take care.

JUSTICE RUTH BADER GINSBURG

Associate Justice, U.S. Supreme Court

"Up until the start of the '70s, it simply wasn't possible to move courts in the direction of recognizing women as people of equal citizenship stature."

"All of us revere the institution for which we work, and we want to leave it in as good shape as we found it."

Of the 114 justices who have served on the Supreme Court, none of them have achieved the level of public acclaim that Justice Ruth Bader Ginsburg has in recent years. What accounts for this enormous, unprecedented popular acclaim for a diminutive, soft-spoken, scholarly justice (just the second woman to serve on the court)?

There are several reasons:

First, Justice Ginsburg's trailblazing efforts as a law professor and a

public-service litigator in the area of gender equality—she cofounded
the successful ACLU Women's Rights Project—have increasingly been
recognized (through movies and books) by the public, particularly
younger generations of women.

Second, during her more than forty years on the bench (thirteen-
plus years on the Court of Appeals for the D.C. Circuit and more than
twenty-seven years on the Supreme Court), she has been a consistent
and articulate supporter of gender equality, contraceptive and abortion
rights, and other positions supported by "liberal" or "progressive" organizations and groups. Often her views, when not in the majority, are
communicated through forceful dissenting opinions (and the opinions
are often seen as masterpieces of legal craftsmanship).

Third, over the past decade or so, a great deal of attention has been
focused on her public persona by the media, making her workout regi-
mens and love of opera endearing parts of her appeal to many.

And further, her several bouts with cancer and other illnesses, and
her determination to remain on the court, even into her late eighties,
are seen as a sign of her personal grit and determination (and perhaps of
her determination to have a Democratic president select her successor).

Anyone who attends a Justice Ginsburg lecture, interview, or appearance witnesses her rock-star appeal. She draws up to twenty thousand people at events, and regularly gets long standing ovations when
publicly introduced at events she simply attends. I have seen this many
times firsthand at gatherings where I have introduced or interviewed
Justice Ginsburg, whom I have come to know over the years through
Kennedy Center events—she is a devoted attendee of our operas—or at
social events in the Washington area.

This particular interview occurred in front of a live audience at the
92nd Street Y in New York in September 2019, and was oversubscribed
many times over. The interview demonstrates her precise use of language, her well-developed sense of humor, and her willingness to discuss openly the discrimination she suffered as a woman. It also shows
her commitment, even at this stage of her life, to seeking to end injus-
tices that she feels still exist for women.

How did Justice Ginsburg become such a leader and, later, such a
role model? The answers come through in the interview: her extraordinary intellect (she was near the top of her class at both Harvard and
Columbia Law Schools), her persistence in fighting for her causes, and

her ability to work with (and charm) those who have disagreed with her, such as her opera-loving close friend the late Justice Antonin Scalia.

And Justice Ginsburg has also found a way to be a leader who is unique within the court: her public appearances and persona have clearly affected public opinion on many of her key issues. And the court, while a creation of legal precedent and scholarship, does reflect the views of this tenth justice: public opinion.

DAVID RUBENSTEIN (DR): How does it feel to get up in the morning and know that 330 million Americans want to know the state of your health that day?

RUTH BADER GINSBURG (RBG): How does it feel? Encouraging. As cancer survivors know, that dread disease is a challenge. It helps to know that people are rooting for you.

Now, it's not universal. When I had pancreatic cancer in 2009, a senator whose name I don't recall said I would be dead within six months. That senator is now no longer alive. [It was Senator Jim Bunning, who died in 2017.]

DR: As long as you're healthy and able to do the job, you intend to stay on the court. Is that correct?

RBG: As long as I'm healthy, and mentally agile.

DR: Justice Stevens and Justice Oliver Wendell Holmes retired when they were ninety. Would you like to break their record?

RBG: I spent the first week in July with Justice Stevens at a conference in Lisbon. It turned out to be the last week of his life. He was remarkable. He was ninety-nine years old. Since he left the court at age ninety, he has written four books. So, yes, he's my role model.

DR: Today many people think that the court is very political—that people appointed to the court by Democratic presidents and those appointed by Republican presidents tend to follow the political desires of the Republican or Democratic Party. Do you think that's a fair assessment?

RBG: People have that view because agreement isn't interesting; disagreement is. So the press tends to play up our five-to-four or our five-to-three decisions. But take just last term as a typical example: We released sixty-eight decisions after full briefing and argument. Of those, twenty were five-to-four or five-to-three decisions, but twenty-nine were unanimous.

So we agree more often than we sharply disagree. The divisions, yes, they are on some very important questions. But our agreement rate is always higher than our disagreement rate.

DR: If you have a five-to-four prospective decision, does one of the justices go to another justice and say, "Why don't you change your mind?"

RBG: No. There's no horse trading at the court.

DR: Nobody says, "If you vote for me on this one, I'll vote for you on that one"?

RBG: It never happens. But we are constantly trying to persuade each other. Most often we do it through our writing. Every time I write a dissent for four, I am hopeful that I can pick up a fifth vote. It once happened that I was assigned a dissent by my senior colleague; the court divided at conference seven to two. But in the fullness of time, the decision came out six to three. The two had swelled to six, and the seven had shrunk to three.

DR: That was your opinion?

RBG: Yes.

DR: Very persuasive. Many people in Washington and around the country are surprised at the civility that exists between justices, even though they write not such favorable things about each other. Justice Scalia used to say not such wonderful things about your views, and you still went to the opera with him. Was that a little awkward or hard to do?

RBG: Not at all. Justice Scalia and I became friends when we were buddies on the D.C. Circuit. What did I love most about him? His infectious sense of humor. When we were together on three-judge panels on the court of appeals, he'd sometimes whisper something to me. It would crack me up. I had all I could do to contain hysterical laughter.

But we had much in common. True, our styles were very different. But both of us cared a lot about writing opinions so that at least other lawyers and judges will understand what we were saying. Justice Scalia was an expert grammarian. His father had been a Latin professor at Brooklyn College, and his mother had been a grade school teacher. So he knew grammar very well.

Every once in a while he'd come to chambers, or he'd call me on the phone, and say, "Ruth, you made a grammatical error." He never did it in writing to embarrass me before my colleagues. Sometimes I would say to him, "Your opinion draft is so strident. You would be more persuasive if you toned it down." That was advice he never, never took.

DR: Both of you were, and you still are, great opera lovers. Where did you get your love of opera?

RBG: My love of opera began when I was eleven years old. I was in grade school in Brooklyn, New York. My aunt, who was a junior high school English teacher, took me to a high school in Brooklyn to attend an opera performance. It was *La Gioconda*, not a likely choice for a child's first opera.

There was a man at the time named Dean Dixon whose mission in life was to turn children on to beautiful music. He had an all-city orchestra. He staged opera performances and took them around to various schools, condensed them into one hour, narrated in between. There were costumes, bare staging. My introduction to opera was thanks to Dean Dixon in 1944.

In 1948, Dean Dixon left the United States because, he said, in all the years he'd been conducting, no one ever called him *maestro*. He was African American. He went off to Europe where he was everybody's darling. And he came back to the United States in the late '60s, some twenty years after he'd left. By that time, every major symphony orchestra in the States wanted him as a guest conductor.

He was the Jackie Robinson of conducting. That difference between the '40s, when he left, and the late '60s, when he visited, is one sign of the progress that had been made in the United States.

I was once on the Metropolitan Opera intermission feature. Usually there's a quiz at intermission, and I'm not in that league. But if there are two intermissions, they sometimes have a conversation with an amateur who loves opera. I spoke about Dean Dixon. I don't know how many e-mails I received from people across the country saying that they had been introduced to opera by that remarkable man.

DR: You go to the opera every time you can. In Washington, D.C., you go to the movies to watch the Met; on weekends, you come up to the Met sometimes in New York. What is your favorite opera, after all these years of watching opera?

RBG: On most days, I will say *The Marriage of Figaro*. On occasional days, I will say *Don Giovanni*. What those two have in common is they're both Mozart with librettos by Da Ponte. They were a powerhouse as a combination, Mozart and Da Ponte.

DR: It's like a five-to-four decision in your mind about which one it should be? You actually have performed in operas, is that right?

RBG: At the Washington National Opera, where I was a super in *Ariadne auf Naxos* along with Justice Scalia, and in *Fledermaus*, along with Justice Kennedy and Justice Breyer. But my crowning achievement was when I had an actual part in an opera.

The opera was *Daughter of the Regiment*. There is a small speaking part, no singing, in it. Very few operas have speaking-not-singing parts. I was the Duchess of Krakenthorp. And I wrote my own lines for her. It was great fun.

DR: You were born and bred in Brooklyn. You have still a bit of a Brooklyn accent, you might admit. You were played in the movie by Felicity Jones, who is not Jewish or from Brooklyn. How do you think she did?

RBG: I thought she was fantastic. When I first met Felicity, I said, "You speak the queen's English. How are you going to sound like a girl born and bred in Brooklyn?" She listened to many tapes of my speeches and my arguments at the court. And she was wonderful.

DR: In recent years, you've also gotten a lot of attention for your exercise routine. When did that start? You have your own trainer. Are you still lifting weights or whatever you're doing?

RBG: As recently as Tuesday. I have had the same personal trainer since 1999, the year of my first cancer bout. I had colorectal cancer. After I had gone through surgery, chemotherapy, radiation, my dear husband said, "You look like an Auschwitz survivor, you must do something to build yourself up. Get a personal trainer."

That's when I started, in 1999. Sometimes I get so absorbed in my work, I just don't want to let go. But when it comes time to meet my trainer, I drop everything. As tired as I may be in the beginning, I always feel better when we finish.

DR: You were married for fifty-six years. You met your husband, Marty, at Cornell, is that right?

RBG: Yes. We met when I was seventeen and he was eighteen.

DR: What is the likelihood of a woman at Cornell meeting somebody she marries, and that person wants to take care of child-rearing and cooking as well as sharing all the other burdens of being married? Is that a very common thing, in your observation?

RBG: It was extraordinary at any time, but particularly in the 1950s. Cornell, by the way, had a four-to-one ratio—four men to every woman. It was the place parents wanted to send their daughters. If you couldn't find your man at Cornell, you were hopeless.

Marty was, in fact, the first boy I ever knew who cared that I had a brain. He was always my biggest booster.

He attributed his skill in the kitchen to two women: his mother and his wife. His mother, I think that was an unfair judgment, but he was certainly right about me. I had one cookbook. It was called *The 60-Minute Chef*. From when you entered the apartment until food was on the table, the time lapse was no more than sixty minutes. I made seven dishes, and when we got to number seven, we went back to number one.

DR: Did Marty's mother ever give you any advice about how to be happily married?

RBG: She gave me some wonderful advice. We were married in her home. She said, just before the ceremony started, "Dear, I'd like to tell you the secret of a happy marriage." "I'd love to hear it. What is it?" "Every now and then," she said, "it helps to be a little deaf." I've followed that sage advice assiduously to this very day, in dealing with my colleagues. If an unkind or thoughtless word is said, I just tune out.

DR: When you went to Cornell, your grades were obviously very good. You got into Harvard Law School. Was the class half women and half men at that time?

RBG: Oh, no. In those ancient days—I went to law school from '56 to '59—there were over five hundred in my entering class at Harvard Law School. Nine of us were women. A big jump from Marty's class. He was a year ahead of me; there were five women in his class. Today the Harvard Law School has about 50 percent women.

DR: You did extremely well and you got onto the *Harvard Law Review*. You were near the top of your class, maybe first or tied for first. When your husband needed to move to New York, you wanted to transfer to Columbia Law School. The dean of the Harvard Law School didn't think that was such a great idea, if you wanted to be a Harvard graduate?

RBG: He said I had to spend my third year at Harvard. The reason I didn't, Marty was diagnosed with having testicular cancer in his third year of law school. Those were early days for cancer cures. There was no chemotherapy, there was only massive radiation. We didn't know whether he would survive. I didn't want to be a single mom. Jane, our daughter, was fourteen months when I started law school. We wanted to stay together as a family.

Marty had a good job with a firm in New York. I asked the dean—I thought there would be an easy answer—"If I successfully complete my legal education at Columbia, may I have a Harvard degree?" "Absolutely not. You must spend the third year here."

I had the perfect rebuttal. A Cornell classmate of mine had finished her first year of law school at Penn. She transferred into our second-year class. I said to the dean, "Well, Mrs. Isselbacher will have her second and third year and will earn a Harvard degree. But it's, I think, universally understood that the first year of law school is by far the most important. She will have year two and three, I have year one and two. It should make no difference." But I was told, "A rule is a rule," and that was that.

DR: You went to Columbia Law School, and your law degree is from Columbia. You did extremely well there. You were on the law review there as well. Having been on the *Harvard Law Review* and the *Columbia Law Review*, you were flooded with job offers from the major law firms?

RBG: There wasn't a single firm in the entire city of New York that would take a chance on me. I have said I had three strikes against me. One, I was Jewish, and the Wall Street firms were just beginning to welcome Jews. Then I was a woman. But the absolute killer—I was a mother. My daughter was four years old when I graduated from law school. Employers who might take a chance on a woman were not prepared to take a chance on a mother.

DR: One of your law professors, Professor [Gerald] Gunther, got you a clerkship with Judge [Edmund] Palmieri. Was that easy to do for him?

RBG: He had no qualms about a woman. He had had a woman as a law clerk before. But he was concerned. The Southern District of New York is a busy court, and sometimes he would need a law clerk's aid even on a Sunday. He was fearful that I would not be able to do the job that needed to be done.

Professor Gunther—I found out about this years later, I didn't know at the time—said to Judge Palmieri, "Give her a chance. If she doesn't work out, there's a young man in her class who's going to a downtown firm. He will jump in and take over."

That was the carrot. There was also a stick. The stick was, "If you don't give her a chance, I will never recommend another Columbia student to you."

That's how it was for women of my vintage. Getting the first job was powerfully hard. You know how Justice Sandra Day O'Connor got her first job? She was very high in her class at Stanford Law School, yet she received no offer for legal employment. So she volunteered to work for a county attorney four months without pay, and said, "If at the end of four months you think I'm worth it, you can put me on the payroll." And of course, after four months, it was clear that she was worth it.

It was getting your foot in the door, getting that first job that was a huge hurdle. When a woman got the job, she did it at least as well as the men. So the second job was not the same obstacle.

DR: After your clerkship, you ultimately got a position as a law professor at Rutgers?

RBG: Yes. I was interviewed by Rutgers when I was working for the Columbia Law School Project on International Procedure.

DR: How did you get connected to the ACLU and your trailblazing efforts in gender discrimination and gender law?

RBG: It came about first by demand from my students at Rutgers, who wanted a course on women and the law. So I repaired to the library, and inside of a month, I had read every federal decision ever written about gender-based distinctions in the law. There was precious little.

At the same time, new complaints were coming into the New Jersey affiliate of the ACLU, complaints of a kind the ACLU had not seen before. One group of complainants were public school teachers who were put on so-called maternity leave when their pregnancy began to show, because the school district worried, "We don't want the little children to think their teacher swallowed a watermelon." The leave was unpaid, and there was no guaranteed right to return. The pregnant teachers began to complain.

Then there were blue-collar workers who wanted to get health insurance for their families and were told, "Family coverage is available to male workers, not to female workers." A female worker could cover herself, but not her family. So the two things came together, the students wanting to learn about women's status under the law, and these new complainants coming to the ACLU.

For me, it was a tremendous stroke of good fortune because, up until the start of the '70s, it simply wasn't possible to move courts in the direction of recognizing women as people of equal citizenship stature.

DR: You won a number of cases for the ACLU on gender discrimination and became quite well known. You later taught at Columbia. You were asked to go onto the U.S. Court of Appeals in the District of Columbia by President Jimmy Carter. Were you surprised to get that appointment? Did you want to be a judge, or were you happy to be a professor?

RBG: President Carter deserves enormous credit for what the federal bench looks like today. When he became president, he noticed that the federal judges all looked like him. That is, they were all white and they were all male. Carter appreciated that that's not how the great United States looks.

So he was determined to put women and members of minority groups on the federal courts in numbers, not as one-at-a-time curiosities. I think he appointed over twenty-five women to district court judgeships and eleven women to courts of appeals. I was the last of the eleven.

DR: You served thirteen years on the Court of Appeals for the District of Columbia. After thirteen years, did you think you had a chance to be on the Supreme Court?

RBG: No one thinks "My aim in life is to be a Supreme Court justice." It just isn't realistic. There are only nine of us. Luck has a lot to do with who are the particular nine at a particular time. Growing up, I never thought of being any kind of a judge. As I said, women were barely there on the bench.

When Carter became president, there was only one woman on a federal court of appeals. She was Shirley Hufstedler, on the Ninth Circuit. He made her the first-ever secretary of education. Then there were none, again. Carter changed that, and no president ever went back to the way it was.

Reagan didn't want to be outdone by Carter, so he was determined to put the first woman on the U.S. Supreme Court. He made a nationwide search and came up with a spectacular choice in Justice Sandra Day O'Connor.

DR: President Carter had no appointments to the Supreme Court. He has said subsequently that he would have put on Shirley Hufstedler. Who really knows?

When President Clinton became president, you were obviously somebody being considered. Then President Clinton talked to somebody who was pushing for your appointment, Daniel Patrick Moynihan.

Clinton said, "Well, women don't want her." How could that have been the case when you were the leading lawyer in gender discrimination? Why would some women not have wanted you on the Supreme Court?

RBG: Just some women. Most women were overwhelmingly supportive of my nomination. But I had written a comment on *Roe v. Wade* and it was not 100 percent applauding that decision. What I said was, the court had an easy target because the Texas law was the most extreme in the nation. Abortion could be had only if necessary to save the woman's life. Doesn't matter that her health would be ruined, that she was the victim of rape or incest. I thought *Roe v. Wade* was an easy case, and the Supreme Court could have held that most extreme law unconstitutional and put down its pen.

Instead, the court wrote an opinion that made every abortion restriction in the country illegal in one fell swoop. That was not the way the court ordinarily operates. It waits till the next case, and the next case. Anyway, some women felt that I should have been 100 percent in favor of *Roe v. Wade*.

DR: So President Clinton met with you. Obviously you had a good meeting, and he offered you the appointment. The confirmation went pretty well, would you say?

RBG: Ninety-six to three? Yes, I'd say.

DR: You've now been on the [Supreme] Court for twenty-six years. In total, you've been on the federal judiciary for thirty-nine years. When you first got on the Supreme Court, were the other justices saying, "We're happy to see you here. Let's go have dinner together. Let's socialize"? Or were they just kind of standoffish? What was your relationship with Sandra Day O'Connor like as the second woman on the court?

RBG: The court wasn't an unknown territory to me. I worked at the court of appeals just a few blocks down the road. And every once in a while, Judge David Bazelon, who was quite senior, would call me and say, "Ruth, we're going to Kronheim's for lunch." Who was Kronheim? He was the biggest liquor distributor in the D.C. area.

Before we went to his warehouse for lunch, we would stop at the

Supreme Court and pick up Justice Brennan and Justice Marshall. I knew Justice Scalia from our court of appeals days together. I knew Justice Clarence Thomas. He was also on the D.C. Circuit. But Sandra was as close as I came to having a big sister. You know, I did have a big sister but she died in my infancy, so I never knew her.

Justice O'Connor was the most welcoming. She gave me some very good advice. Not only when I was a new justice, but during my first cancer bout. Because she had survived breast cancer and was on the bench nine days after her cancer surgery. She was very clear about what I had to do. She said, "Ruth, have your chemotherapy on Fridays. That way you'll get over it during the weekend and be back in court on Monday."

DR: Now, the best way to win a case, if you're arguing one before the Supreme Court, is to write a great brief? To be a great oral advocate? Does the oral argument or the brief really make a difference?

RBG: Having a case that's strong on the merits counts most. An oral argument at the court is not a debate won by the best arguer. I'd say of the two components of appellate advocacy, the brief is by far the most important. It's what we start with and what we end up with when we go back to chambers.

Oral argument is fleeting. At the Supreme Court, it's exactly half an hour a side. So you can't do much more with an oral argument than to make the judges want to rule in your favor. But the brief is what does the heavy lifting.

DR: After an oral argument, the justices twice a week will meet and decide how they want to vote, or at least talk about it. Who decides who writes what opinion?

RBG: The chief, whenever he's in the majority, will assign the opinion. When he's not in the majority, the most senior justice who is assigns the majority opinion. Last term, I assigned three majority opinions. That meant that the chief and Justice Thomas were on the other side, so I was the most senior.

DR: The court meets from October to June, more or less. What do the justices do in July and August? Do they sit around reading briefs, or they do other things?

RBG: One matter that follows us all over the world throughout the year is the death penalty, which the court treats like a firing squad. Very often, when an execution date is set, there's an eleventh-hour application for a stay.

No one justice is responsible for the final vote. We all are polled, wherever we are in the world. I also try to keep up with the petitions for review during the summer so when we come back—our opening conference is at the end of September—I don't have a huge accumulation to deal with.

In addition, most of us take some time off to teach. Many U.S. law schools have summer programs abroad. Sometimes I participate in an exchange with judges from other systems. This summer, I started out in Lisbon with Justice Stevens and Justice Sotomayor. It was a conference sponsored by NYU Law School.

DR: Today, what is it that gives you the greatest hope for the future about the court and the way it works? I assume you're optimistic about the way the court generally works, and you're reasonably pleased with the way the justices work with each other?

RBG: All of us revere the institution for which we work, and we want to leave it in as good shape as we found it.

DR: Each justice gets, I think, four clerks. If somebody wants to be a Supreme Court clerk, they just send in a letter applying? How does that work?

RBG: We get hundreds and hundreds of applications. My best source for law clerks are other federal judges. Law professors tend to write glowing letters of recommendation. Everyone is "the best and the brightest student that ever graduated from this law school." But my colleagues on other federal courts will tell me the straight story.

Very often, I'll get a call from another federal judge saying, "I have a clerk this year who I think would be just right for you." Those are my best recommenders.

In the days when Justice Kagan was dean of the Harvard Law School, she picked one of my clerks, and the dean of Columbia Law School picked one of my clerks. Remaining clerks came to me dominantly from clerkships with district judges or court of appeals judges.

DR: If you could change one thing about the Constitution, what would it be and why? If you were a Founding Father, a Founding Mother, what might you have put into the Constitution that didn't quite get in there?

RBG: I would add an Equal Rights Amendment to the Constitution.

I explain it this way. When I take out my pocket Constitution to show my granddaughters, I can show them the First Amendment that guarantees freedom of speech and of the press, but I can't point to anything that says, "Women and men are persons of equal citizenship stature."

Every constitution in the world written since the year 1950 has an equivalent of that statement: men and women are persons equal in stature before the law. I would now like my great-grandchild to have a constitution that includes a statement of that kind, recognizing that it is a fundamental premise of our society just as freedom of thought and expression is.

DR: What gives you the most hope for the future?

RBG: My granddaughters. I'm very proud of my eldest granddaughter, who is a lawyer. She cares a great deal about our country, and about its highest values. She and other young people like her will help us get back on track.

DR: What do you think is the biggest threat to our democracy?

RBG: A public that doesn't care about preserving the rights we have. In a great speech on liberty, renowned Judge Learned Hand said, "If the fire dies in the hearts of people, no constitution and no judge can restore it." My faith is in the spirit of liberty.

MASTERS

Jack Nicklaus

Mike "Coach K" Krzyzewski

Renée Fleming

Yo-Yo Ma

Lorne Michaels

JACK NICKLAUS

Golf Legend

"My record is good. But you could always be
better. That's the neat thing about the game of golf. No matter
how good you get at something, you could be better."

"Your mind is a big part of it. You've got to believe in
what you can do. You've got to learn to play within yourself—
in all walks of life. I don't care what business you're in,
you need to work within yourself."

"Records are all made to be broken."

I am not a golfer—it's too time-consuming and frustrating, given my
lack of athletic talent—but I always admired from afar Jack Nicklaus,
widely seen during his career as history's greatest golfer. His ability to
win so regularly, in the most important tournaments particularly, and
to do so with a humble, low-key demeanor struck me as the model of

athletic leadership—performing in a manner that peers and fans alike admired and respected.

His golf achievements are legendary: a record eighteen professional majors, seventy-three PGA tour wins, a Masters tournament win at age forty-six. Just as legendary is his commitment to his family: five children, twenty-two grandchildren, a wife, Barbara, of sixty years, and his resolve to never be away from his family for more than two weeks at a time, which is quite hard to do as a globe-trotting professional golfer, course designer, businessman, and ambassador.

How did Jack Nicklaus become the world's finest golfer and, in midcareer, a leading golf course designer, while maintaining a close-knit family and pursuing a philanthropic concern for children in need of medical treatment? And how did he also become the most admired golfer—indeed the exalted public image of his sport?

Jack attributes his success in these disparate areas to his belief in himself and in what he could achieve. He makes clear that any successful person must believe in what he or she is trying to accomplish if success is going to be the result, i.e., a high degree of self-confidence.

Athletic success does not always guarantee public admiration. But Jack Nicklaus's modest, all-American personality and commitment to family life have kept him in high public esteem for more than a half century.

I spoke a few years ago at a philanthropic event at the Bear's Club (Nicklaus's home club in Florida), and Jack Nicklaus was in the audience. I did not understand what he thought he could learn from me, but soon found out from him that he is now devoting a large part of his life to philanthropic projects, especially those related to children's health. The main children's hospital in Miami is now named the Nicklaus Children's Hospital, and there are at least seventeen outpatient centers and urgent-care facilities spread across Florida as part of the Nicklaus Children's Health System. He and Barbara spend a fair amount of their time raising money for the Nicklaus Children's Health Care Foundation, which supports these facilities and offers initiatives throughout North America.

I asked if I could interview him about his career and current life. He readily agreed.

This interview was held at the Bloomberg studios in New York in front of a live audience in June 2019. I did not leave the interview thinking that, had I believed in myself, I could have become a great golfer, but I did see how Jack Nicklaus became one—and much more.

DAVID RUBENSTEIN (DR): I am not a golfer, I have to be honest with you. I took it up when I was nine; I quit when I was ten.

JACK NICKLAUS (JN): I'm not one anymore either.

DR: Well, you're pretty famous in golf.

Here's what I couldn't understand. Why is it that so many people are addicted to something so humiliating and frustrating for so many people all the time? The ball never goes where it's supposed to go.

JN: A never-ending pursuit of an unattainable goal is what it really is. Nobody has ever mastered the game. Almost all athletes in all other sports love to play golf because it's difficult. It challenges them at whatever level they play. That's why I enjoyed it, because no matter how good I got, I could always be better.

DR: Your father was the one who got you into golf initially. Was he a good golfer himself?

JN: He was a decent golfer as a kid. Then he quit for fifteen years, and was a pharmacist. He broke his ankle playing volleyball. He ended up having three operations and had it fused. The doctor said, "Charlie, if you don't want to end up in a wheelchair, you better start walking again."

So we moved out to the suburbs, to Upper Arlington [a suburb of Columbus, Ohio], near Scioto Country Club. He joined there, took me along to carry the bag. That particular year, a fellow named Jack Grout came to Scioto, and the PGA Championship came to Scioto that year. I got all that in my first year of playing golf. It just sort of got me charged up to learn the sport.

My dad was my best friend and my idol. I loved my dad and he just did everything with me. He gave up everything for me.

DR: In those days, it wasn't clear that you could make a big career financially as a professional golfer. So you were thinking of getting a degree as an accountant or a pharmacist?

JN: Most kids want to be what their dad was. My dad was a pharmacist, so I went through pre-pharmacy. I hated afternoon labs. My dad, before I went into pharmacy school, talked me into doing something else. So I started selling insurance. I loved selling life insurance to my fraternity brothers. (Said with ample sarcasm.) They really needed it. I did pretty well at it. (More sarcasm.) I was making good money. I got married, and had a first child. But I really wanted to play golf. So that's what I did.

DR: In those days, you were thinking of becoming a professional, but you weren't sure. You met with Bob Jones, the most famous amateur golfer of them all. How did you come to meet him?

JN: He was a speaker at the banquet at my first U.S. Amateur, when I was fifteen years old.

He saw me play in the last practice round. Then he said, "Young man, I'm going to come out and watch you play a little bit tomorrow." Here I am, a fifteen-year-old kid playing in my first U.S. Amateur, and the greatest player who had ever lived, Bob Jones, is going to come out and watch me play.

He came out, and I immediately went bogey, bogey, double bogey, lost my match. But it was a great experience. He became a good friend, and he was a great counsel. He was really a good man.

DR: You decided ultimately to turn professional in the year after you won your second U.S. Amateur. After you had done that, you decided you'd make a career out of it?

JN: I didn't have any more goals or anything more to do in amateur golf. I wanted to be the best I could be at playing golf. So I said, "The only way I could do that is to play against the best. The only way to do that is to play against the pros." That's why I turned pro.

DR: In those days, the compensation was good, but not compared to today.

JN: I was making as much money selling insurance as I would have won playing golf.

DR: How'd you do in your first year as a pro?

JN: My first year as a pro, I won four tournaments. I won the U.S. Open. I won, I don't know, $15,000 or so. I was third on the money list. Arnold Palmer was the leading money winner. He won, like, $64,000 official money, and I won, like, $61,000. But I won what's called the World Series of Golf, which was the first big tournament, and that was a $50,000 first prize.

DR: As you went on, you had a rivalry with Arnold Palmer. He was the leading golfer when you came into the pros, then you surpassed him in many ways. What was it like in the early days when you were rising and he was at the top?

JN: I wasn't real popular, because I started beating Arnold. I wasn't popular with myself, because I was an Arnold Palmer fan. Arnold was a good guy. We got to be very close friends. Our wives got to be very close friends.

Arnold used to come over from Latrobe [Pennsylvania] and pick me up in Columbus, and we flew all over the country playing exhibitions. We had a lot of fun together. He never really seemed to mind that I beat him more than he beat me. I'm sure he probably did inside, but he never let me know it. He took me under his wing. He was ten years older than I was, and he was great to me. I have nothing but love for Arnold Palmer.

DR: In your career, you won eighteen majors, which is the most of anybody. Tiger Woods has now won—with his most recent Masters win—fifteen. But many people think that trying to beat your record is almost impossible.

JN: I don't know. Tiger's pretty good.

DR: You won the Masters six times. Is that your favorite tournament?

JN: Probably so, yes.

DR: You've won the U.S. Open four times, the British Open three times, and the PGA Championship five times. That's pretty good. In the course of your career, you've won some one hundred and twenty tournaments including eighteen majors. You were the leading money winner eight times, the lowest scoring average for a year eight times. There's no record in golf you haven't achieved. Is that right?

JN: I don't know that there's any record I haven't achieved. My record is good. But you could always be better. That's the neat thing about the game of golf. No matter how good you get at something, you could be better.

DR: What is the key that makes somebody a great golfer? Is it concentration? Is it physical ability? A combination of those things?

JN: Your mind is a big part of it. You've got to believe in what you can do. You've got to learn to play within yourself—in all walks of life. I don't care what business you're in, you need to work within yourself.

And then you need to do what you can do, not what somebody else can do. You start believing in that. Winning breeds winning. I was lucky my first year, I won the U.S. Open. I won the biggest tournament in golf my first year out. I believed that I could play. All of a sudden, they started coming in a little easier for me.

DR: One of the most enjoyable tournaments, people say, to ever have watched was the 1986 Masters, when you were an old, old man of forty-six.

JN: Yeah, that's a really old man, isn't it?

DR: In those days, that seemed like an old man. Today, to me, it doesn't seem that old.

JN: It's very young today, David.

DR: No one had ever won the Masters over the age of maybe forty-one or forty-two at that time. Tiger won the Masters at forty-three. Forty-six was considered ready for a golf cart or a wheelchair. You were not leading that tournament until near the end. You were four shots behind with the final nine holes to go. Did you actually think you could win?

JN: I birdied nine, I birdied ten, I birdied eleven. I messed up twelve a little bit and bogeyed, but that actually got me refocused. Then I birdied thirteen. And when I eagled fifteen and birdied sixteen and birdied seventeen, yeah, I thought I could win.

DR: Was that the most emotional win you've ever had?

JN: It's kind of funny, because I'd really finished playing golf by then. I'd won two majors when I was forty years old. I really just enjoyed playing golf, and I wanted to be part of the game. I caught lightning in a bottle that week.

I got around to that last nine or ten holes, and I remembered how to play. You get yourself into contention—much like what happened to Tiger at the Masters this year, when I saw the fellows start to fill up at Rae's Creek, which is in front of the twelfth hole, and he took this pretty little shot out, cut it into the middle of the green. I said, "Tournament's over. Because for the rest of the day he will remember how to play."

That's what I did. I remembered how to play, and I remembered how to finish. That was really fun, being able to do that.

DR: The most important club in golf is the putter, would you say?

JN: That and the driver.

DR: What is it that some players get—"the yips"? They get nervous?

JN: I really don't want to know what it is. I've never had it. But I see guys that have it. They've lost confidence, and their nerves get such that they just jump at the ball. It's really a sad thing to watch it happen to people. Henry Longhurst used to say—he's an old great golf writer and commentator—"Once you get the yips, you die with the yips." It's not a good thing.

DR: After you play a round of golf at the Masters, you go out to the practice tee again, you go out and hit balls? After the day is over, you still go out and practice?

JN: I used to. Now I'm just trying to get through eighteen holes. I practice probably 98 percent of the time after I play.

DR: When you go into a tournament, do you prepare a couple of days in advance?

JN: I went in a week ahead of time, because the majors were always the most difficult tests. Maybe the easiest tournaments to win, because most people got scared of them. But they were the most difficult tests, so you had to be prepared.

My wife has a saying: there's no excuse for not being properly prepared. She's absolutely dead right. I went in to make sure that I knew how the speed of the greens was going to be, the width of the fairways, the depth of the rough, how firm the greens were, what conditions were going to be, and so forth and so on. You learn everything. So all I had to do the week of the tournament was play golf.

DR: One of your records was just broken. It was a fifty-nine-year-old record. You had the lowest score ever for an amateur in the U.S. Open. A young player broke that, Viktor Hovland. [He turned pro after the tournament.] Did you ever think a fifty-nine-year-old record was actually going to be broken by somebody?

JN: Records are all made to be broken.

DR: Over the years, has equipment changed the game a great deal?

JN: I'll put it in terms of the golf ball. From about 1930 to 1995, the average distance for the golf ball grew to about six to seven yards longer, only because of the way they made the golf ball, which was a little bit better. From 1995 to 2005, the range of a golf ball increased about fifty yards in distance.

That's the biggest change. When they switched from a wound ball to a composite ball, the golf ball exploded. They should have changed the rules. But then they changed equipment.

And golfers, over the last ten or fifteen years, have gotten bigger. Everybody's gotten bigger, in all sports. We've got a bunch of big, athletic guys with equipment that hits the ball a long way and they are just absolutely taking apart golf courses.

DR: In the old days, thirty, forty years ago, golfers didn't exercise a lot. Now they do work out?

JN: I think they do. We worked out. I was not a gym rat, but I ran. In the off-season, I did weights and so forth. Gary Player is an amazing guy. He's eighty-three years old, and he is at the gym every day.

Gary can still really play golf. He's really good. I'm amazed that guys would do that [work out]. I've just never been motivated to do that. When we were playing, not even the football players were lifting weights.

DR: How did course design change the most over the years? By becoming longer or more difficult?

JN: The courses have changed to accommodate the golf ball and the equipment. Fifty years ago, your U.S. Open might have been a 6,800- or 6,700-yard golf course. Now it's a 7,700- or 7,800-yard golf course. It's just to accommodate equipment.

DR: Professional golfers are trained to never cheat. They're very careful about the rules.

JN: They better be. People watch them on television, and say, "Hey, that guy did something wrong."

DR: Professional golfers are probably, of all the professional athletes, the most honest about the rules. There's no cheating at all?

JN: They're their own referees.

DR: You, early in your career, decided that you wanted to be involved in golf course design. You have personally designed about 310 courses, and your company has designed over 400 or so. About a thousand tournaments have been held on these courses, in forty-six different countries and forty different states. That's pretty impressive. What is the secret to course design? How did you get into that?

JN: I got into it by way of a fellow named Pete Dye. Pete has been sort of the premier golf course designer over the last thirty years or so. One day he called me—this is in the mid-'60s—and said, "Jack, I'm doing a new course for a fellow named Fred Jones, and I want you to come out and see what it is. I want you to critique it for me." I said, "Pete, I don't know anything about design." He said, "Oh, you know more than you think you know." So I went out, and I looked through the golf course.

Then he asked me a couple of things. I said, "I don't know anything about that." He said, "Yeah you do. Just tell me what you would like to see." And I did it. It piqued my interest.

I got a call in 1968 from Charles Fraser at Sea Pines Plantation, down in Hilton Head Island. He said, "Jack, I'd like to have you do a golf course for us." I said, "I don't know anything about it, but there's a young guy, named Pete Dye, I think I'd like to work with."

I made twenty-three visits there with Pete. It got my juices flowing as far as creativity. I didn't know I was creative at all. But I seemed to be able to come and look at a piece of ground, and I could pick how I think a golf hole should fit on there, and how it should play, and how to do that. I designed by, you might say, the seat of my pants. I've played a lot of golf, and I've seen a lot of places, and there's nothing really new in golf course design. It's just how you apply it to each piece of ground.

DR: Talking about golf courses, what's your favorite course to play, other than ones you might have designed?

JN: If I had one round of golf to play, I'd probably go out to Pebble Beach [California]. I love Pebble Beach. I won the U.S. Amateur there, won the U.S. Open there, won three Crosbys out there. But my two favorite places in the game are probably Augusta National [Georgia] and St. Andrews [in Scotland].

DR: The reason you like St. Andrews so much?

JN: It's the home of golf. And because of what it stands for, and what it has meant to the game, and all the people who have won there and have played there through centuries.

DR: When you finished your professional career in 2005, your last tournament was the British Open at St. Andrews. Was that pretty emotional?

JN: Yeah. I had my family there. They were all there. My son Steve caddied for me during that week. We stopped at what's called the Swilcan Bridge, which is a bridge across from the eighteenth fairway. We didn't get a decent picture. Steve was crying too much.

They're all emotional. I'm trying to figure out how to finish the golf tournament, and they're out there crying on me. We had a great time, though. It was fun. I loved it.

I didn't want to finish on Friday, but I did finish on Friday.

DR: Your last hole was a birdie?

JN: It's kind of funny, because I wanted to make the cut that day. After I three-putted from the front edge of seventeen trying to make birdie, I got to the eighteenth hole, and I hit the ball to about fourteen feet behind the hole.

Now, the ball had not gotten anywhere near the hole all day. With that putt, because the tournament was over, I knew, no matter where I hit it, the hole was going to move in front of it. And that's what it did. And I made my last putt. I started my career in major championships in 1957 with a birdie on the first hole I played, and I finished it on St. Andrews with a fourteen-foot putt for birdie.

DR: You've played with many prominent individuals and prominent golfers over the years. If you could pick any golfer to be your partner in a twosome, who would you want to have?

JN: I think I'll have to pick Tiger today. I never got to play with Bob Jones, even though I knew him and I really loved the man. I would love to have played with Jones. I played quite a bit of golf with [Ben] Hogan. Hogan was fantastic. You could give me any one of those.

DR: You've also played with a number of presidents of the United States. Which one's the best in playing golf?

JN: Of the ones I've played with, Trump is probably the best player. Trump plays pretty well. He plays a little bit like I do. He doesn't really ever finish many holes, but he can hit the ball, and he just goes out and plays and just enjoys it. He's won several club championships.

Gerald Ford—I must have played fifty rounds with Ford. He was about a 13 handicap, but he played to a 13 handicap. Clinton? I never knew what Clinton might do. Clinton would play to a 10, or he might play to a 30. But he had a nice golf swing.

All these guys enjoyed playing golf. I don't think any of them really was very serious about the game, but they all enjoyed playing it. It's good for the game of golf to have the president of the United States say, "You know, this is my game."

DR: If you look back at your career, what's the thing you're most proud of doing?

JN: You know, to me, golf is a game. The most important thing to me was my family. I've got five kids, who all know me. My wife made sure that my kids grew up knowing me. I spent a lot of time with them. She'd bring them to tournaments all over the country to make sure that they knew their father.

I've got twenty-two grandkids who are great. I do things with all of them all the time. Now *that*, to me, is far more important. Golf's a game. I love the game of golf, and I'm proud of my major championships, obviously. But they're still just part of the game.

DR: You had a rule you didn't want to be away from home for more than two weeks.

JN: Never away more than two weeks the whole time I played.

DR: Was it difficult for your sons to grow up with a famous golfer as their father? Could they possibly live up to that?

JN: I didn't push them into the game. It probably was a mistake. Three of them ended up being golf pros, and the other one ended up being close to a scratch player. Not because of Dad. I didn't want them to play golf because I wanted them to play golf; I wanted them to play golf if they wanted to play golf.

Two of them particularly said, "Dad, why didn't you push us more when we were younger?" I said, "I didn't want to push you away from the game. All I can do is introduce you to it." I see a lot of parents pushing their kids into games, and I think it's wrong.

You can lead them there. You can introduce them. You can support them. But you can't play it for them. They've got to want to do it. And then, if they really go after it, they'll be good.

DR: Is there anything left you would like to accomplish professionally or in the philanthropic world? What is your greatest goal at this point in life?

JN: My greatest goal is just to see my kids continue to progress and my grandkids grow and be on the right path.

I don't have any professional goals to achieve. I enjoy designing golf courses. I enjoy going to different parts of the world, and meeting different people and different cultures, and seeing how golf can fit into their game. I enjoy going and meeting different people around the country. We play a few little golf tournaments—the guys they call the "golf greats." We don't ever have to make a score. We just go out and hit and have fun and giggle. I don't have any real goals. My goal has always been family, and it's going to stay family.

MIKE "COACH K" KRZYZEWSKI

Head Coach, Duke University Men's Basketball; Former Head Coach, U.S. Men's Olympic Basketball

---

"You're not going to get there alone. Be on a team. Surround yourself with good people and learn how to listen. You're not going to learn with you just talking. And when you do talk, converse. Don't make excuses. Figure out the solution."

Mike Krzyzewski, best known as Coach K, is widely considered the greatest living basketball coach, having won five NCAA Division I men's titles and three Olympic gold medals as head coach—not to mention his more than 1,100 victories as the head coach of the Army and Duke teams over the past forty-four years.

As a Duke graduate, an ardent follower of its men's basketball team, and for four years the chair of Duke's board of trustees, I came to know and greatly admire Coach K in recent years. His head-coaching record is as impressive as it gets, but his commitment to preparing his extraordinary athletes, many of whom will be NBA players, is remarkable.

Mike's demeanor, like that of so many other truly great leaders, belies his achievements. He is modest, focusing always on his players and on the importance of disciplined teamwork (values no doubt instilled during his years at West Point as a player and later a coach), not on himself. But like other great coaches in any sport, Mike is an intense competitor, always concentrating on how to motivate his players, to get them to focus on team rather than individual performance, to become part of what is now called at Duke "the Brotherhood."

He recognizes that the Duke program is both very popular (because of its long-term success) and also, with more than a few, very unpopular (also because of its long-term success). Coach K has come to accept this reality, and to accept that to remain competitive at the upper ranks of college basketball, he needs to recruit the one-and-done high school players—those who will be talented enough to play in the NBA after just one year of college play.

That has required him to spend much more time recruiting than in the earlier years, and to be continuously coaching teams led by freshman players. While constantly recruiting seventeen-year-olds may not be the most gratifying part of coaching college basketball at its highest levels, Coach K enjoys shaping young athletes into young men and into national champions. That has been more appealing than coaching NBA teams—which he could have done many times. (Famously, Coach K turned down the late Kobe Bryant's efforts to get Mike to coach the Lakers, at many times his Duke salary.)

To what would he attribute his success over more than four decades—a long time to be at the top of any profession? What has made him such an enduring leader?

Mike gives three answers in this interview that are particularly worth noting: 1) changing and updating what you are doing to reflect changes in whatever world you are operating in; 2) figuring out how to make the requisite changes by talking to others and listening to them;

and 3) surrounding yourself with good people—those who can help you when you need advice and support.

I have interviewed Coach K many times over the years, and always learn something new about his views on what it takes to be successful. This interview was held in his office at Duke in January 2017, immediately following a radio interview that he did with me for his Sirius radio show, *Basketball and Beyond with Coach K.*

DAVID RUBENSTEIN (DR): Let's talk about how you got into basketball. You grew up in Chicago. Your father was a fireman?

COACH K (CK): No, he was an elevator operator. My brother was a fireman.

DR: When you were growing up, did you say, "I'm going to be a great basketball coach"? Were you a basketball player as a young kid?

CK: I was an All-State player, and I went to Catholic schools. I was the leading scorer in the Catholic league in Chicago for two years and was recruited.

My mom never went to high school. My dad went two years, so when I was recruited by West Point, they could not imagine that a Polish kid from Chicago was going to go to a school where presidents went.

I didn't really want to go to West Point. I wanted to dribble behind my back, throw bounce passes that were fancy. I didn't want to carry a rifle, but my parents kept putting pressure on me. They would speak in Polish in the kitchen. We never had a house, but we had a flat, and they would talk in Polish.

DR: And you didn't know Polish?

CK: I did not. They would never want me to. I didn't know this till later. They didn't want me to talk Polish in grade school and high school so that I wouldn't have an accent.

DR: When you went to West Point, were the players a better level than you thought they were?

CK: We were good. Bob Knight, the legendary coach, was the coach. We were a top-twenty team, and I got to be a point guard and captain of the team. Going to West Point is the foundation of everything I am now as a man.

DR: Did people come along and say, "Well, you have to go into the military, but you're good enough to play in the NBA"?

CK: I was not good enough to play in the NBA.

DR: Did you know that?

CK: Yeah. And it wasn't like that was everyone's dream at that time. My dream, coming out of high school, was to be a teacher and a coach.

DR: When you go to West Point, you have a commitment of five years. You finished your commitment, then you got into coaching. Where did you first coach?

CK: I went to Indiana and was a graduate assistant. I was getting my MBA at Indiana. Coach Knight was there. I was there for one year and didn't finish my MBA. And I was fortunate to go back to my alma mater at the age of twenty-eight and coach at West Point. We took over a program that had seven wins and forty-four losses in two years. I got the best start that you could get going there.

DR: So you coached there, then Duke was looking for a coach. They interviewed you, and your coaching record the year before you were hired was, I think, nine and sixteen?

CK: Nine and seventeen.

DR: So it wasn't that auspicious. Why did they hire you?

CK: They wanted to make a great decision. In your business, a lot of times if you look at one line item, it doesn't tell the full story. We took over a program that was seven and forty-four, and after five years we were seventy-three and fifty-nine. The last year, we lost six players to academic honor and injury.

We were still able to play Virginia, Purdue, Illinois, St. John's. We should have been, like, three and twenty, and we were nine and seventeen. So, to be quite frank, it was one of our better coaching jobs—but to the public it wasn't. It produces a certain amount of toughness when you have to go through a period where every game, every possession is important.

DR: The athletic director at Duke then was Tom Butters, and he took a chance on somebody he didn't really know. Your record was explainable but not great. Did he know how to pronounce your name?

CK: He did. I hit it off with him right away. I was ready to leave West Point. When I was interviewing for the job at Duke, I was already offered the head job at Iowa State.

I wasn't a leading candidate at Duke. A lot of people said, "Just take Iowa State." I told the people at Iowa State, "You should look for someone else. Don't wait for me. I'm going for it whether I get it or not. I'm going to go for Duke."

DR: So you got it, and then the first couple years were not wonderful.

CK: No.

DR: And after three years, you had a losing record.

CK: Thirty-eight and forty-seven. A lot of people were calling for my firing. We have a fund-raising element here called the Iron Dukes. During my first three years, I was able to establish a new fund-raising element called the Concerned Iron Dukes. They were concerned about me being their coach.

But my athletic director, Tom Butters, and the president at that time, Terry Sanford, said when I was hired, "You have a lot of work to do. There's a lot of rebuilding here. Just keep doing it." So I was never worried, whether I was naïve or whatever.

The next year we turned it around, and then it went crazy. It's one of the reasons I've stayed at Duke. They were loyal to me. I love Duke, but I'm a big people guy, you know. If you are honest with me, you trust me, you believe in me, I'm going to be committed to you. And that's how I felt about this university.

DR: You turned it around. From 1986 or so, you had a very good team. You didn't win the national championship, but you came reasonably close. And then you won the national championship the first time in 1991. To do that, you had to beat a team that had crushed you in the 1990 Final Four—UNLV. You play the same team, essentially, the next year [again in the Final Four], and you beat them. What was it like preparing your team for that?

CK: They had won forty-five in a row going in. A lot of people felt they were one of the greatest teams in the history of sport. And they were, but we were good too. We wouldn't have gotten to the national championship game the year before without having good players.

Then the two best players, [Bobby] Hurley and [Christian] Laettner, stayed on the team. In Grant Hill, we added a player who was better than anybody.

Psychologically, to get our guys ready for that game was huge. Because UNLV had beaten us by so much, I'm not sure they had the edge that we did. We ended up winning one of the greatest games in the history of college basketball, but it was not the championship game.

Then we had to get ready in forty-eight hours and beat Kansas. We were able to turn that around to where the players were thinking of Kansas. And we won our first national championship.

DR: You won your first championship and vindication for you and everybody else who stayed behind you and supported you. The next year, you had pretty much the same team and you came back. People thought you'd win the national championship, maybe not readily, but somewhat easily. Then you came up against Kentucky in a semifinal. That became one of the greatest games ever played. Can you recount what actually happened at the end?

CK: Rick Pitino—one of the great coaches, a Hall of Fame coach—was building that Kentucky program back. It was really a back-and-forth game. They went ahead 102 to 101 on a bank shot from the right—eight feet, ten feet in front. It was a lucky shot.

At that time, the clock didn't stop in the last couple minutes of overtime of the game. Our guys called a time-out with 2.1 seconds.

We were down by a point. The very first thing a leader has to show is strength, so I met them as they were coming to the bench, and I said, "We're going to win. We are going to win."

I don't know if I really believed that, but I kept saying it. Then we sat down.

A lot of times it's good to ask a guy to do something instead of telling him. I said to Grant Hill, "Can you throw the ball seventy-five feet?" He was going to inbound the ball. He said, "Yeah, I can do that." And I said, "Well, I want you to throw the ball, and I'm going to bring Laettner up to the top of the key."

I looked to Laettner, who was very confident, very cocky, and I said, "Can you catch it?" He said, "Coach, if Grant throws a good pass, I'll catch the ball." And I said, "Well, he throws it, you catch it, and I'm going to have two guys run this way. If you don't have a shot, hit one of them and let's see what happens." So he threw it and Laettner caught it.

He dribbled once—which, you know, your heart sinks, because—

DR: —he's not a famous dribbler?

CK: No, but there was only 2.1 seconds. He had enough courage and knowledge about where he put it in, and then he shot the ball and it went in. Now, it was the twentieth shot he took that day. He had ten free throws. He made all ten of them. What most people don't know is that he was ten for ten from the field. He had a perfect game, to include the game-winning twenty for twenty.

DR: So you won the game, and you went on to win a national championship. In 2001, you won another national championship with a team that had Shane Battier and Jay Williams on it. What was that team like?

CK: That team was as good a team as we've ever had—that and the 1992 team—because it had a number of NBA players. Battier's really the best leader on the court and off the court that we had, and he was college player of the year. Jason Williams was also a national player of the year.

That team could really score. One of the biggest games we won was in the semifinals against Maryland. You know, Maryland was terrific, and they were ahead of us thirty-nine to seventeen in the first half.

Our guys were like—I can remember the time-out—"What do you do?" I just told them, "Guys, it's Saturday afternoon. You guys are playing scared. Make believe it's a pickup game and just go out and play." Boom. We won by eleven points. It was a thirty-four- or thirty-five-point turnaround.

Those are the games that people don't remember. They remember the championship games.

DR: You say that very calmly. You don't curse or yell a little bit?

CK: At times you do, but at the time that wouldn't have done anything. What do you have to lose? We'd be down by twenty-two and I'd say, "Look, just play ball." And they could play ball. They were really good players. They were playing for the wrong reasons.

DR: You won the championship that year, then you went a couple years without winning. Then you won again in 2010 with a team that hadn't been expected to win the national championship. Is that right?

CK: It was an unusual team for us, because it was a real big team. We had a lot of big guys. [Brian] Zoubek was seven foot one, Lance Thomas six eight. But they were a real together group. Sometimes in college a guy hits a spurt that all of a sudden propels you, and that was Zoubek.

Zoubek was good player but had a lot of injuries for four years. And finally—this is senior year—he's seven one. He's a huge guy, 260 pounds. In the middle of February, we're playing Maryland here, and he has a game of nineteen points and fifteen rebounds. I said, "Whoa, where did that come from?" From that point on, he was a top-ten player in the country. Where did that come from? I don't know.

DR: It wasn't the coaching?

CK: I don't know what it was. Maybe we changed training meals or something. What I'm saying is that at times a guy just hits something. He gets it, and it hits him. Zoubek was the cornerstone for our team for the next month and a half, and we won.

DR: The last championship you won—the fifth one, in 2015—that was a team where you were basically playing freshmen. You had recruited a number of very good freshmen. The team won with four freshmen on the floor. How did that happen?

CK: It was a most unusual year. College basketball had changed. There are still really good old teams, but there are a lot of teams that aren't old. If you can combine a couple of old players with new talent and they mesh, sometimes you can hit it.

We got down to eight guys who could play, so everybody felt important, and they meshed. The leadership of Quinn Cook, our only senior, was amazing. Three freshmen who went pro after that. They went early, they were one-and-done, they really didn't care about their own stats. [Jahlil] Okafor, [Justise] Winslow, and Tyus Jones, they just wanted to win, and they knew how to win.

DR: Let's talk about recruiting. In the old days, when you first started, it was still competitive. Today, they get these one-and-done players, it's extraordinarily competitive. You're now sixty-nine years old, trying to convince a seventeen-year-old to come to your school. What is it like?

CK: I work harder at recruiting now than I've ever worked, because you have to do it more often. The top players—you don't know if they're going to be one-and-done, but you know that the really good ones are going to go early. So that means you have to do it over and over.

DR: Now you have the situation where Duke is considered royalty in college basketball. As a result of that, because you're so successful, a lot of people root against you. Is that a problem for you? Do you take that personally?

CK: No, I never take any of that personally. It's useless to do that. If you're really good, there are a lot of people who don't like you because you've made a lot of money and you have a lot of influence. You can't run your life based on that. Those people respect you, though. And they respect me and my program.

There are many more people who love our program than hate it. In the last ten years, we've been voted nine times America's favorite program and seven or eight times America's most hated program. I don't know how you do both.

But, you know, our sport's a very intimate sport. You're playing in your shorts and people can see you. They're right on top of you. It's not what the papers say as much as during a game where people can say the worst things imaginable. I can't say them on this show. And the players have to be hard-nosed enough to take that. I get that too, but I'm older. I can laugh it off. I can see five guys in the front row of some of the arenas who look like doctors or lawyers, and they're giving you the finger sign and telling you different things, and you're saying, "Whoa, where did that come from?"

DR: As you've been coaching over the years, what would you say are the most important lessons of leadership you've learned? The things that you really want to impart to your players?

CK: The very first thing is that in order to get better, you change limits. And when you change limits, you're going to look bad and you're going to fail. At West Point, I learned that failure was never a destination. In other words, figure out why, and then change.

The other thing is that you're not going to get there alone. Be on a team. Surround yourself with good people and learn how to listen. You're not going to learn with you just talking. And when you do talk, converse. Don't make excuses. Figure out the solution. You don't have to figure it out yourself. That's what we've tried to build our program on for the forty-two years now that I've been a coach.

DR: What would you like to have as your legacy?

CK: I'll let other people define that. I just like to work hard every day. I love what I do and make every day like it's my first day, but with the experience of forty-two years.

And that I was hungry every day. And that I gave everybody my best shot. I always wanted to be a part of a team. I wanted to lead that team. And what an interesting life it is to be a leader.

RENÉE FLEMING

Singer, National Medal
of Arts Recipient

"I do share with you this wonder
at the realm of possibilities that we have as
Americans. My grandfather was a coal miner
in Pennsylvania. I have performed for and dined
with royalty. And I always stop and say, 'Isn't this
amazing?' That, in two generations, I have this
ability to experience the world at the
most extraordinary level."

"I don't have a wish list. What I do have is
an open mind, and a belief in the future. I absolutely
believe that things come to us if we work hard,
we're dedicated, we love what
we're doing, and we're passionate."

R enée Fleming is one of the world's most talented, most respected, and best-known classical singers. Contrary to the image of many leading sopranos, Renée is not a prima donna. Far from it. She is one of the most gracious and charming individuals that I have ever met—and not just in the performing arts world.

Her friendly and warm nature has been observed by all who have been fortunate to know her during her determined, committed quest for artistic perfection—whether she is performing in an opera or as a concert soloist, Broadway singer, or jazz artist. Careers in the performing arts are always challenging (rejection is all too common), but few arts present as many challenges as opera: there are few opportunities; performances are not generally in one's native language; audiences can be brutally difficult; the global travel schedule is unrelenting; and one's voice must always be in perfect shape.

Renée overcame these challenges by working with skilled voice and singing coaches; learning foreign languages; being willing to travel extensively around the world (often taking her young children with her); and learning an extraordinary number of different operatic roles. The career of a typical opera star is generally not too long; the voice often gives out and the travel fatigue can be overwhelming. But Renée Fleming is not typical. She has expanded her repertoire by singing in many other musical forms, and she devotes an enormous amount of her time to helping prospective opera stars and to supporting philanthropic activities, most especially her work with the National Institutes of Health to have music provide its therapeutic and healing effects to those with illnesses.

I have come to know Renée in recent years through my work at the John F. Kennedy Center for the Performing Arts, where she is an artistic advisor, and through other performing arts forums and activities. In those settings, and in many others outside the U.S.—she is also in great demand as a performer abroad—Renée is as concerned with teaching the next generation of opera performers as she is with performing.

Perhaps this interest comes from the fact that both of Renée's parents were music teachers. (One actually still teaches voice.) Since I am tone-deaf, I have long known that Renée's master classes will not ever make my voice fit for public consumption. So I have contented myself over the years with interviewing her. This particular interview occurred at the Bloomberg studios in New York in April 2018.

DAVID RUBENSTEIN (DR): Let's talk about how you became a very famous soprano, perhaps the most famous in the world. You grew up in upstate New York.

RENÉE FLEMING (RF): I did. Rochester, New York.

DR: And your parents were music teachers. Did they always say to you, "You should grow up to be a great opera singer"? Or they never bothered you to do that?

RF: No, no, they were absolutely shocked. They said, "Forget about that—that's just too impossible. You get a teaching degree." You can imagine their surprise. My mother's still teaching voice. She loves it, she's very passionate about teaching. A performing career takes an incredible amount of drive and resilience, because it's hugely competitive.

DR: So when you applied to college, you wanted to go to a school that had a very good music program. You got into Oberlin. But your parents couldn't afford for you to go there, so you went to a New York state university.

RF: Right, right—SUNY Potsdam.

DR: It turned out, that was a pretty good thing for you, because they had a very good school of music. Is that right?

RF: Yes, the Crane School of Music. And a great voice teacher. One of the key components for success is having someone who can help you develop your voice. It's not easy. It's very individual. When you think about it, every instrument is different. It's internal, the voice, and each bone structure, each physical structure, requires a slightly different set of rules for technique.

DR: When did you realize that you actually were good enough to maybe be a professional singer?

RF: I just kept going along. It wasn't as if I made a decision. When I had the Fulbright scholarship, that was a big turning point for me—to be in Europe, to be steeped in a foreign language, and studying. I loved that.

DR: How did you actually break through?

RF: Somebody has to take a chance. You just have to have one person, one impresario, who says, "I don't care what other people think, I like this soprano, and I'm going to give her a break."

DR: And how did that come about? Somebody called you and said, "Somebody got sick, and can you come and perform?"

RF: Exactly. I had auditioned for Houston Grand Opera's Young Artist Program. A few months later they called and said, "We had a cancelation for a leading role in a main-stage production."

DR: When you're singing opera, you sing more from the chest and not from the throat?

RF: We use an optimal breath expansion—an intake, and then support. Support is really a key thing that optimizes the amount of sound you can make without using pressure, without actually tiring yourself.

Somebody can go to a sports event and shout and they're hoarse the next day. When you hear that, you say, "Were you at a rock concert, were you at a sports event? Where were you? Were you out dancing?" You can hear the toll on their voice. We, on the other hand, can sing for three hours, which is just as extreme in terms of how we're using our voice, and the next day we can do it again without any hoarseness or loss of quality.

DR: When you sing an opera and you don't know the language, is that very difficult?

RF: I sing in eight to nine languages, if you include *The Lord of the Rings*. I only speak, really, three of them. Four, if you include English. Learning everything else, whether Russian or Czech, is by rote. It's memorizing sounds. You have to sound authentic, and you also have to memorize what everyone else is saying. It's very time-consuming.

DR: Today you do opera, and you're also doing other kinds of music.

RF: I mostly concertize. That's what I've been doing for fifteen years. I'd say I spend 80 percent of my performing time on the concert stage, which enables me to travel the world. I enjoy creating the Renée Fleming show—a mixture, usually, of repertoire I love, that I think the audience will enjoy the most. I love meeting new audiences where they are and feeling that connection.

DR: Famous sopranos are sometimes labeled divas or prima donnas, Maria Callas being a good example of that. But you don't have that reputation. So how did you avoid that?

RF: I wanted to nurture that reputation a little bit, so I could be the subject of dinner conversations, but I just couldn't do it. I've never been good at it.

DR: In other words, the ego that's involved with being a great soprano gets to a lot of people.

RF: I think it comes from a huge anxiety about performance pressure. Let's not diminish what performance pressure means. It is really challenging. If you make it to the top, even staying at the top is terribly difficult.

I have internalized the pressure that I have felt over the years, and that's not really ideal either, because it's so stressful. But other people externalize it, and they take it out on whoever's around them. Then they go onstage and they're great.

DR: Because of the pressure of being an opera singer, sometimes you need an outlet. What did you do for an outlet?

RF: I am a culture fanatic. I'm a lifelong learner. So I'm always going to museums and theater. I absolutely love theater. And I love beauty in nature, very much so. I'm enjoying nurturing young talent, and I hope to continue doing that in a more meaningful way in the future.

DR: When young performers come up to you and say, "I want to be a famous opera singer," what is the advice you give them?

RF: I really advise people, first and foremost, not to accept any limitations. Now you not only have to sing fabulously, have a super technique, and really be able to trust your voice; you also have to look fabulous, look like the character you're playing, act amazingly well, and have a great social media game. A lot of this has developed since I started singing, and I'm sure the demands will be even greater in the future.

DR: If I wanted to learn how to be an opera singer, it's late in life. You have to learn early. You can't start late in life, right?

RF: Typically not.

DR: When you go to master classes and teach people, do you ever see anybody and think, "This person really is talented"?

RF: Absolutely. I find there are a lot of diamonds in the rough out there. We also say, "The greatest singers in the world probably don't even know they have a voice."

DR: If you had to pay to watch opera, who would you want to pay to listen to? Who are the great male and female opera performers you would have paid to hear?

RF: Oh gosh. First would be Leontyne Price, whose voice is exquisitely beautiful and who has mentored me. I would have loved to have heard Maria Callas, because of her musicianship. I still go to her records all the time. Victoria de los Ángeles is another. I don't think I ever heard her sing live. I'm a huge fan of her singing. Elisabeth Schwarzkopf. I did a master class with her, but I never heard her sing live.

We belong to a tapestry that is really historic. I love celebrating that connection to what's come before. I love celebrating that. That's something we are losing in our culture right now because of the rapidity of change, and the focus on the here and now.

DR: You have two daughters. Do they want to be singers?

RF: They're wonderful singers. My running joke is that they know too much. Neither of them wants to pursue singing. The lifestyle is challenging. I travel so much—there are periods when I'm on a plane every three days.

DR: When your daughters were younger, you've written that you would pack them up and take them on the road with you and get tutors. Was that complicated?

RF: Yes, but worth it. Totally worth it. I really believed that it was most important to be together—that their home was with the people who loved them. That's worked out well. They've turned into fabulous young women.

DR: If you had the chance to sing only one opera for the rest of your life, what opera would you want to be in?

RF: *Der Rosenkavalier* was absolutely my favorite. The Marschallin is the most interesting woman, the most complex, three-dimensional character, which you don't find very often in a historic art form like opera, where women are victimized right and left, as the chattel of men. That's why the Marschallin, who has power and is complex, is so interesting to me.

DR: You've done Broadway, done opera, classical music. Is there something you haven't done that you would like to do?

RF: Gosh, you know what, David, it's already so much richer than I ever could have imagined. If you told me that I would be in a musical on Broadway, I would've said, "Unlikely, unlikely." I don't have a wish list. What I do have is an open mind, and a belief in the future. I absolutely believe that things come to us if we work hard, we're dedicated, we love what we're doing, and we're passionate.

DR: When you're an opera singer, you can't yell at anybody or at anything, because you could ruin your voice. Do you ever worry about that?

RF: I made that mistake once. Ugh. One of my daughters was upstairs, and in the moment I shouted at her, I felt it go. I went, "Uh-oh." I had to cancel three performances at the Met—in a production that was built for me. That was really unfortunate.

DR: I'm not a good singer, as I mentioned. I'm completely tone-deaf. But I can sing in the shower, and nobody objects. Can an opera singer sing in the shower?

RF: It's great to sing in the shower. It's a good place to warm up, you have all that moisture. You know, one could become a better singer in the shower.

DR: Other than raising two very talented young women, your daughters, what would you say you've achieved that's given you the most pride? Is it coming from very modest circumstances to becoming one of the most famous people in the opera world?

RF: I do share with you this wonder at the realm of possibilities that we have as Americans. My grandfather was a coal miner in Pennsylvania. I have performed for and dined with royalty. And I always stop and say, "Isn't this amazing? That, in two generations, I have this ability to experience the world at the most extraordinary level."

DR: And the legacy that you would like people to think about you—let's say twenty years from now, when people look back?

RF: I hope people will acknowledge that I forged my own path. I think I expanded possibilities for singers who came after me, by singing in multiple genres, by singing jazz, by making a rock album, and also singing in musical theater. When I started, people discouraged that very heavily. They said, "You're going to ruin your legacy, the way in which you're viewed critically. You must not step out of the box. In fact, the more specialized you are, the better." I thought, "I'm too curious. I want to try new things." So I just ignored that advice.

DR: When you go out for a bow, it can go on for ten minutes, twenty minutes. How long do you go out before you realize it's finally time to leave the stage?

RF: Bowing in opera is an art form unto itself. It's another performance. Some people do it extremely well. And the audience loves it. They need it. I have friends who have yelled at me through my whole career, "Stay onstage. The audience wants to show their appreciation." That doesn't come naturally to me.

YO-YO MA

Cellist, Citizen of the World, Recipient of the Presidential Medal of Freedom

"The greater pleasure is the energy in the audience. Again, we're talking about who you're playing for. Music, live music, is a communion. You don't have to be there. I don't have to be there. If we're going to spend time together, let's make it count. If it doesn't count, if you forget what you did today tomorrow, and if I forget what I did today tomorrow, what's the purpose of doing it?"

For a good many years now, Yo-Yo Ma has been the world's most visible and acclaimed classical musician. In recent years, while maintaining his continuous global performing schedule, he has spent much of his public time as a cultural ambassador—i.e., as someone who works to educate audiences of all ages about the importance of the arts to our education, our humanity, and our civilization's progress.

As he has pursued that role, I have come to know him better, for the Kennedy Center's mandate includes arts education. Toward that end, he has been an arts ambassador for the center, and I have had an opportunity to work and travel with him as part of its efforts to have individuals learn more about and better appreciate the importance of the performing arts in our lives.

As anyone who has been fortunate to spend time with Yo-Yo Ma knows, he is a force of nature. Beyond his extraordinary skills as a cellist—he is the true successor to the legendary Pablo Casals—he is passionate about so much of life: his friendships, his role as cultural ambassador, and his role as a teacher and educator.

Born in Paris to Chinese parents, he came to the U.S. as a young boy, becoming a child prodigy performer (for President Kennedy, among others), and a gifted student and performer at Juilliard and Harvard. Although I had spent time with him over the years, I had actually not interviewed him prior to the *Peer to Peer* session we had at the Kennedy Center in April 2017.

So how does one become a Yo-Yo Ma? There is no simple answer, but he recognizes that his artistry and renown are due to his ability to focus with great concentration on what he is doing. And he sees his ability to both perform and educate as his contribution to cultural life. Making those contributions is critical to his very being.

But no doubt his ability to be heard on cultural issues of concern to him rests on his credibility as a virtuoso performer—one who is recognized and admired for his artistry around the world. And that level of artistry has matured from the child prodigy stage to the world master stage. (Many child prodigies do not reach the ultimate stage; they often burn out.)

The world-master level of performing skill is, of course, due in part to endless and almost daily practice sessions over many decades. But it is due as well to the intense, unmatched passion for music and perfection that Yo-Yo Ma brings to every performance—and to his life.

DAVID RUBENSTEIN (DR): You were born in France and grew up there for a couple years. Is that right?

YO-YO MA (YM): I was born in the coldest winter in France for decades. I had to spend the first month of my existence in a hotel because there was no heat.

DR: Your native language was Chinese?

YM: Chinese and French.

DR: You have an older sister who plays the violin. Your father, who was a music teacher, said, "Why don't you play the violin as well?" Why did you not become a violinist?

YM: My sister played much better than I did. There is something, I think, in each person that is innate in terms of the kinds of sounds you like. For example, I somehow didn't think I could make a good sound on the violin.

I didn't play any other instrument for a while. I didn't even hear the sound of a double bass, but I saw one. And I thought, as a four-year-old, "That's a big, big, giant instrument. I want to play it." As four-year-olds might do, I started saying, "Please give me a double bass. I want to play it." There was no double bass I could play. Cello was the next best instrument.

DR: You go to New York, where your father is trying to talk his brother out of moving back to China. Your father said, "This might be a better place for my son to learn how to play the cello."

YM: What happened was that by total coincidence, my sister, who played very well, and I did a small performance someplace in Manhattan on our last stop. This Franco-American lady who had founded an elementary school in New York was looking for a music teacher and had heard about this person, Dr. Ma.

DR: Your father.

YM: She came to the concert and then decided on the spot to ask him to teach at her school. Had we not met this lady, we would have gone back to France.

DR: You were already well known because you had met Pablo Casals, whom many people consider the greatest cellist of the twentieth century— at least the first half of the twentieth century. How did you meet Pablo Casals, and what did he think of your playing as a young boy?

YM: I was taken to play for him at age seven. And I have him writing something in my autograph book. I played for him, and he said, "Very good. But you should always also go play baseball." Which was very interesting, because Casals at that time was in his upper eighties, probably. I remember his saying, maybe in that autobiography or in an interview, "I think of myself as a human being first, a musician second, and a cellist third."

I thought that was really interesting. Where do we place our identity? For guys, often it's what do you do? What's your profession? Most people think of me as a cellist. But the human being part for Casals was the most important thing. That was something I always thought about.

DR: And he recommended you to Leonard Bernstein for an event in Washington. You performed at the age of seven in front of a live TV audience, and President Kennedy was there. What was that like? Fairly intimidating?

YM: We were newly arrived people. Immigrants. Did I know exactly who President Kennedy was? Probably not. Did I know he was an incredibly important person? Yes. Did I think about this for the rest of my life, about who this person was? Absolutely.

DR: You went to Juilliard. Then you decided to go to college at Harvard.

YM: The fields I was most interested in were anthropology and archae-ology. And you may ask why.

DR: Because they both start with an *a* and you like the *a*'s?

YM: Exactly. You're so clever! The thing is, I was a very confused child. When you move, all the things that you hold to be solid and true—visually and emotionally, but certainly in terms of habits and people—it all changes. The rules are different.

People say different things. A lot of our French friends couldn't understand why we would move to the United States. Certainly a lot of Americans thought this is the best country in the world. My parents kept telling me, "Chinese culture, so incredibly important."

So I was kind of befuddled, because not everybody can be right all the time. Anthropology gave me a way of studying values in cultures, where slight shifts in values create the society and become expressive in their arts as well as in all of their various other expressions.

DR: When you get to Harvard, you realize there are a lot of smart people there. Were there many who said, "I want to be the leading cellist in the world"? Were you unique?

YM: I don't even know that anybody, myself included, wanted to be something like that. One thing that's interesting in music is that you are striving for mastering an instrument that is there to serve the purpose of expression.

The purpose of doing something in music is to find your voice. In music, there is no such thing as this is the greatest anything. It's about learning forever and finding the most concise way of expressing something as precisely as possible.

DR: You have now recorded ninety-some albums. Or maybe more than that.

YM: I don't know. I don't keep track.

DR: You've won twenty-some Grammys or something like that. You've become the most well-known figure in the classical music world. Does that put a lot of pressure on you to perform up to the highest standard every single time? Can you ever relax a little bit?

YM: You know the phrase that you're only as good as your last performance, right? Some of that is true. What you are talking about—and I don't want to belittle that—is external recognition. Being a musician is about internal development.

You collect art. What makes one person that artist and nobody else? What makes you David Rubenstein and nobody else? What makes the sounds that I make only possible because of some wish to hear certain sounds a certain way? That's what I spend my life on. Winning awards is fabulous because it gives you more chances to do something that you might wish to do.

But with awards we're talking about external recognition versus internal satisfaction, fulfillment. What I've learned is that you go for an external goal, and if you achieve it, the pleasure is momentary. It's sort of like, "Great. You got an award. Fantastic. Now what?"

There are different levels of pleasure, right? There are levels of deep fulfillment, and this is where the loose term I'm going to use—*culture*—comes along. If you do things in arts and sciences, in culture, your wish is to build something that's a strong enough building block that someone else can build on top of it.

DR: Today you have a life playing around the world. You're in great demand. You could spend 365 days playing concerts or symphonies. How do you pick where to go every year?

YM: I really don't mind what I play and where I play, but I care about who I play for and with. I decided early on that whether I play in New York or Jakarta or Peoria or Waco, Texas, doesn't matter.

The most important thing I can do is to be totally present and totally engaged. There's nothing more important. If I play for a group of people, whether it's kindergarteners at an inner-city school or at the White House, you think about what you're trying to say, who you're saying it to. The only thing that's important is that they remember something that will make them perform an action afterward. It's living material.

DR: Do you ever have the problem that you're thinking about one thing when you're playing a piece?

YM: When I'm playing, it's about absolute concentration. Nothing interferes with that. I can sometimes feel mental lapses come and go.

DR: Do you ever forget a piece?

YM: I do sometimes, and sometimes I don't. What I tell people is, if you want to memorize pieces, do that before you're twenty-one years old. Whatever you learn before twenty-one, you remember forever. After you're forty, forget it.

DR: What about where you play? Is there one music hall that you think is better than the others for acoustics?

YM: Some people say, "Okay, this is the greatest hall. Therefore it must be fantastic to play." Yes, that gives a certain amount of pleasure. But the greater pleasure is the energy in the audience. Again, we're talking about who you're playing for. Music, live music, is a communion.

You don't have to be there. I don't have to be there. If we're going to spend time together, let's make it count. Because if it doesn't count, if you forget what you did today tomorrow, and if I forget what I did today tomorrow, what's the purpose of doing it?

DR: You obviously made a decision in your career to do more than classical music.

YM: Music to me is expression of ideas, thoughts, and feelings, spatial structures in sound. I do not think of classical music as separate from the rest of the world. I would like to think that classical music is part of world music. It is not thought of as world music, but I think that classical music is one of the best things the world has invented. To make that category different really upsets me.

DR: You are seen as a symbol of the importance of culture. And is this an important part of your life and your legacy—to convince people that music and other kinds of artistic performances are very valuable for society?

YM: It's back to the old question. Who are people? Why do people do what they do? How do people learn? What is the meaning of why we live?

It's not a theoretical thing for me. If I have to play a performance on four hours' sleep and I have to leave my family two-thirds of the time that we've had children growing up, you better have a good reason why you're doing that. So you get to that existential level. You have to care. You have to have the reasons of why it's important. As I get older and as I observe what you're doing, you get more and more involved in societal issues.

You think about patriotism. You think about civilization. You think about *civitas*. I think so too, but from my angle, from playing little notes. You say, "Why should that matter when other things are going on?" I have to prove it to myself, let alone to the rest of society, that something is worthwhile, that my humanity or my playing three notes on the cello means something.

LORNE MICHAELS

Creator and Executive Producer, *Saturday Night Live*

"Because of my own experience, I know you don't want someone standing over your shoulder. You can't hold creative people without loose reins. It's just the nature of how you manage creative people. So you're there, and you're present and you're available, but you're not always in the room."

"When you are in a room with really talented people, you don't make many suggestions. Almost everything that you're going to suggest has been covered by someone. You lead by example. It's what you stand for and what your taste is, and mostly it's about being right more often than you're not."

O n October 11, 1975, television history was made: a comedy show unlike any other, *Saturday Night Live* (then called *NBC's Saturday Night*), began its forty-five-year run as the showcase and arbiter of American humor. *SNL* became the training ground for such legendary comedians as Chevy Chase, Gilda Radner, Bill Murray, John Belushi, Eddie Murphy, Will Ferrell, Tina Fey, Billy Crystal, Martin Short, Chris Rock, Julia Louis-Dreyfus, Amy Poehler, and scores of others who came to dominate the American humor world for nearly half a century.

The man who produced the first episode, and is still producing the show, is Lorne Michaels, a Canadian-born writer, comedic performer, and producer who was tasked with creating *SNL* at the age of just thirty.

How did he get that assignment, and how has Lorne Michaels continued for more than four decades to discern what will be funny, and who will be funny, when America's taste for humor is always evolving (as is its taste for popular music—also an element of the show's long success)? He addressed those questions, among others, in an interview for *Peer to Peer* that I had with him at the Bloomberg studios in New York in June 2019.

At that time, I had only met Lorne briefly a few times—though he did invite me a few weeks before the interview to stand and talk with him as one of the *SNL* shows was being broadcast. How a ninety-minute live show with so many performers, skits, and set changes is brought together and done live, week after week, is a dizzying and eye-opening marvel to watch unfold.

Lorne Michaels does not do many interviews. He is understandably reluctant to compare *SNL*'s various performers or the political impact of many of its comedy pieces. (In recent years, President Trump has been the visible subject of some of the political humor, though all presidents, beginning with Gerald Ford in 1975, have been targets for the show's humor.)

Discussing how he has been able to lead such a visible, popular show for so long and survive the critics—and there have been some—Lorne Michaels says the key is being open to new ideas, to changing his mind, and to accepting the best ideas from wherever they come. He also believes that he has been able to lead not by reminding everyone that he is in charge, but by always doing what he thinks is best for the show—not for himself or any individual performer. And he believes that by clearly placing the show ahead of anything else, including egos, he has demonstrated a type of leadership by example. He puts the show first, and expects all of the others involved in its production to do so as well.

So far, that approach has obviously worked. It will no doubt continue to work for *Saturday Night Live* for as long as Lorne Michaels continues to produce it—hopefully for at least another decade or so. And maybe during that decade, Lorne will realize his only failing has been not having a private equity investor serve as an *SNL* host.

DAVID RUBENSTEIN (DR): The show started October 11, 1975. Did you think at the beginning that you were going to change television history and the history of comedy when you were starting *SNL*?

LORNE MICHAELS (LM): I don't think I thought of it in those terms. I thought that if we actually got on the air and did the show, that the kinds of people who were doing the show would stay home to watch. I thought there were enough people like us, because we'd all pretty much come from the audience. I was probably the person who'd had the most experience in television. For most of the people involved, it was the first time they'd been on television.

DR: But you were only thirty years old?

LM: Yes. Dan Aykroyd was twenty-three. John Belushi was twenty-six. Gilda Radner was twenty-nine. Chevy Chase was a little older than me.

DR: Why did all of a sudden NBC say, "We need to have a late-night live TV show"?

LM: We replaced a show called *The Best of Carson*—Johnny Carson of *The Tonight Show*. His show had a timeliness to it. He didn't like it in repeat, so he asked for it to be taken off the air. Herb Schlosser, who was running the network then—and who was in New York and remembered the heyday of live television here—had a lot of empty studios, because the business had migrated to Los Angeles.

He thought it would be great to do a live television show. "Live" was a big part of it. I'd never done live, but I'd done stage and sort of knew what that was about. Dick Ebersol, whom he hired to run late-night [programming], interviewed a lot of people, and was originally thinking he'd do a series of different shows.

Then he and I met, and we got along. I told him what I wanted to be doing and how I would do it. The decision was made that it would just be one show as opposed to many shows. Then it came down to making the decision as to which of them it was going to be. And then it turned out to be mine.

We were originally announced as *Saturday Night Live*. Then Roone Arledge, who was a big industry figure at ABC, announced a show in June called *Saturday Night Live with Howard Cosell*, so we had to fall back on *NBC's Saturday Night*. When Cosell's show got canceled the following year, I wrote to him and asked if he'd mind if we had our title back. He said he didn't have a problem with that.

DR: Why would a thirty-year-old be picked to produce this show? What was your background that enabled someone to think you would have experience to do this?

LM: First and foremost, late night was very low stakes. It was no one's real responsibility. Carson was on five nights a week, and that was doing really well.

I'd done television in Los Angeles, both in the late '60s and then when I moved back in 1972. The more ambitious things that I would suggest or go in and meet about, they'd say it wouldn't work in prime time. In those days you needed a forty share of the audience to stay on the air.

DR: "Forty share" means—

LM: Forty percent of the audience is watching you. They'd say, "It won't work" or "It'll just work on the coasts." I was from Canada—kind of in between the coasts. I thought there were plenty of people like me out there, and it was a different generation. We were the beginning of the baby boom.

I'd worked on shows like *Laugh-In* as a writer. I'd done shows with Lily Tomlin and Richard Pryor, which were always specials. I'd done enough that I sort of knew how you do it. It was a question of putting together a show that was, on some level, new wine in old bottles. I took elements of various variety shows and knew that we'd be different because we'd be doing it.

DR: There had been a lot of variety shows in the United States in the 1950s and '60s—Sid Caesar and so forth. They kind of died out by the mid-'70s.

LM: Yes. It was more of a New York thing than an L.A. thing. But they'd morphed into a different kind of show like *Laugh-In* or *The Smothers Brothers*.

DR: You grew up in Toronto. Did you say, "I want to be a lawyer or doctor" like all young Jewish boys in those days?

LM: No. My grandparents owned a movie theater. If asked in the third grade what I wanted to do, I probably would have said "lawyer" because that's what you said. But I would have wanted to be in the movies.

DR: You got to the University of Toronto, and you majored in English. Then you decided to get into the entertainment world. Were you a performer initially, or a writer?

LM: I'd been writing and performing and directing from high school on in various forms. I did it at University of Toronto as well.

DR: Did you at one point say, "I want to make my career in Canada"? Or the big time was really the United States?

LM: [The year] 1967 was the hundredth birthday of Canada—the centennial. There was a new spirit in the country, and I thought, "I'd be perfectly happy to be here the rest of my life." Then I got an opportunity to do a show in California called *The Beautiful Phyllis Diller Show*. A variety show.

I was working with a partner then, Hart Pomerantz. We'd write and perform. We wrote some stand-up for Woody Allen, Joan Rivers, and people like that. Not that we influenced their careers, but we'd had enough experience, and we'd perform.

So we got a job in California, and that led to a couple of other shows—*The Dean Martin Summer Show* and *Laugh-In*. Then the Canadian Broadcasting Corporation asked us if we wanted to come back and do our own show, which we did for three years.

DR: Ultimately, in October 1975, as I mentioned, you get *NBC's Saturday Night* on the air. Did you interview all the people who were going to be the cast of characters there? Did you say in the beginning, "Dan Aykroyd's going be great, John Belushi's going be great"?

LM: I was the first employee. When I came to look at office space, Rockefeller Center in 1975 had, like, deer running through the halls. There was nothing but space.

We were put on the seventeenth floor. We're still there. I hired an assistant, Tom Schiller, and I'd asked for a bunch of time for preproduction. I signed April 1, which in comedy is sort of an auspicious date.

I used three months to put the team together. I interviewed and met with hundreds and hundreds of people. When I found somebody that, for whatever reason, just felt right, or was funny in a different kind of way, I put them together.

DR: In the early days, the cast of characters was called the Not Ready for Prime Time Players?

LM: Which was Herb Sargent's title, yeah.

DR: You picked a number of the people who went on to great fame and fortune. When the first show went on, right when it was over, were you convinced you had a great hit?

LM: My lot in life is that I only see the mistakes. By the end of the show, there's been enough of them that I can focus on that. Not to the point of obsession, but that's the thing I'll be dealing with—that moment got missed, there was a late camera cut on that. It's never going to be perfect, which is why I'm still there.

That night, we got through it. I knew, when we were beginning— I've said this often—that I had all the ingredients, I just didn't have the recipe.

Between the first show and the second show, we changed. The second show was Paul Simon. Third show was Rob Reiner with Penny Marshall. By the fourth show, with Candy Bergen, we'd found the show that resembles the show today.

DR: The original idea was to have a cast of characters—the Not Ready for Prime Time Players—and a host.

LM: A different host every week. There was a show called *The Holly-wood Palace* that a guy named Nick Vanoff produced, and it had a different host every week.

DR: Who was your host the first week? The first show?

LM: George Carlin.

DR: Was he so funny in those days you knew it'd be a hit? Or was he too complicated?

LM: I knew he had monologues that would work, and I thought he was funny. The biggest controversy in that first show was that the network wanted him to wear a suit. A jacket and tie. He didn't want to. He wanted to wear a T-shirt.

It was not the biggest thing in my life. I let him wear what he wanted. But the compromise, which took up a lot of time on show day, was that he wore a suit with a T-shirt, which was the perfect solution.

I had two musical guests. I dropped a lot of the parody commercials, which we shot in preproduction, between real commercials, which led to some confusion. It just sort of went on, and George Carlin did three or four monologues.

DR: For people who may not remember this, in those days there wasn't as much live TV as there had been in, say, the '50s or '60s.

LM: Only sports.

DR: So, for example, Johnny Carson would tape a show live in front of an audience, but since it would be taped, he could make some changes if he wanted.

You go on live. You can't make any changes. You're really live. Did you have to have a censor for words that might not be appropriate?

LM: There was a lot of discussion about what we could do and what we couldn't do, and what you could do at eleven-thirty and what you could do at midnight. We were all those phrases from the '70s—*cutting edge* and *pushing the envelope.*

We were just trying to reflect life as we were living it. Also, 1975 was the end of the Vietnam War. The president resigned. New York City was bankrupt. It was a little window that opened where it wasn't business as usual. We were the least of it.

DR: "Weekend Update" was a regular feature of the show from the beginning?

LM: Originally, because I'd done a similar thing in Canada, the thought was that I would do that. Then, when I thought it over, I decided I would be cutting everybody else's stuff and leaving my own in, and that wouldn't be the right spirit.

DR: You produced the show from 1975 to 1980, and then you decided to become a movie producer.

LM: I left because people moved on. Because it's a grueling pace, and also because opportunities open for people. The show was such a hit there was no way that the network would let me rebuild the new cast with enough time. We weren't a priority. I'd been holding this group together. No one was fired in five years. It was just time to go. There were lots of other things that I wanted to do.

DR: So you started producing some movies and television shows.

LM: Did that. I did a bunch of music shows. I built a house. I built a garden.

DR: Then in 1985 you came back. And you've been producing from 1985 all the way through 2019?

LM: To a few weeks ago, yeah.

DR: It doesn't get tiring, doing the same thing for now forty-plus years?

LM: No. Tiring on a physical level, yes. It's just what I do.

DR: Since the late '70s or early '80s, how has humor changed? Do people laugh at the same kinds of things? Are there certain things you can make fun of now you couldn't then, or vice versa?

LM: There's almost nothing we did in the '70s that I could do now. Gilda Radner would not be able to play Roseanne Roseannadanna. John Belushi would not be able to play Japanese. Garrett Morris doing "News for the Hard of Hearing" would have been making fun of a handicap. Values change. Between the movie *Arthur* and the movie *Arthur 2*, alcoholism became a disease and no one wanted to laugh at drunks anymore. Whereas for two hundred years they laughed at drunks.

DR: Let's take people through how the show is actually produced. On a Monday, do you recover from the previous week or do you actually go to work?

LM: We have to show up Monday. I have a meeting beginning at five on Mondays, which has all the writing staff, all the cast, the host. People from the music department. People from the film department.

We all gather in my office. They gather, I'm behind a desk. I go around the room and ask everybody what their idea is. Normally it isn't an inspiring meeting. Most of the ideas are—they know they have to say something. Quite often it'll just be a joke.

Once in 1978 or '79, Bill Murray took out a piece of paper and he said, "Paint store." He said, "I'm not sure whether I'm supposed to go to the paint store or it's an idea for a sketch."

You can't keep talking about last week's show. We have a show this week, and this person sitting here is going to be hosting it, and we have to start.

DR: Do people call you and say, "I'd be a really good guest host"?

LM: Some people do that, but mostly it's agents and managers. In the '70s, it was more who you said no to than anything else.

DR: So Monday you come up with a few ideas. Then Tuesday and Wednesday they do the writing?

LM: What will happen is someone will hear somebody else's idea in the meeting, and there will be a lot of cross-pollination, and people say, "I'll work on that." The read-through on Wednesday starts around four, so things have to be in. They're taken from people's hands by two.

Tuesday night, most people work through the night. I take members of the cast and some of the writers to dinner with the host. The most anxious part for the host is Monday to Wednesday, because there's absolutely nothing written, so they don't know what they're going to be doing. They have to trust that we know what we're doing. Which was harder at the beginning.

DR: Thursday and Friday you do dress rehearsals?

LM: We choose the show on Wednesday. We read forty to forty-five pieces, looking for thirteen or fourteen. Once those are chosen, the designers begin designing the sets, then those plans go out to the shop late that night and they start building. The film unit goes off to figure out how they're going to shoot the two or three pieces we're shooting. We are always assessing who has not as much to do as we'd like. We've left the opening of the show and generally one or two spots open for anything that happens between then and showtime.

DR: Have you ever gotten worried that you picked a guest host who really isn't up to the task?

LM: Yeah.

DR: How do you coach them? "Maybe you could do a better job"?

LM: We can get almost anyone through it. It's an odd hybrid, because you're onstage—there are lots of people who are very good at that—but then there's also cameras, and the script is constantly changing up to the last minute. It takes a level of focus. There's a point at which the host really just gives up and goes, "You just have to trust at this point that it will all come together."

DR: Then Saturday you do a final rehearsal?

LM: No. What happens is on Thursday music comes in. They rehearse first. At the same time, sets are arriving. There's two rewrite tables working on the pieces we've chosen. The film unit is prepping—either they're going to shoot Thursday night or very early Friday morning. Then they'll also do another film shoot after from eleven to three or four in the morning.

DR: Are there cases where you think you got a really funny sketch or script, and all of a sudden people aren't laughing in the studio? Or where you're not sure it's that funny, and all of a sudden it becomes very funny?

LM: Yes. You choose the pieces on Wednesday. You rehearse them Thursday and Friday, and again Saturday afternoon in costume and makeup. Then you do a dress rehearsal, which is the first time that three hundred or four hundred people come in and see it. Whatever you thought, if they disagree, they're right.

We adjust from that. Things that you thought were surefire don't play. A lot of it is placement—where they are in the show. If it's a harder piece, if you play it early it probably won't work. It's where you play things—running order—and also topicality.

DR: Have you ever picked people to be in your regular cast who you weren't sure really were that funny and they turn out to be superstars? Or the reverse?

LM: No. There's too much of an audition process. If you're in a room with somebody who's not funny, there's an early-warning system on that.

DR: You are pretty famous as the producer, for almost forty-five years now, of this show. You have a great legacy, even if you were to leave tomorrow. But you plan to keep doing it for as long as you can?

LM: Physically, yes.

DR: What would you see as your great accomplishment in your life, then? That you remade comedy on television?

LM: I just am always thinking about what we're doing next week. There's not a moment where I go, "Wow, I've really done some important things." It doesn't go that way.

DR: Do you have any outside hobbies or interests beyond the show? What do you do to relax?

LM: We finish the season, which is grueling. It's basically the school year. It starts in September, it ends in May.

I have a rule based on experience: don't make any decisions in June. One, because generally I don't want to see anybody I've worked with all year ever again. And also I have no perspective on it. So I tend to go away. I tend to travel, or I go up to the country. My mode of thinking is walking, so I go for long walks and things get clearer after a while.

DR: When you're not doing *Saturday Night Live*, you're also producing some other television shows.

LM: I do *The Tonight Show* and *Seth Meyers*, the late-night show.

Tina Fey was a brilliant head writer on *SNL*, and then cast member, and did "Weekend Update." We did *Mean Girls* together as a movie. She wanted to do a television series. It ended up being *30 Rock*.

What I will do is I'll be all over something at the beginning, to know for sure that it's both on track and that it's the best version of what it can be. Once it's going or going well enough, I will tiptoe out of the room and go back to my other job, which is *Saturday Night Live*.

Because of my own experience, I know you don't want someone standing over your shoulder. You can't hold creative people without loose reins. It's just the nature of how you manage creative people. So you're there, and you're present and available, but you're not always in the room.

DR: Is there anything that makes you laugh so uproariously you can't control your own laughing?

LM: There's always something in the show that I'm really proud of. Comedy is a disruptive thing. People don't plan to laugh. They're taught when to applaud, but they're not taught when to laugh. So there's something that's always surprising. When you see the pairing of really good writing and a brilliant performance, when they're locked in, it's thrilling.

DR: When people are made famous by your show and then go on to great fame and fortune beyond it, do they ever call you up and say, "Thank you for everything you did for me. I couldn't have done it without you"?

LM: There's very strong feelings on both sides of it. When we did the fortieth anniversary a couple of years ago, all the people were invited who worked on the show, plus people who'd hosted the show. I think when people looked around the room and saw all the different genera-tions who'd done it, they realized that what we'd done is important.

DR: Was it hard to get all these people to show up? Did you say, "Leave your egos somewhere else"?

LM: Everybody was just happy to see each other. It was hard, because there's only the 350 seats.

DR: Any regrets about this incredible career?

LM: Millions of regrets. Regrets specifically about what?

DR: Something you wish you had achieved that you haven't achieved? The show has been so successful. Is there anything you wish you had done differently with the show or with your life?

LM: There are so many things—when something doesn't work and it comes out mean, or when something doesn't work because so-and-so entered differently and the camera cut was late, and then the thing unraveled. When it doesn't work, it's just quiet. Very quiet. The cast know it. We all know it.

There's no idea that somebody brilliant isn't able to figure out and pull off. So you're always just hopeful on that front.

DR: Are there things you would like to do with the show that you haven't done yet?

LM: The show just continues to morph. Since the last election, it's been much more political, because the audience can follow it. There were times in the mid-'90s where if you'd ask one of the cast members who the Senate majority leader was, they wouldn't know.

Obviously, post-Watergate politics was very important, and to the baby boom generation remained important. In good times, it sort of recedes. We're always doing what's topical. It might be politics. Right now it is.

DR: If somebody said, "I really want to be like Lorne Michaels. I want to be a successful producer—"

LM: I'd say, "Why?"

DR: To be a master of television, what are the qualities that this person should have? Hard work? Good sense of humor? Know how to get along with people? Motivate people? What qualities are the most important ones?

LM: I wouldn't advise anybody on it. But leadership in this particular field is the ability to change your mind, and change your mind quite often. If a better idea comes in from a first-year writer, we'll go with that.

It's a culture that thrives on that. It isn't status or hierarchy that determine it.

There isn't a week where someone's not seriously unhappy. It's not fun walking past people just after you've cut their piece because we're running long and that's the piece that got cut. But there's always next week, and you just keep moving forward. You try to create a culture where everyone feels they're heard.

DR: Very often I ask people, "What does it take to be a leader?" You're obviously a leader in your area. From your observation of other people, or in your own life, what qualities have you seen that really make people effective leaders?

LM: If you're in power, everybody knows it, so you don't ever have to explain you're in power. When you are in a room with really talented people, you don't make many suggestions. Almost everything that you're going to suggest has been covered by someone.

You lead by example. It's what you stand for and what your taste is, and mostly it's about being right more often than you're not. Also pushing people forward, because in my case, people know that all that matters to me is whether the show is good or not.

And I am going to be ruthless in the search for that. If you haven't caught up with it on some level, why I'm doing something, I really won't have time to explain. But after a while, you'll see a pattern. We have forty-five minutes between dress and air to just figure it out.

I go round the room and go, "What do you think? What do you think? What do you think? What about if we put this here?" Everybody speaks. The decision is technically mine, but you can feel consensus, and they're all people who just want it to be good.

Acknowledgments

There are a good many people who made this book possible, and I would like to thank them for all of their assistance and help.

My publisher, Simon & Schuster, supported this book from the inception, and I want to thank Jonathan Karp, Simon & Schuster's gifted CEO, for this support. I would like to express my appreciation as well for my editor, Stuart Roberts, who was quite skillful in editing my drafts and in suggesting numerous ways to improve the book.

My counsel and friend from law school, Bob Barnett, served as my indispensable legal advisor and as my representative in all business and legal matters with Simon & Schuster.

Of course I want to thank all of the interviewees included here for both letting me interview them and allowing me to publish edited transcripts of our conversations.

I also want to thank Sharon Rockefeller, the president of WETA, the public television channel in the Washington area, for arranging to have *Peer to Peer* broadcast on WETA and other PBS channels around the country.

I would also like to thank Chris Ullman for his considerable help with the public relations associated with this book.

The interviews in this book were made possible through the support of the Economic Club of Washington, D.C., and Bloomberg TV. The executive director of the Economic Club, Mary Brady, did everything possible to facilitate the interviews held in front of the club's members. She was helped by the club's media director, Judi Irastorza.

At Bloomberg, I am indebted to a number of people who made *Peer to Peer* possible. The idea for the show was originally that of Juleanna Glover, who was a member of the Economic Club; she suggested it to Justin Smith, also a member of the club as well as the executive in charge of media at Bloomberg. His support of the show from the beginning has been extraordinary. Mike Bloomberg approved of the idea for the show as well, and I appreciate his longtime friendship and support.

Overseeing the show has been Al Mayers, the head of Bloomberg TV, and his support of the show has also greatly helped its success.

At the show's beginning, the producer was Matt Saal, an experienced television producer, and his hard work and skill helped to get the show off to a strong start. Matt also began the process of editing these interviews for publication.

When Matt left Bloomberg TV to work for Governor Andrew Cuomo, he was succeeded by Laura Chapman, an experienced professional at Bloomberg TV. Laura too helped make the show work well, before leaving to work on the Bloomberg presidential campaign.

Laura was succeeded by another experienced Bloomberg TV producer, Kelly Belknap, who returned to New York from Bloomberg's TV operations in Hong Kong in order to produce the show. Kelly has been extremely helpful in enhancing the show, and in obtaining and reviewing the television transcripts from which this book is drawn. Producer Samantha Shivraj and Bloomberg Media counsel Patricia Suh helped arrange permission to use the transcripts.

In my office, a number of individuals have been quite helpful in the preparation of this book: Mary Pat Decker, my longtime chief of staff, who juggled my schedule sufficiently to ensure that the interviews in this book could occur; Laura Boring, who helped with the many and frequent changes in the manuscript; Amanda Mangum, who worked with Laura on the manuscript's preparation; and Robert Haben, who helped me with all of the research needed to prepare for the interviews.

I particularly want to thank Jennifer Howard, who did the yeoman's work of reviewing and editing the interview transcripts, and of editing my own summaries of each of these interviews. Jennifer performed the same role in my previous book, and continued to show with this book that she is a skilled and thoughtful editor, writer, and wordsmith.

All of the proceeds that would normally accrue to the author from a book such as this one will be given to the Johns Hopkins Children's Center. I am on the Johns Hopkins Medicine Board of Trustees and have been a longtime supporter of its Children's Center.

I am sure that I have made some mistakes in this book. The mistakes are solely my responsibility.

About the Contributors

JAMES A. BAKER III is the only person to serve as secretary of state, secretary of the treasury, and twice as White House chief of staff—for Presidents Ronald Reagan and George H. W. Bush. As secretary of the treasury under Reagan, Baker played a key role in the Tax Reform Act that simplified the nation's tax code. During his tenure as secretary of state, Baker laid the diplomatic groundwork for the unification of Germany and forged the international coalition that forced Saddam Hussein's troops from Kuwait. After he left the government, he founded the James A. Baker III Institute for Public Policy at Rice University, was personal envoy of the United Nations to seek a political solution to the conflict over Western Sahara, and was special presidential envoy to restructure Iraq's sovereign debt. He is a senior partner with the law firm Baker Botts. He and his wife, Susan Garrett Baker, have eight children and nineteen grandchildren.

JEFF BEZOS founded Amazon.com in 1994. Amazon's mission is to be earth's most customer-centric company. Amazon offers low prices and fast delivery on millions of items, provides thousands of movies and TV shows through Prime Video, designs and builds the best-selling Kindle, Fire, and Echo devices and Alexa voice-recognition service, and empowers companies and governments in over 190 countries around the world with the leading cloud-computing infrastructure through Amazon Web Services. Bezos is also the founder of aerospace company Blue Origin, which is working to lower the cost and increase the safety of spaceflight, and he is owner of the *Washington Post*. In 2018, he founded the Bezos Day One Fund, which focuses on funding nonprofits that help homeless families, and on creating a network of tier-one preschools in low-income communities. Bezos graduated summa cum laude, Phi Beta Kappa, in electrical engineering and computer science from Princeton University in 1986, and was named *Time* magazine's Person of the Year in 1999.

SIR RICHARD BRANSON is founder of the Virgin Group. Conceived in 1970, the Virgin Group has gone on to grow successful businesses in sectors including mobile telephony, travel and transportation, financial services, leisure and entertainment, and health and wellness. Virgin is a leading international investment group and one of the world's most recognized and respected brands. Since starting youth culture magazine *Student* at the age of sixteen, Richard has found entrepreneurial ways to drive positive change in the world. In 2004, Richard established Virgin Unite, the nonprofit foundation of the Virgin Group. Most of his time is now spent building businesses that will make a positive difference in the world and working with Virgin Unite and organizations it has incubated, such as the Elders, the B Team, and Ocean Unite. He lives on Necker Island with his wife, Joan, and has two children, Holly and Sam, and five grandchildren.

WARREN E. BUFFETT was born in Omaha, Nebraska, on August 30, 1930. He is chairman of the board and CEO of the holding company Berkshire Hathaway Inc. Berkshire Hathaway has eighty-nine operating businesses and is number five on *Fortune*'s list of the World's Most Admired Companies. Along with Bill and Melinda Gates, Mr. Buffett is a cofounder of the Giving Pledge, which encourages wealthy Americans to devote at least 50 percent of their net worth to philanthropy. Mr. Buffett has pledged that all of his shares in Berkshire Hathaway—about 99 percent of his net worth—will be given to philanthropic endeavors. Mr. Buffett attended the Wharton School of Business at University of Pennsylvania, and in 1950 received his BS from the University of Nebraska. He earned his MS in economics from Columbia University in 1951. Mr. Buffett was married to Susan T. Buffett until her death in 2004. They had three children: Susan, Howard, and Peter. In 2006, he married Astrid Menks.

GEORGE W. BUSH served as the forty-third president of the United States of America from 2001 to 2009. Following the terrorist attacks on September 11, 2001, President Bush responded with a comprehensive strategy to protect the American people. Under his leadership, the United States built global coalitions to remove violent regimes in Afghanistan and Iraq, and provided unprecedented support for young democracies and dissidents around the world. President Bush also launched global HIV/AIDS and malaria initiatives that have saved millions of lives. Prior to serving as president, he was the forty-sixth governor of Texas from 1995 to 2000. After the presidency, President Bush and former First Lady Laura Bush founded the George W. Bush Presidential Center in Dallas, Texas, home to the George W. Bush Presidential Library and Museum and the George W. Bush Institute, a nonpartisan public policy and leadership development center. He and Laura have twin daughters, Barbara and Jenna, and three grandchildren.

WILLIAM JEFFERSON CLINTON, the first Democratic president in six decades to be elected twice, led the United States to what was then the longest economic expansion in American history, including the creation of more than twenty-two million jobs. After leaving the White House, President Clinton established the Clinton Foundation in order to continue working on the causes he cared about. Since its founding, the foundation has endeavored to help build more resilient communities by developing and implementing programs that improve people's health, strengthen local economies, and protect the environment.

In addition to his foundation work, President Clinton served as the top United Nations envoy for the Indian Ocean tsunami recovery effort, and as the U.N. special envoy to Haiti—and has partnered numerous times with Presidents George H. W. Bush and George W. Bush to support relief efforts for communities devastated by natural disasters.

President Clinton was born on August 19, 1946, in Hope, Arkansas. He and his wife, Secretary Hillary Rodham Clinton, live in Chappaqua, New York. They have one daughter, Chelsea, and three grandchildren, Charlotte, Aidan, and Jasper.

TIM COOK is the CEO of Apple and serves on its board of directors. Before being named CEO in August 2011, Tim was Apple's COO and was responsible for all of the company's worldwide sales and operations, including end-to-end management of Apple's supply chain, sales activities, and service and support. He also headed Apple's Macintosh division and played a key role in the continued development of strategic reseller and supplier relationships. Prior to joining Apple, Tim was vice president of corporate materials for Compaq and was responsible for procuring and managing all of Compaq's product inventory. Tim also spent twelve years with IBM, most recently as director of North American fulfillment where he led manufacturing and distribution functions for IBM's Personal Computer Company in North and Latin America. Tim earned an MBA from Duke University, where he was a Fuqua Scholar, and a BS in industrial engineering from Auburn University.

JAMIE DIMON is chairman of the board and CEO of JPMorgan Chase & Co., a global financial-services firm with assets of $3.1 trillion and operations worldwide. Dimon became CEO on January 1, 2006. He began his career at American Express Company, and served as CFO and then president at Commercial Credit. He served as president and COO of Travelers from 1990 through 1998 while concurrently serving as chief operating officer of its Smith Barney Inc. subsidiary before becoming cochairman and co-CEO of Smith Barney and Salomon Brothers after their merger. In 1998, he was named president of Citigroup Inc. He joined Bank One as chairman and CEO in 2000. Dimon earned his bachelor's degree from Tufts University and holds an MBA from Harvard Business School. He serves on the boards of a number of institutions including the Business Roundtable, Bank Policy Institute, and Harvard Business School.

ANTHONY S. FAUCI, MD, is director of the National Institute of Allergy and Infectious Diseases (NIAID) at the U.S. National Institutes of Health, where he oversees an extensive research portfolio devoted to preventing, diagnosing, and treating infectious and immune-mediated diseases. Dr. Fauci has been a key advisor to six presidents and their administrations on global AIDS issues, and on initiatives to bolster medical and public health preparedness against emerging infectious disease threats, including Ebola, Zika, and, most recently, Coronavirus Disease 2019 (COVID-19). He was one of the principal architects of the President's Emergency Plan for AIDS Relief (PEPFAR), which has helped save millions of lives throughout the developing world. Dr. Fauci is a member of the U.S. National Academy of Sciences and the U.S. National Academy of Medicine and is the recipient of numerous prestigious awards for his scientific and global health accomplishments, including the Presidential Medal of Freedom.

RENÉE FLEMING is one of the most highly acclaimed singers of our time, performing on the stages of the world's greatest opera houses, concert halls, and theaters. Winner of four Grammy Awards and the U.S. National Medal of Arts, Renée has sung for momentous occasions from the Nobel Peace Prize ceremony to the Diamond Jubilee Concert for HM Queen Elizabeth II at Buckingham Palace. In 2014, Renée became the first classical artist ever to sing the U.S. National Anthem at the Super Bowl. As artistic advisor to the John F. Kennedy Center for the Performing Arts, Renée launched a collaboration with the U.S. National Institutes of Health, with participation by the National Endowment for the Arts, focused on the science connecting music, health, and the brain. Her many awards include the Fulbright Lifetime Achievement Medal, Germany's Cross of the Order of Merit, and France's Chevalier de la Légion d'honneur. She is the author of the memoir *The Inner Voice*.

BILL GATES is cochair of the Bill & Melinda Gates Foundation. In 1975, Bill Gates founded Microsoft with Paul Allen and led the company to become the worldwide leader in business and personal software and services. In 2008, Bill transitioned to focus full-time on his foundation's work to expand opportunity to the world's most disadvantaged people. Along with cochair Melinda Gates, he leads the foundation's development of strategies and sets the overall direction of the organization. In 2010, Bill, Melinda, and Warren Buffett founded the Giving Pledge, an effort to encourage the wealthiest families and individuals to publicly commit at least half of their wealth to philanthropic causes and charitable organizations during their lifetime or in their will. In 2015, Bill created the Breakthrough Energy Coalition, a group of individuals and entities committed to clean energy innovation, followed by Breakthrough Energy Ventures in 2016, an investor-led fund focused on providing patient capital to support cutting-edge clean energy companies.

MELINDA FRENCH GATES is a philanthropist, businesswoman, and global advocate for women and girls. As the cochair of the Bill & Melinda Gates Foundation, Melinda sets the direction and priorities of the world's largest philanthropy. She is also the founder of Pivotal Ventures, an investment and incubation company working to drive social progress for women and families in the United States, and the author of the best-selling book *The Moment of Lift*. Melinda grew up in Dallas, Texas.

She received a bachelor's degree in computer science from Duke University and an MBA from Duke's Fuqua School. Melinda spent the first decade of her career developing multimedia products at Microsoft before leaving the company to focus on her family and philanthropic work. She lives in Seattle, Washington, with her husband, Bill. They have three children, Jenn, Rory, and Phoebe.

JUSTICE RUTH BADER GINSBURG, associate justice of the Supreme Court of the United States, was born in Brooklyn, New York, March 15, 1933. She married Martin D. Ginsburg in 1954, and has a daughter, Jane, and a son, James. She received her BA from Cornell University, attended Harvard Law School, and received her LLB from Columbia Law School. From 1961 to 1963, she was a research associate and then associate director of the Columbia Law School Project on International Procedure. She was a professor of law at Rutgers University School of Law from 1963 to 1972 and at Columbia Law School from 1972 to 1980. In 1971, she was instrumental in launching the women's rights project of the American Civil Liberties Union (ACLU), and served as the ACLU's general counsel from 1973 to 1980. She was appointed a judge of the United States Court of Appeals for the District of Columbia Circuit in 1980 by President Jimmy Carter. President Bill Clinton nominated her as an associate justice of the Supreme Court, and she took her seat August 10, 1993.

KEN GRIFFIN started trading in 1987 as a nineteen-year-old sophomore from his dorm room at Harvard University using a fax machine, a personal computer, and a telephone. He caught the attention of hedge fund pioneer and cofounder of Chicago-based Glenwood Partners Frank Meyer, earning him the opportunity to establish what would one day become Citadel. Ken founded Citadel in 1990 and has since served as the firm's CEO. He is a passionate philanthropist and has given over $1 billion to numerous organizations, including the University of Chicago, the Ann & Robert H. Lurie Children's Hospital of Chicago, the Field Museum of Natural History, the Art Institute of Chicago, the Museum of Modern Art, and the American Museum of Natural History. Ken earned his bachelor's degree from Harvard University and is a proud supporter of his alma mater. In 2014, he donated $150 million to support need-based financial aid at Harvard, the largest gift in school history at the time.

MARILLYN HEWSON is executive chairman of Lockheed Martin Corporation. She transitioned to the role of executive chairman in June 2020, after serving as Lockheed Martin's chairman, president, and CEO for over seven years, leading the corporation during one of the most successful chapters in the company's history. Ms. Hewson joined Lockheed Martin in 1983 as an industrial engineer. *Time* magazine has identified her as one of the 100 Most Influential People in the World, and she has been ranked by *Fortune* magazine as number one on its list of 50 Most Powerful Women in Business for two years in a row. Previously, she was named Chief Executive of the Year by *Chief Executive* magazine, a Top 10 Businessperson of the Year by *Fortune* magazine, and one of the World's 100 Most Powerful Women by *Forbes*. Ms. Hewson earned her BS degree in business administration and her MA degree in economics from the University of Alabama.

PHIL KNIGHT, a director since 1968, is chairman emeritus of the board of directors of Nike, Inc. Knight is a cofounder of the company and led Nike from a partnership founded on a handshake and $500 to the world's largest athletic footwear, apparel, and equipment company. Except for June 1983 through September 1984, he served as its president and CEO from 1968 to 1990, and from June 2000 to December 2004. Knight earned a bachelor's degree in business in 1959 from the University of Oregon, where he was a middle-distance runner on the varsity track team under famed coach Bill Bowerman. He then received an MBA from the Stanford University Graduate School of Business in 1962. He remains devoted to both universities, and has contributed substantially to their academic and athletic programs. Knight is also the author of *Shoe Dog*, the best-selling memoir of the creation of Nike. The Knights and their family live in Oregon.

MIKE "COACH K" KRZYZEWSKI is the head coach of men's basketball at Duke University. In forty seasons at Duke, Krzyzewski—a Naismith Hall of Fame coach, five-time national champion, and twelve-time Final Four participant—has built a dynasty that few programs in the history of the game can match. Krzyzewski owns a 1,157-350 record in forty-five years as a head coach. From his first career win as head coach at Army on November 28, 1975, to his most recent—the 1,157th over North Carolina on March 7, 2020—Krzyzewski has set the standard for winning in Division I men's basketball. He was inducted into the Naismith Basketball Hall of Fame in 2001. Following his appointment as head coach of the United States Men's National Basketball Team on October 26, 2005, Coach K presided over one of the golden eras of USA Basketball, during which the team won three Olympic gold medals. A graduate of West Point, he enrolled in the U.S. Military Academy to receive a quality education, play basketball, and become a U.S. Army officer.

CHRISTINE LAGARDE has been president of the European Central Bank since November 1, 2019. A French national, Lagarde graduated from law school at University Paris X, and obtained a master's degree from the Political Science Institute in Aix-en-Provence. Lagarde joined the international law firm Baker & McKenzie and after twenty years of legal practice was elected global chairman. She was called to the French government in June 2005 as minister for foreign trade, and in June 2007 became the first woman to hold the post of finance and economy minister of a G7 country. In July 2011, she was elected director of the International Monetary Fund (IMF), the first woman to hold that position. She resigned from the IMF in September 2019 following her nomination as president of the European Central Bank. In 2019, Lagarde was ranked the second most influential woman in the world by *Forbes* magazine. An *officier* of the Légion d'honneur and a former member of the French national team for synchronized swimming, Lagarde has two sons.

YO-YO MA, perhaps the world's most famous living cellist, was born in 1955 to Chinese parents living in Paris. He began to study the cello with his father at age four, and three years later moved with his family to New York City. There, he continued his studies at the Juilliard School. After his conservatory training, he sought out a liberal arts education and graduated from Harvard with a degree in anthropology. Yo-Yo's career is testament to his faith in culture's power to generate the trust and understanding essential to a strong society. This belief inspired Yo-Yo to establish the global cultural collective Silkroad, and, more recently, to set out on the Bach Project—a six-continent tour of J. S. Bach's suites for solo cello and an invitation to a larger conversation about culture, society, and the themes that connect us all.

LORNE MICHAELS is an Emmy Award–winning producer and writer, best known as the creator and executive producer of *Saturday Night Live*. *SNL* is the longest-running and most Emmy-nominated weekly late-night television program in TV history. Michaels is also executive producer of the Emmy-nominated *The Tonight Show Starring Jimmy Fallon* and *Late Night with Seth Meyers* on NBC, among other shows. His previous television credits include *Portlandia*, *Late Night with Jimmy Fallon*, *30 Rock*, and *Late Night with Conan O'Brien*. His motion-picture credits as a producer include *Mean Girls*, *Wayne's World*, and *Whiskey Tango Foxtrot*. Michaels has personally won eighteen Emmys as a writer and producer of television. In 2016, he was awarded a Presidential Medal of Freedom, the nation's highest civilian honor, for his significant cultural contributions to the country. In 2008 and 2015, he was named one of *Time* magazine's *Time* 100, and in 2013 he earned the rare honor of an individual Peabody Award.

JACK NICKLAUS is globally recognized as the greatest champion in golf history. He was named Individual Male Athlete of the Twentieth Century by *Sports Illustrated* and one of the Ten Greatest Athletes of the Century by ESPN.com. Jack has one hundred and twenty professional tournament victories worldwide, including a record eighteen major championship titles. Using his success as a platform for a greater good, he became just the fourth person in history and the first sports figure to be honored with the Presidential Medal of Freedom, the Congressional Gold Medal, and the Lincoln Medal. In 1962, he founded the Nicklaus Companies and one of the game's most recognized global brands. He has personally designed more than 310 courses worldwide. Jack and his wife, Barbara, created the Nicklaus Children's Health Care Foundation, with a goal to provide access to world-class health care for all children and support innovative programs focused on diagnosis, treatment, and prevention of childhood illnesses.

INDRA NOOYI is the former chairman and CEO of PepsiCo (2006 to 2019). She was the chief architect of Performance with Purpose, PepsiCo's pledge to do what's right for the business by being responsive to the needs of the world around us. During her tenure, PepsiCo grew net revenue more than 80 percent, and its total shareholder return was 162 percent. Before joining PepsiCo in 1994, Mrs. Nooyi held senior positions at the Boston Consulting Group, Motorola, and Asea Brown Boveri. Currently, she is a member of the board of Amazon, an independent director of the International Cricket Council, and a member of the American Academy of Arts & Sciences. In 2007, she was named an Outstanding American by Choice by the U.S. State Department. She holds a BS from Madras Christian College, an MBA from the Indian Institute of Management in Calcutta, and a master's of public and private management degree from Yale University. Mrs. Nooyi is married and has two daughters.

NANCY PELOSI is the 52nd Speaker of the House of Representatives, having made history in 2007 when she was the first woman to be elected to the office. For thirty-three years, Speaker Pelosi has represented San Francisco, California's Twelfth District, in Congress. She has led the House Democrats for seventeen years and previously served as House Democratic whip. Pelosi brings to her leadership position a distinguished record of legislative accomplishment. She led the Congress in passing historic health insurance reform, key investments in college aid, clean energy, and innovation, and initiatives to help small businesses and veterans. She has been a powerful voice for civil rights and human rights around the world for decades. Pelosi comes from a strong family tradition of public service in Baltimore. Married to Paul Pelosi, she is a mother of five and grandmother of nine.

GENERAL DAVID H. PETRAEUS (U.S. Army, Ret.) is one of the most prominent military leaders of the post-9/11 era. His extraordinary service has taken him from battlefields and academia to leadership in government and the investment world. General Petraeus's military career of over thirty-seven years culminated in six consecutive commands, including the Surges in Iraq and Afghanistan. Following his retirement from the military, he served as director of the CIA. He is now a partner in the global investment firm KKR and chairman of the KKR Global Institute. A graduate with distinction from the U.S. Military Academy, he also earned a PhD from Princeton University's Woodrow Wilson School of Public and International Affairs. Over the past fifteen years, General Petraeus has been named one of America's 25 Best Leaders by *U.S. News & World Report*, a *Time* 100 selectee, and a finalist for *Time* magazine's Person of the Year. General Petraeus's numerous awards and decorations include four awards of the Defense Distinguished Service Medal; the Bronze Star Medal for Valor; and the Combat Action Badge.

GENERAL COLIN L. POWELL (U.S. Army, Ret.) has devoted his life to public service for over fifty years, having held senior military and diplomatic positions across four presidential administrations. He served as the sixty-fifth U.S. secretary of state from 2001 to 2005. General Powell served thirty-five years in the U.S. Army, rising to the rank of four-star general, and served as chairman of the Joint Chiefs of Staff from 1989 to 1993. He also served as national security advisor to President Ronald Reagan. He is the chair of the Board of Visitors for the Colin Powell School for Civic and Global Leadership at his alma mater, the City College of New York. He is the founder and chairman emeritus of the America's Promise Alliance. General Powell is the author of two best sellers, *My American Journey* and *It Worked for Me: In Life and Leadership*.

CONDOLEEZZA RICE is the Denning professor in global business and the economy at the Stanford Graduate School of Business, the Thomas and Barbara Stephenson senior fellow on public policy at the Hoover Institution, and a professor of political science at Stanford University. She is also a founding partner at Rice, Hadley, Gates & Manuel LLC, an international strategic consulting firm. From 2005 to 2009, Rice served as the sixty-sixth secretary of state of the United States; she also served as President George W. Bush's national security advisor from 2001 to 2005. Rice has authored and coauthored numerous books, most recently *To Build a Better World: Choices to End the Cold War and Create a Global Commonwealth* (2019), coauthored with Philip Zelikow, and *Political Risk: How Businesses and Organizations Can Anticipate Global Insecurity* (2018), coauthored with Amy B. Zegart. Among her other volumes are the best sellers *Democracy: Stories from the Long Road to Freedom* (2017) and *Extraordinary, Ordinary People: A Memoir of Family* (2010).

VIRGINIA M. (GINNI) ROMETTY is executive chairman of IBM. She was previously chairman, president, and CEO from 2012 to 2020. During her tenure, she made bold changes to reposition IBM for the future, reinventing more than 50 percent of IBM's portfolio, building a $21 billion hybrid cloud business, and establishing IBM's leadership in AI, quantum computing, and blockchain. Ginni also established IBM as the model of responsible stewardship in the digital age. She was the industry's leading voice on technology ethics and a champion of diversity and inclusion. This pioneering work was recognized in 2018 by the prestigious Catalyst Award for advancing diversity and women's initiatives. Beginning her career with IBM in 1981, Ginni held a series of leadership positions across the company and led the successful integration of PricewaterhouseCoopers Consulting. Ginni has a BS with high honors in computer science and electrical engineering from Northwestern University.

ERIC SCHMIDT is technical advisor to Alphabet Inc., where he advises its leaders on technology, business, and policy issues. Eric joined Google in 2001 and helped grow the company from a Silicon Valley start-up to a global leader in technology. He served as Google's CEO from 2001 to 2011, and executive chairman from 2011 to 2018, alongside founders Sergey Brin and Larry Page. Eric serves on the boards of the Mayo Clinic and the Broad Institute, among others. His philanthropic efforts through the Schmidt Family Foundation focus on climate change, including support of ocean and marine life studies at sea, as well as education, specifically cutting-edge research and technology in the natural sciences and engineering. He is founder of Schmidt Futures, which helps exceptional people do more for others by applying science and technology thoughtfully and working together across fields. He is the coauthor of *The New Digital Age*, *How Google Works*, and the new book *Trillion Dollar Coach: The Leadership Playbook of Silicon Valley's Bill Campbell*.

ADAM SILVER was unanimously elected NBA commissioner in 2014 by the NBA Board of Governors. Silver presides over a global sports and media business built around four professional sports leagues: the National Basketball Association, the Women's National Basketball Association, the NBA G League, and the NBA 2K League. Silver was named *Sports Business Journal*'s Executive of the Decade and has been ranked number one on the publication's annual list of the 50 Most Influential People in Sports Business. He was also named to *Time*'s 100 Most Influential People, *Fortune*'s World's 50 Greatest Leaders, and *Bloomberg Businessweek*'s list of 50 people who defined global business. Prior to becoming commissioner, Silver served as NBA deputy commissioner and COO. He has been instrumental to many of the league's signature achievements, including the negotiation of three collective bargaining agreements with the National Basketball Players Association; the development of the WNBA, NBA G League, NBA 2K League, and the Basketball Africa League; and the creation of NBA China.

ROBERT F. SMITH is the founder, chairman, and CEO of Vista Equity Partners. Vista currently manages equity capital commitments of over $57 billion and oversees a portfolio of over sixty enterprise software, data, and technology-enabled companies. In 2017, Smith was named by *Forbes* as one of the 100 Greatest Living Business Minds. Born in Colorado to two parents with PhDs, Mr. Smith trained as an engineer at Cornell University, earning his BS in chemical engineering. He received his MBA from Columbia Business School with honors. Smith is the founding director and president of the Fund II Foundation, dedicated to preserving the African American experience and sustaining critical American values. In 2017, Smith signed on to the Giving Pledge, the only African American to do so. His gift of $20 million was the largest by an individual donor to the National Museum of African American History and Culture. In 2019, Smith made headlines by announcing he would cover the student loans of nearly four hundred Morehouse College graduates.

OPRAH WINFREY is a global media leader, producer, and actress. Winfrey is also a dedicated philanthropist. During a December 2002 visit with Nelson Mandela, she pledged to build a school in South Africa and has contributed more than $200 million toward providing education for academically gifted girls from disadvantaged backgrounds. In 2019, Ms. Winfrey made a donation to Morehouse College in support of her Morehouse Scholars Program, bringing her total donation to men's education to $20 million. Additionally, Winfrey is a founding donor of the Smithsonian's National Museum of African American History and Culture. In June of 2018, the museum opened "Watching Oprah: *The Oprah Winfrey Show* and American Culture," an exhibit exploring Winfrey's life and her talk show's impact featuring artifacts from the set, costumes from her movies, and interactive interviews. In 2013, Winfrey was awarded the Presidential Medal of Freedom, the nation's highest civilian honor. In 2018, she was honored with the Cecil B. deMille Award by the Hollywood Foreign Press Association.

Index

About the Author

David M. Rubenstein is a cofounder and coexecutive chairman of The Carlyle Group, one of the world's largest and most successful private investment firms.

Mr. Rubenstein is chairman of the boards of trustees of the John F. Kennedy Center for the Performing Arts and the Council on Foreign Relations; a fellow of the Harvard Corporation; a regent of the Smithsonian Institution; a trustee of the National Gallery of Art, the University of Chicago, Memorial Sloan Kettering Cancer Center, Johns Hopkins Medicine, the Institute for Advanced Study, the National Constitution Center, the Brookings Institution, and the World Economic Forum; a director of the Lincoln Center for the Performing Arts and the American Academy of Arts and Sciences; and president of the Economic Club of Washington, D.C.

Mr. Rubenstein has served as chairman of the board of trustees of Duke University and the Smithsonian Institution, and cochairman of the board of the Brookings Institution.

Mr. Rubenstein is an original signer of the Giving Pledge and a recipient of the Carnegie Medal of Philanthropy.

Mr. Rubenstein is the host of *The David Rubenstein Show: Peer to Peer Conversations* on Bloomberg TV and PBS, and the author of *The American Story: Conversations with Master Historians* (Simon & Schuster, 2019).

Mr. Rubenstein, a native of Baltimore, is a 1970 magna cum laude graduate of Duke University, where he was elected Phi Beta Kappa. Following Duke, he graduated from the University of Chicago Law School in 1973. Prior to cofounding Carlyle in 1987, Mr. Rubenstein practiced law in New York and in Washington, and during the Carter administration he was deputy assistant to the president for domestic policy.